The Family,
Civil Society,
and the State

The Family,
Civil Society,
and the State

edited by
Christopher Wolfe

ROWMAN & LITTLEFIELD PUBLISHERS, INC.
Lanham • Boulder • New York • Oxford

ROWMAN & LITTLEFIELD PUBLISHERS, INC.

Published in the United States of America
by Rowman & Littlefield Publishers, Inc.
4720 Boston Way, Lanham, Maryland 20706

12 Hid's Copse Road
Cumnor Hill, Oxford OX2 9JJ, England

British Library Cataloguing in Publication Information Available

Library of Congress Cataloging-in-Publication Data

The family, civil society, and the state / edited by Christopher
Wolfe.
    p.   cm.
    Includes bibliographical references and index.
    ISBN 0-8476-9224-8 (cloth : alk. paper). — ISBN 0-8476-9225-6
(paper : alk. paper)
    1. Family—Congresses.   2. Family policy—Congresses.   I. Wolfe,
Christopher.
HQ7.F297   1998
306.85—dc21   98–22522
                                                                  CIP
Printed in the United States of America

♾™ The paper used in this publication meets the minimum requirements of American National
Standard for Information Sciences—Permanence of Paper for Printed Library Materials, ANSI
Z39.48–1984.

Contents

Introduction

Christopher Wolfe

The family consisting of a husband, a wife, and children, united in permanent bonds of love, is an ideal that almost all Americans embrace. But in our age, many have come to regard it as a hopelessly unattainable ideal, for themselves or for large numbers of their fellow citizens. Phenomena such as elevated divorce rates and a growing number of births outside of marriage require us, it is said, to be aware of the fact that there is no "family," but rather many forms of "families." Given the social problems associated with the family forms encouraged by these contemporary trends, however, it hardly seems reasonable simply to give up and accept them as inevitable.

Perhaps the most important practical question that today's generation of young Americans must face—a question that the generation preceding it has unfortunately failed to confront—is: *why does our society seem to be incapable of sustaining genuinely stable and happy family life?* A second question, equally important, is: *what can we do about it?*

At least part of the answer may be that many people in our society—especially its intellectuals and those whom they influence—have come to believe that the political community ought to be "neutral" on questions about the good human life. It should confine itself to the less exalted, but safer, task of protecting human rights. This disposition manifests itself especially in the promotion of a more rigid separation of church and state and in the creation and expansion of a "privacy" doctrine that insulates important moral questions (such as abortion and active homosexuality) from public decisionmaking. In a society that is pluralistic—that is, deeply divided over fundamental questions of how to live well—this contracted public sphere is said to be an essential condition for public peace and security.

It *is* sensible, of course, to maintain limits on government power to intervene in matters that most directly affect the individuals involved. But that does not mean that our society can afford to ignore the *substantial though indirect* effects of the quality of family life on the well-being of the nation. It is true that the two people most interested in a marriage are the husband and wife. Yet it is also true that, especially in cases where that relationship breaks down and where children are involved, there can be enormous implications for society at large.

Traditionally, American liberal democracy has understood this fact, and, like other societies, given marriage a privileged status. It has, in direct and indirect ways, provided support for the family by promoting moral and social norms that tie marriage, family, and sexuality closely together. For example, this understanding has provided grounds for social norms against, and for the legal prohibition of, adultery, fornication, sodomy, and prostitution and for important limits on divorce.

One way to characterize this tradition is to say that liberal democracy, like other forms of government, must manifest some serious concern for the character of its citizenry and promote a respect for certain fundamental human duties—such as fidelity to spouse and commitment to one's children, even when these require self-sacrifice and perseverance in the face of difficulties. This explicit focus on human duties was more characteristic of earlier forms of political thought, such as the classical natural right thought of Plato and Aristotle and the natural law thought of medieval Christendom, than of liberal political theory. But, despite the shift in emphasis from duties to rights in earlier modern thinkers, such as Hobbes and Locke, classical liberals maintained some sense of the need for a moral framework for society.

The intellectual development of liberalism from Locke and Hobbes through Mill and down to John Rawls today has seen a declining concern for the moral framework that might be viewed as a kind of legacy to modern liberalism from natural right and natural law thought. A contemporary liberal such as David A. J. Richards can "appreciate" Locke by seeing him as a somewhat inconsistent harbinger of contemporary liberalism, with its more consistent and more radical separation of personal morality and legal and social norms. Indeed, much of contemporary liberalism can be viewed as an effort to "purify" liberal democracy of the remnants of premodern social norms of morality.

But it may be that the well-being of modern liberal democracies depends precisely on that moral framework it inherited from premodern thought. If so, efforts to "purify" liberalism and render it more "consistent" may end up wounding it deeply. It may be that modern liberal democracies may depend on the natural right and natural law traditions for essential prerequisites for their own well-being.

This does not mean, of course, that the clock can or should be turned back centuries according to some nostalgic view of idyllic family life in the past. There was much in the past that we have rightly left behind. But at the same time, there were other elements in the Judeo-Christian tradition— above all, the social norm of a permanent conjugal bond oriented especially to the well-being of the family (a genuine norm, though it was often not honored in practice)—that we ought to maintain.

The exact place of the family in a healthy political community, and the appropriate ways to sustain it, are profoundly complicated and difficult questions. The contributors to this book cannot aspire to give complete answers to them. They do try to provide us with some of the essential elements of the right answers.

The first section of the book asks about what is distinctive in the current situation of the family. One response to the family crisis of the late twentieth century has been to deny that there is a crisis and to assert that what we confront is "business as usual." Our dismay at current family life is merely the result of a nostalgic and fundamentally mythical view of family stability in bygone eras. When we understand the past for what it was, some say, we discover that family life today is different only in certain shades from family life in the past; in the past, too, there was no "family" but rather many diverse forms of "families."

Elizabeth Fox-Genovese provides us with some thoughts on the history of the family that challenge academic views that emphasize past diversity of family forms so much that they overlook the underlying common elements of marriage and family. In fact, this failure to recognize common elements helps us to understand what is truly distinctive about ideas regarding the family in our own time.

Lawrence Stone, in his response to Fox-Genovese's paper, gives a pessimistic assessment of the current situation of the family, noting the various social pathologies linked to the breakdown of the nuclear family and observing that "we do not know how to get out of the mess we are in," and, even if we did know, are unlikely "to pay the high cost of putting it right."

Gertrude Himmelfarb is marginally less pessimistic, though not for lack of a keen eye for current problems. She supplements Fox-Genovese's points about current family life with observations from Europe, providing a striking picture of "elegant, urbane cynicism" about the family. Despite this bleak picture, however, there are some intimations of the spiritual-moral revival that would be a precondition for mending the family.

The delegitimization of the family is not merely a recent phenomenon, says David Wagner, but can be traced in some measure to the intellectual founders of liberalism, Thomas Hobbes and John Locke. In these influential thinkers, we find a transition from the family as a natural institution to the family as a conventional and legal institution, and as "a mere instrumentality for child-rearing, implicitly replaceable by others. The family was thus delegitimized, opening the way for its enemies of today."

Allan Carlson emphasizes, contra certain historians, the strength of the family in the early history of America (1775-1825) and identifies some of its key features in that era. He goes on to explore the challenge to the family from the Leviathan state through several episodes in American history: two in the nineteenth century (the rise of public education and the emergence of the *parens patriae* doctrine), and two in the twentieth (the substitution of the welfare state for husbands and the displacement of generational bonds by the Social Security system).

Celia Wolf-Devine rounds out the theoretical and historical section of the book with an analysis of family critiques in existentialist and radical feminism in the work of a contemporary liberal, John Rawls, and of a liberal feminist, Susan Moller Okin. She demonstrates some of the ways in which both feminism and liberalism tend to dissolve the bonds on which the family rests.

Part two provides a look at the family today. David Popenoe reviews a wealth of demographic information in order to explain the instability of family life today. Factors such as increasing divorce rates and rates of illegitimacy can be traced, he argues, in great measure to the philosophy of radical individualism that attained such influence in the 1960s. Whatever the other effects of these changes, the effects on children of the collapse of the married, two-parent family have been devastating.

David Blankenhorn details some of the social pathologies associated with family breakdown and focuses in particular on the question of the role of the father. Sons learn the meaning of masculinity from fathers, and daughters develop self-confidence and learn the meaning of a healthy relationship with a man. Our society is endangered by the loss and absence of many fathers and the loss of the very idea of fatherhood. A cultural movement to restore the importance of fatherhood is necessary, and the seeds for it have been planted.

Mary Ann Glendon takes up a question that many people wonder about: Is the economic emancipation of women today contrary to a healthy, functioning family? She asks whether the movement of women into the workforce today is properly described as "emancipation" and points out that many women do not experience it that way. She rejects the conservative vision that expects women simply to withdraw from the world of work into the family and she rejects the feminist vision of motherhood as oppression. The problem, she suggests, may lie more in the organization of the world of work. Economic values must be subordinated to human values, including the need to support the family, which is essential for the social capital on which the market depends. Capitalism, like liberalism, needs to worry about whether it is eroding its own supports in civil society. Promoting women's exercise of all their talents, rights, and responsibilities without undermining their roles within the family will require calling not only husbands and fathers to their family responsibilities but also governments and private employers to their social duties.

Part three offers analysis of the family and American law, especially the law of divorce. Bruce Hafen describes the current status of the family in American law. He finds that the personal relationships most protected by U.S. state and federal laws are still limited—at least at the formal level—to those that arise from kinship, adoption, and heterosexual marriage. But there is a contrary trend, observable especially in the movements toward easier divorce and same-sex marriage. These trends reinforce the emerging tendency to view marriage as a private contract, rather than viewing it, as our legal tradition has, as a social institution.

Gerry Bradley analyzes current church-state and privacy law in the United States, showing that the way the Supreme Court conceives of religious and moral ideals as necessarily private choices provides an intellectual foundation for denying the traditional family any public status.

Maggie Gallagher goes further, arguing that *de facto* marriage as a formal, legal institution has already been abolished by no-fault divorce laws. The right to leave a marriage is judged so compelling that it must override our right to make (and be held responsible for) our commitments. But recent studies—contrary to the earlier academic wisdom—conclude that some of the changes in divorce law did increase the divorce rate in some jurisdictions. Contrary to counsels of despair—"this is the new family, and there's no going back"—we should aim at two simple goals: to stabilize marriage, so that the majority of lovers who marry succeed in making a permanent union, and to reconnect marriage and childbearing, so that each year more and more (rather than fewer and fewer) American babies begin their lives under the protection of a couple publicly joined in marriage.

Diane Medved points out some of the "ruinous ripples" of divorce, extending from the couple itself, out to those who are close to them (children, parents, and friends), and then to society at large. She then examines some of the causes of divorce: economic (the many tangible benefits accruing to various professions from divorce), cultural (especially the influence of images promoted in movies and on television), and personal (the triumph of "heart" over "head," for example). But there are ways to resist these forces and to strengthen marriage, she argues.

Part four deals with the relationship between the family and two profoundly important facets of the structural framework of American life: our capitalist economic system and the cultural power of the media.

Doug Bandow looks at the question of capitalism and the family. He looks at some key characteristics of capitalism, its philosophical underpinnings, and its outcomes, and evaluates their impact on the family. While recognizing that different elements of capitalism have different effects on the family—some positive, some negative—he concludes that, on balance, the family is better off under a capitalist economic system than under any of its major competitors.

Michael Medved abstracts from the question of the particular content of television and makes a powerful argument that television as a medium has important effects undermining the family. Above all, it encourages impatience, depression, and selfishness, all of which are harmful to family life. If we want to improve the quality of family life, the answer is not so much "change TV content" as "turn off the TV."

The values of the "media elite" can best be described as those of "expressive individualism," say Robert Lerner and Althea Nagai. So we should not be surprised that comparisons of media elite and public attitudes on questions such as adultery, teenage sex, and homosexuality show stark contrasts. Lerner and Nagai also offer some persuasive arguments for the impact of the media in "defining deviancy down."

The fifth and last part of the book surveys various areas of public policy and concludes by asking what, if anything, public policy can do for the family. William Mattox, Jr. and John Mueller discuss the impact of the American system of taxation on the family, and they offer new ways of conceiving principles of taxation that might reduce its burden.

Marvin Olasky and John DiIulio discuss welfare and its effect on the family, finding interesting areas of agreement and disagreement. Olasky argues that government is the problem, not the solution. The only effective means for dealing with poverty and welfare—means that avoid the destructive impact of government welfare on the family—are faith-based initiatives that have the capacity for transforming people's lives. DiIulio, while similarly emphasizing the enormous benefits of faith-based activity to help the poor, remains convinced that—given the limited capacities of private charity—government must continue to play an important role in providing financial support for the poor.

Charles Glenn examines the question of parents, schools, and government in the education of children. While recognizing the legitimate roles of schools and government, Glenn argues compellingly that they must not displace the family, as they often do. Schools cannot be reduced to mere agencies of the government, or even of the family, but a policy of parental choice of schools is the most effective way to "help families to act more effectively by operating as though what families do is significant—whatever their social class."

Lawrence Criner details the facts and the problems involved in myriad forms of sex education in America today. The most powerful institutions controlling sex education, with the active support of government bureaucracies and funds, are committed to policies that take as given (and, in some cases, regard as desirable) a high level of sexual activity among the young. These organizations not only downplay, but, to a surprising extent, aggressively oppose education that emphasizes the need for abstinence.

William Galston and William Kristol, two thoughtful commentators—academics by training and also leading political actors on different sides of the political spectrum—round out the volume by asking what public policy can do for the family. They concur in the importance of the two-parent family, on the wisdom of the age-old principle "first, do no harm," and on a range of limited and sensible policy proposals that would benefit the family. But in the end they are divided by divergent attitudes toward certain social changes, perhaps especially those associated with feminism.

This book is based on a conference sponsored by the American Public Philosophy Institute, a group of scholars sharing a commitment to natural law theory, broadly conceived. We believe that principles of practical reason, which include a recognition of objective human goods and moral norms rooted in them, can effectively be brought to bear on important social and political problems. Indeed, attempts to deal with the varied social pathologies of our time will inevitably be unavailing, unless they respect these fundamental truths about human life.

The family—understood as husband, wife, and children—is among the most fundamental features of human life, being itself a human good of the highest order and also an irreplaceable means to achieve a wide range of other human goods. At the same time, many aspects of family life are variable—the relationship between family life and various forms of work, for example. Discerning what is the permanent core of family life, and what are the variable forms of it, are among the key questions that all societies must confront. Our hope is that this volume will be a valuable contribution to the ongoing reflection on these questions.

Acknowledgments

Grateful acknowledgment is due the support that made possible the conference on which this book is based. In particular, we would like to thank Richard Larry and the Carthage Foundation, the University of Notre Dame Law School, and Richard John Neuhaus and the Institute on Religion and Public Life.

I owe many thanks to the members of the coordinating committee that devised the themes and organization of the conference: Mary Ann Glendon of Harvard Law School, Russell Hittinger of the University of Tulsa, and Robert George of Princeton University.

David Blankenhorn's paper is from *Reclaiming America's Moral and Cultural Heritage* (Tallahassee, Fl.: James Madison Institute, 1998). We are grateful for the permission to reprint it.

The assistance of Bill Muck at Marquette University, who helped greatly in putting the manuscript into final form, was invaluable.

Finally, I want to express my appreciation to Jon Sisk and Steve Wrinn of Rowman & Littlefield for their editorial support, and to managing editor Julie Kirsch for her efficient and cheerful help in producing the final manuscript.

Part One

What Is Distinctive in the Current Situation of the Family?

1

Thoughts on the History of the Family

Elizabeth Fox-Genovese

Since the 1950s, but especially since the 1970s, contemporary concerns about the family have generated intense interest in the variety of family forms in different times and places. Recent decades have especially witnessed a veritable explosion of family history, ranging from oral histories of specific families to massive scholarly monographs on the family in specific periods to general interpretations and overviews. This work, at its best, has yielded fascinating results that have decisively expanded our sensitivity to the myriad forms which the purported trans-historical monolith of "the family" may take. Much of it, however, may fairly be viewed as suspect, if only because it was written to serve a specific political or ideological agenda. Above all, for what should be obvious reasons, many of the historical studies of the family originated in a desire to disclose the distinctive, if not unique, features of the family during the period under consideration and thereby to emphasize the difference rather than the similarity among families in different societies and centuries.

Not for nothing has the family captured the attention of historians: How better to expose an institution as the product of human choice rather than natural or divine order than to call attention to its historical variation? Indeed, during the years following World War II, and especially since the 1960s, historians have explored the multiplicity of family forms as well as the changing patterns of family formation and dynamics. Following the pioneering path traced by the work of the French historian Philippe Ariès, they have, for example, rejected the idea of childhood as a distinct and universal stage of development, insisting that the idea only took shape in Europe during the early modern period. In earlier times, Ariès insisted, children had been viewed as miniature adults.[1] Others, following the lead of Lawrence Stone, have focused upon the changing character of marriage and its relation to the socialization of the young, beginning with childrearing practices.[2] Most historians of the family, notwithstanding differences among them, have tended to follow the lead of Ariès and Stone in insisting upon the close association among the appearance of the idea of childhood and the emergence of the nuclear family, companionate marriage, and, especially, the modern idea of motherhood.[3]

Drawing freely upon psychology, sociology, and anthropology, historians of the family have, on the whole, emphasized the functional or economic character of marital and family relations. The broad functional perspective might be summarized as, "Each society gets the forms of marriage and family it deserves or which best serve its purposes." The economic perspective, which shares many assumptions with the functional, shifts the emphasis to the limits that economic possibilities place upon marriage and family, concluding that the nature of both are shaped by economic forces. Both the functional and economic perspectives converge in their emphasis upon the differences among families according to century, location, or social class. Both have, in this respect, paved the way for the contemporary or postmodern emphasis upon the malleability of family composition and the endless variety of family forms.[4]

The emergence of the contemporary infatuation with the infinite plasticity of "the family" helps to explain the fascination with family history. Having, in our own time, called the very notion of the two-parent heterosexual family into question, we seem compelled to prove that it has never been either naturally or divinely sanctioned and, if anything more important, that most people throughout history have been unwilling or unable to observe its norms.[5] Thus the dominant tendency in family history seems to suggest that there have been as many kinds of families as there have been societies or even individuals. The logical conclusion to be drawn from this work is accordingly that the family, like marriage in which it is anchored, constitutes a relation into which people enter and that they frequently leave according to shifting individual preferences and interests.

In fairness, it is entirely possible that the attitudes toward the family and marriage that many scholars project upon the past may have triumphed in our own time. But, if we are to make any sense of the current debates about marriage and the family, we must understand that the situation of marriage and the family in our time is not merely new but unprecedented. For, until the very recent past, marriage and the family have been universally viewed as the necessary foundation of specific societies and of civilization in general—as the source and manifestation of human and divine order. This understanding of marriage and the family as the most important and abiding system of human relations, as simultaneously necessary to individuals and to society as a whole, has persisted throughout human history. Beneath the surface of changing patterns of marriage and family, the ubiquitous insistence upon the intrinsic value of marriage and family as fundamental goods for the individual and society has endowed the various manifestations and practices with a common character and meaning.[6]

Marriage and the family do change in response to the broad social, economic, and cultural changes as well as in response to political and legal change. To take an easy example, where antimiscegenation laws prevail, a man and woman of different race do not marry, even if they cohabit, and consequently their children enjoy no legal identity as members of their family. Similarly, slaves in the antebellum South could not legally marry although they frequently entered into binding relations with a person of the opposite sex, sometimes with the blessing of a minister. And because these marriages had no legal standing, the children they produced were not legally the children of their biological procreators.[7]

The case of slave marriage throws into relief some of the central features of marriage and the family as legally or religiously constituted institutions. Today, many primarily consider marriage and the family from the subjective perspective of the individual: Do they or do they not further the individual's happiness and fulfillment? Yet if, from the perspective of the individual, marriage and family constitute a subjective story, from the perspective of society they primarily constitute an objective story. Thus, the anthropologist Robin Fox reminds us that marriage figures as a central and enduring feature of "the network of relationships that bind individuals to each other in the web of kinship." And he argues that this network, like marriage itself, has functioned as "the pivot on which most interaction, most claims and obligations, most loyalties and sentiments [have] turned."[8] In other words, notwithstanding variations in form, marriage and the family have served as the primary link between the individual and society or the polity—the essential and irreducible social unit. In this role, marriage and the family typically secured the mutual rights and responsibilities of women and men, recognized the right and responsibility of parents to shape the future of their offspring, and secured the ownership and transfer of property. Until very recently, they preceded and outranked the individual, who was socially and politically defined by them rather than by personal attributes or status. Indeed, in the most important respects, marriage and the family, throughout most of history, have grounded and defined the identity of the individual, who is placed at high risk without their legitimization.[9]

At an accelerating rate during the late nineteenth and twentieth centuries, marital and family ties have increasingly come to be viewed as secular contractual relations, which primarily concern the state, if indeed they concern anyone other than the immediate participants. Throughout history, however, marriage and the family have been of primary concern to the Church or religious authorities, who have viewed them as inherently sacramental. Until the French Revolution, for example, the records of marriages, births, and deaths were not kept by the state, but by the clergy, who inscribed them in the parish registers from which historians have drawn such valuable information. Throughout history, religious authorities have displayed a special interest in marriage, presumably because they, like political authorities, have viewed marriage and the family as fundamental agents and sites of the ordering of human life. And most societies have ascribed a primary role to the family in the religious and moral education of the next generation.[10]

Today, many dismiss the interest of religious and political authorities in the regularization of marriage and the family as further evidence of the curtailment of individual desire by illegitimate authorities. Others, seemingly in growing numbers, demand that religious and political authorities acknowledge, sanctify, or legitimize whatever unions between individuals or groupings of individuals as valid forms of marriage or family.[11] The mistrust of marriage and the family has especially bedeviled feminists, who are wont to charge both with primary responsibility for the subordination and exploitation of women. And there can be no doubt that the feminist movement has decisively contributed to the dismantling of marriage and the family during recent decades.[12] Yet religious and political interest in marriage and the family testifies less to the determination to oppress women and children than to a deep understanding that marriage and the family have everywhere constituted the fundamental social unit—the fulcrum of civilization, the threshold between nature and culture. The core of the religious and political authorities' interest in marriage and the family may, then, be presumed to have derived from their understanding that these are the relations through which people recognize themselves as human beings, through which people define themselves. The question was less one of their imposing marriage and the family upon naturally recalcitrant individuals than of their gaining legitimacy by associating political and religious authority with the fundamental social units into which people grouped themselves.

With respect to the bonds between marriage and family on the one hand and religious and political authority on the other, it is worth noting that both religious and political authority themselves long borrowed heavily from the language of family relations, presumably because that language was taken to be the one that seemed most natural and legitimate to most people. The familial imagery that pervades Christianity begins with God the Father and includes not merely His Son, but the Blessed Mother, and the Holy Family. This same imagery pervaded and structured the early forms of European political authority, which, for centuries, depicted the monarch or the tsar as the father of his people. This form of political authority came appropriately to be known as patriarchalism. In its classic formulation by the British political theorist Sir Robert Filmer, it justified the authority of the monarch as a direct inheritance from Adam, the father of the human race.[13]

In theory, patriarchalism proclaimed a perfect symmetry between the governance of families and the governance of states—-both understood to honor and obey the divinely sanctioned authority of the father. But variants of patriarchalism prevailed in societies that restricted its authority to the private realm and did not take it to justify the governance of public affairs. The leading example may well be ancient Rome, which endowed the father of the family with the power of life and death over family members and slaves. The power of the father in the Roman Republic thus exceeded even that of the power of the father in ancient regime France, who still had the authority to demand that the king imprison a son who dared to defy his wishes.[14] Even after the English had forcefully repudiated public patriarchalism and beheaded Charles I, the king who embodied it, they retained traces of its legacy in the assumption that a father would govern the family for which he was responsible, including his adult wife. Thus, in the eighteenth century, when Sir William Blackstone produced his great treatise on English common law, he insisted that in marriage the husband and wife must be one, and that one must be the husband. Blackstone was articulating the law of coverture, according to which the wife lived under the covering wing of her husband, who was held to protect her, govern her, and represent her in the public realm.[15]

The assumption that men naturally govern families, including their wives, has prevailed throughout most of history, although most premodern societies have granted more power to the family as a whole than to the specific husband and father, whom they have tended to view as the delegate of the family—that is, as the steward of an authority that provides for the proper ordering of the family as a whole, which transcends him as an individual. In such a world, it was frequently possible for a woman to step into that role and speak in the name of the family as a whole. Had that not been the case, Elizabeth I would never have succeeded to the throne of her father, and, although questions about the effect her marriage might have upon her role as sovereign persisted throughout her reign and may well have accounted for her never having married, as ruler she proved no more tolerant of challenges to her authority than he.[16]

Not all societies proved as faithful to the principles of delegation as the British, and to avoid complications, the French precociously established or rediscovered the Salic Law according to which a woman could never succeed to the throne. But elsewhere, notably Russia and Austria, women did govern in the name of their families, the interests of which they were believed to represent. Only during the modern and increasingly bureaucratic period did one country after another deem it prudent to institute explicit laws against women's political participation. And they invariably did so following the triumph of liberal, democratic, or individualistic principles that drew a hard line between public and private realms but also opened the way to women's claims to an individual identity independent of the family. Thus, during the second half of the nineteenth century, the United States and many, if not all, Western European countries explicitly barred—or tacitly excluded—women from activities and occupations. In this respect, a kind of sexual segregation emerged in tandem with the racial segregation that succeeded the northern victory in the American Civil War and the abolition of slavery.[17]

Feminists have frequently been tempted to condemn most, if not all, marital and family relations throughout history as patriarchal. Many even argue that an independent system of patriarchy, grounded in men's presumed universal dominance within the family, has prevailed in all times and places.[18] This charge woefully misjudges the true nature of patriarchy, which has been far from universal. More importantly, it fails to capture the complexity and, above all, the interdependence that have normally characterized the relations between women and men within marriages and families. To grasp the normal state of affairs, we need only remember that the vast majority of human beings have traditionally lived in peasant or farm families in which the contributions, including the labor, of the woman have normally been as important as those of the man.[19] We should also recall that historically most married women have lived under conditions in which the reproduction of the population was the first business of society, in which many pregnancies did not come to term and many babies did not survive infancy, and in which artificial contraception was not—or not generally—available. These were conditions under which the biological difference between the sexes had important consequences and were generally taken to justify significantly different roles for women and men, even when the women also played an important role in provision of the family's resources.[20]

To identify the principal common denominator among the various historical forms of marriage and the family, we could do worse than settle on the widespread belief that marriage and the family articulate the natural sexual division of labor upon which social order and civilization rest. So widespread has agreement been on this matter that, until recently, one would have been hard-pressed to point to a single system of belief, including the great formal religions, a single theory of government, or a single social system that did not regard that "biological" fact as foundational—as an expression of the natural law that underlies and sets limits upon the positive laws of specific states.[21] Only in the very recent past have we witnessed significant opposition to the view of men and women as different and complementary and naturally suited to cooperation within marital and familial bonds upon which the future of the succeeding generation is taken to depend. Indeed, had that purportedly natural relation between the sexes not encountered opposition, we, like other societies, would presumably still regard the family as the natural unit of all human society, notwithstanding differing assumptions about its precise composition and size.

Thus far, I have tried to underscore a few enduring, common elements of marriage and family at the expense of the various forms they may take. But historically, the family, precisely because of its pivotal and indispensable role in linking the individual to society, has demonstrated impressive adaptability: According to circumstances, families may be extended or nuclear, multigenerational or two-generational, matrilineal or patrilineal, matrilocal or patrilocal. They may assuredly be patriarchal, although they have probably never, as Friedrich Engels and others speculated, been genuinely matriarchal.[22] Marriages themselves have varied not merely by monogamy and polygyny, but by whether arranged or freely chosen, whether established on the basis of a bride price or a dowry, and more. Scholars have emphasized the variations, in large measure, to disabuse the complacent assumption that to be legitimate family and marriage must always have observed the model we take for granted. All societies may attempt to ensure their own orderly reproduction through the ways in which they welcome and rear the next generation, but they have not all done so in the same way. Yet the very richness and interest of our new panoramic sense of the diversity of family forms risks obscuring the most important consideration of all. For it may reasonably be argued that none of these seemingly infinite variations matches in significance the sea change that has marked the modern and, especially, the postmodern worlds.[23]

If the modern ideals of companionate marriage and the nuclear family may not claim universal authority, they have nonetheless decisively shaped the ideas of contemporary Americans as well as Western Europeans, and, since World War II, they seem to have exercised some influence within a variety of "modernizing" societies throughout the world. The view of the family as appropriately nuclear and marriage as appropriately the product of the mutual love and choice of the individuals concerned emerged, as Lawrence Stone and others have argued, in Western Europe, notably England, at the dawn of the modern era. Scholars continue to debate the precise origins and causes of the modern ideal of marriage and the family, and most concur that it did not triumph in one fell swoop, much less gain an equal hold upon all social classes or even all regions of a single country. But they increasingly agree that, during the years following 1750, a new ideal of family and marriage was establishing a secure and apparently irreversible foothold among the English upper and upper-middle classes and that inhabitants of Western Europe and the North American colonies were following their lead.

Debates persist about the causes of the change in family size and dynamics toward the end of the early modern period. Some scholars attribute the decisive role to economics and others to ideology, but most concur about the manifestations. The new attitude toward marriage emphasized the importance of individual choice and love rather than the preference for arranged marriage designed to serve the political and economic interest of the larger family. In conformity with this preference for companionship and love between the partners, there emerged a new attitude toward children and motherhood. Elite mothers, who had previously turned their children over to wet-nurses, nannies, and governesses, were now expected to nurse their children themselves and to play a major role in the development of their minds and character. These expectations typically arose more or less in tandem with the first stirrings of political individualism, and they derived from the new interest in children as themselves emergent individuals. Indeed, both political individualism and the new psychology of childhood had a common source in the work of John Locke, in which childhood was viewed[24] as a distinct—and formative—stage of life during which children's impressionable minds and hearts were molded by the loving attention and firm discipline of parents, especially the mother. Whether as effect or cause, these new convictions about marriage, childhood, and family life generally accompanied an older age at first marriage for women and a gradual decline in the number of children per family. And the whole was ensconced in a view of the family as a private sphere, safely removed from the hurly-burly of public life, and informed by the glow of intimacy and love.[25]

Most of us recognize this constellation of attitudes, if only because it prevailed among Europeans and Americans until at least the upheavals of the 1960s and still prevails among many today. What we not so readily recognize is that this view, which so many of us cherish, contained within itself the seeds of its own ultimate destruction. Companionate marriage and the loving, child-centered, private family assured tremendous benefits to many people and to society at large, but they also created an array of problems, including men's abuse of women and children, the personal unhappiness of husbands and wives, and the psychic misery of children. We need not exaggerate the abuses, which have occurred in all families in all times and which may actually have diminished during the nineteenth and early twentieth centuries, but do need to acknowledge them. In recent years, it has become commonplace—in some circles, obligatory—to denounce the repressive and abusive character of the "patriarchal" bourgeois family. But whatever that family was, it was not patriarchal, and it arguably served its members better than any known alternative.

Ironically, the very emphasis upon love and mutuality between husband and wife and among parents and children that fostered the best features of this family also opened the way to its erosion. For example, once one assumes that a marriage must be grounded in love, how does one prohibit divorce when love dies? By the 1920s, divorce had, indeed, become much easier to obtain and was beginning to lose its social stigma. Thereafter, especially in the United States, the divorce rate skyrocketed—all in the name of true love and the fulfillment of individuals. The bonds of the nuclear family were steadily loosening, but the decisive blow came with the extraordinary sexual and economic revolution of the last thirty years.[26] That dual revolution has spawned both unprecedented opportunities for women and the modern feminist movement, and has decisively undercut the social centrality of marriage. These explosive changes have given us no-fault divorce, abortion on demand, rampant unwed motherhood, and "children's rights," and now threaten us with same-sex marriage as well.

The numbers that chronicle the proliferation of divorce, the children born to unwed mothers, the children who live all or a large part of their childhood without a resident biological father, and the other casualties of our current attitudes and practices are staggering. But there is a real danger that single-minded attention to the quantitative magnitude of family disruption will obscure the dramatic significance of the qualitative change. For, seen in historical perspective, our contemporary situation is indeed something new under the sun. To be sure, there are many who deny that qualitative change has occurred, arguing, for example, that the proliferation of divorce more often than not results in the formation of new marriages.[27] And in truth, many, if not most children in the seventeenth-century Chesapeake lost one or both of their parents before they reached their teens. Workers in nineteenth-century Paris frequently lacked the resources to marry and lived in common law marriages, which meant their children lacked legal standing. Until the twentieth century, most people died much younger than they die today, which meant that marriages did not last as long as those of today, and the surviving partner often remarried, which meant that many children grew up without either a biological mother or a biological father in residence. As for the contemporary reliance upon day care and nannies, was such not the experience of countless children throughout history, especially among the well-to-do? All of which and more is true, but the use to which these facts are being put entirely misses the point.

For before the last thirty years or so, no known society has rejected some form of marriage and family as the ideal—and as a norm to which most people were expected to aspire. Exceptions to and violations of the norm were recognized as exceptions and violations. Today, if we credit our senses, we are witnessing a concerted attempt by a portion of the elite to deny the value of the norm. In its place, we are offered marriage as the personal fulfillment of the individual, who must be free to switch partners at will. And we are offered family as "families"—whatever combination of people choose to live together on whatever terms for whatever period of time. It is possible that adults may survive this madness, although one may be permitted to doubt. It is doubtful that any significant number of children will survive it, as the mounting evidence of their distress amply warns. History suggests that, since the dawn of time, one of the principal tasks of civilization has been to bind men to families—to hold them accountable for the children they father and for the children's mother. The modern period slowly eroded elements of that accomplishment, while it introduced some salutary reforms. But it left the ideal intact. Since the 1960s, the postmodern elite has, as if with the snap of the fingers, exploded it. What may emerge from the wreckage is anyone's guess, although the initial signs do not inspire confidence.

Permit me then to conclude with this thought: At first glance the history of marriage and the family may appear to offer a wondrous array of diversity, but that first glance, like others, is more deceptive than trustworthy. For, on closer inspection, history teaches that civilization has always been accompanied by—indeed grounded in—an ideal of marriage and the family that attempts to join the biological difference of men and women in the common project of responsibility for the next generation.

Notes

1. Philippe Ariès, *Centuries of Childhood: A Social History of Family Life*, trans. Robert Baldick (New York: Alfred Knopf, 1962).

2. Lawrence Stone, *The Family, Sex, and Marriage in England, 1500-1800* (New York: Harper & Row, 1977).

3. See, for example, Randolph Trumbach, *The Rise of the Egalitarian Family: Aristocratic Kinship and Domestic Relations in Eighteenth-Century England* (New York: Academic Press, 1978); Elisabeth Badinter, *Émilie, Émilie: L'Ambition féminine au XVIIIème siècle* (Paris: Flammarion, 1983); Jacques Donzelot, *The Policing of Families*, trans. Robert Hurley (New York: Pantheon, 1979); Cissie Fairchild, "Women and Family," in *French Women in the Age of Enlightenment*, ed. Samia I. Spencer (Bloomington: Indiana University Press, 1984), 97-110. See also Elizabeth Fox-Genovese and Eugene D. Genovese, *Fruits of Merchant Capital: Slavery and Bourgeois Property in the Rise and Expansion of Capitalism*, (New York: Oxford University Press, 1983), ch. 11 "The Ideological Bases of Domestic Economy: The Representation of Women and the Family in the Age of Expansion."

4. Initially Talcott Parsons and his students pioneered in applying Weberian theory to family history. See, for example, Neil Smelser, *Social Change in the Industrial Revolution: An Application of Theory to the British Cotton Industry* (London: University of Chicago Press, 1959). Many subsequent histories of family life, including some excellent ones, have adapted a functional perspective to their own purposes. See, for example, David Levine, *Family Formation in an Age of Nascent Capitalism* (New York: Academic Press, 1977); David Levine, ed., *Proletarianization and Family History* (Orlando, FL: Academic Press, 1984); Hans Medick, "The Proto-Industrial Family Economy: The Structural Function of Household and Family during the Transition from Peasant Society to Industrial Capitalism," *Social History* 1, no. 3 (Oct. 1976): 291-315; Michael Anderson, "Family, Household, and Industrial Revolution," in *The American Family in Social-Historical Perspective*, ed.

Michael Gordon, 1st ed. (New York: St. Martin's, 1973); Michael Anderson, *Family Structure in Nineteenth-Century Lancashire* (Cambridge: Cambridge University Press, 1971); Michael Anderson, Frank Bechhofer, and Jonathan Gershuny, eds. *The Social and Political Economy of the Household* (Oxford: Oxford Univ. Press, 1994); Peter Laslett, *Family and Household in Past Time* (Cambridge: Cambridge Univ. Press, 1972). For a general sampling, see *The American Family in Social-Historical Perspective*, ed. Michael Gordon, 2nd. ed. (New York: St. Martin's, 1978) and 3rd. ed. (New York: St. Martin's, 1983). For a more explicit anthropological perspective, see, for example, Jack Goody, *Production and Reproduction* (Cambridge: Cambridge University Press, 1976); Nancie I. Gonzalez, *Black Carib Household Structure: A Study of Migration and Modernization* (Seattle, WA: University of Washington Press, 1969). And, for a critique of functionalism, Christopher Lasch, *Haven in a Heartless World* (New York: Basic Books, 1977).

5. Good examples of this attitude may be found in Louise A.Tilly and Joan W. Scott, *Women, Work, and Family* (New York: Holt, Rinehart & Winston, 1978) and Darret B. Rutman and Anita H. Rutman, *A Place in Time: Middlesex County, Virginia, 1650-1750*, 2 vols. (New York: Norton, 1984).

6. The intrinsic value of marriage and family embodied in the changing forms of both emerges from a wide variety of studies. See, for example, Charles Rosenberg, ed. *The Family in History* (Philadelphia: University of Pennsylvania Press, 1975); Jack Goody, Joan Thirsk, and E. P. Thompson, eds., *Family and Inheritance: Rural Society in Western Europe, 1200-1800* (Cambridge: Cambridge University Press, 1976); Georges Duby, *Le chevalier, la femme et le prêtre: le mariage dans la France féodale* (Paris: Hachette, 1981); Frances and Joseph Gies, *Marriage and the Family in the Middle Ages* (New York: Harper & Row, 1987); Barbara A. Hanawalt, *The Ties That Bound: Peasant Families in Medieval England* (New York: Oxford University Press, 1986); David Herlihy, *Medieval Households* (Cambridge, MA: Harvard University Press, 1985); Ernest Bertin, *Les Marriages dans l'ancienne société française* (Genève: Slatkin, 1975; orig. ed., 1879); Cristiane Klapisch-Zuber, *Women, Family, and Ritual in Renaissance Italy*, trans. Lydia G. Cochrane (Chicago: University of Chicago Press, 1985); Suzanne Fonay Wemple, *Women in Frankish Society: Marriage and the Cloister, 500-900* (Philadelphia: University of Pennsylvania Press, 1981); Herbert G. Gutman, *The Black Family in Slavery and Freedom, 1750-1925* (New York: Pantheon, 1976); J. Hajnal, "European Marriage Patterns in Perspective," in *Population in History: Essays in Historical Demography*, D. V. Glass and D. E. C. Eversley, eds. (London: E. Arnold, 1965); Paul Ourliac and J. de Malafosse, *Le Droit familial*, vol. 3 of *Histoire de droit privé* (Paris: Presses universitaires, 1968); Martine Segalen, *Mari et femme dans la société paysanne* (Paris: Flammarion, 1980); Jean-Louis Flandrin, *Families in Former Times*, trans. Richard Southern (Cambridge: Cambridge University Press, 1979).

7. I offer a more extended discussion in *Within the Plantation Household: Black and White Women of the Old South* (Chapel Hill: University of North Carolina Press, 1988). See also Eugene D. Genovese, *Roll, Jordan, Roll: The World the Slaves Made* (New York: Pantheon, 1975); Gutman, *Black Family*; James Hugo Johnston, *Race Relations in Virginia and Miscegenation in the South, 1766-1860* (Amherst, MA: University of Massachusetts Press, 1970).

8. Robin Fox, *Kinship and Marriage: An Anthropological Perspective* (Harmmondsworth: Penguin, 1974).

9. For a fuller discussion of the issues, especially the relation of individualism to family cohesion, see Elizabeth Fox-Genovese, *Feminism without Illusions: A Critique of Individualism* (Chapel Hill: University of North Carolina Press, 1991).

10. For a fuller discussion, see James Gustafson, *Ethics From a Theocentric Perspective*, 2 vols. (Chicago: University of Chicago Press, 1984), 2: 153-84. See also Duby, *Le chevalier, la femme et le prêtre*; Steven Ozemont, *When Fathers Ruled: Family Life in Reformation Europe* (Cambridge: Harvard University Press, 1983).

11. William N. Eskridge, Jr, *The Case for Same-Sex Marriage: From Sexual Liberty to Civilized Commitment* (New York: Free Press, 1996); Sanford M. Dornbusch and Myra H. Strober, *Feminism, Children, and the New Families* (New York: Guilford Press, 1988); Sharon Elizabeth Rush, "Breaking With Tradition: Surrogacy and Gay Fathers," in *Kindred Matters: Rethinking the Philosophy of the Family*, ed. Diana Tietjens Meyers, Kenneth Kipnis, and Cornelius F. Murphy, Jr. (Ithaca, NY: Cornell University Press, 1993), 102-142. For the opposing position, see, for example, Maggie Gallagher, *The Abolition of Marriage: How We Lost the Right to a Lasting Love* (New York: Regnery Publishing, 1996) and David Popenoe, *Life without Father: Compelling New Evidence that Fatherhood and Marriage Are Indispensable for the Good of Children and Society* (New York: Free Press, 1996).

12. See, for example, Carole Pateman, *The Sexual Contract* (Stanford, CA: Stanford University Press, 1988); Rosalind Coward, *Patriarchal Precedents: Sexuality and Social Relations* (London: Routledge & Kegan Paul, 1983); Ellen Willis, *No More Nice Girls: Countercultural Essays* (Hanover, NH: Wesleyan University Press, 1992); Adrienne Rich, "Compulsory Heterosexuality and the Lesbian Experience," *Signs: Journal of Women in Culture and Society* 4 (1980).

13. Sir Robert Filmer, *Patriarchia and Other Writings*, ed. Peter Laslett (Oxford: Basil Blackwell, 1949). See also Fox-Genovese, *Feminism without Illusions* and my "Property and Patriarchy in Early Bourgeois Political Culture," *Radical History Review* 4, nos. 2 & 3 (Spring/Summer 1977): 35-59. See also Gordon Schochet, *Patriarchalism in Political Thought: The Authoritarian Family and Political Speculation and Attitudes Especially in Seventeenth-Century England* (New York: Basic Books, 1975).

14. Suzanne Dixon, *The Roman Family* (Baltimore: Johns Hopkins University Press, 1992); Judith P. Hallett, *Fathers and Daughters in Roman Society: Women and the Elite Family* (Princeton: Princeton University Press, 1984); Louis de Loménie, Les Mirabeau: Nouvelles études sur la société française au XVIIIè siècle 5 vols. (Paris, 1879-1891).

15. William Blackstone, *Commentaries on the Laws of England*, 4 vols. (Chicago: University of Chicago Press, 1979; orig. ed., 1765-1769). See also, Margaret J. M. Ezell, *The Patriarch's Wife: Literary Evidence and the History of the Family* (Chapel Hill: University of North Carolina Press, 1987).

16. J. E. Neale, *Queen Elizabeth I* (New York: Doubleday-Anchor Books, 1957).

17. See, for example, Carroll Smith Rosenberg, *Disorderly Conduct: Visions of Gender in Victorian America* (New York: Alfred Knopf, 1985); Ellen Carol DuBois, *Feminism and Suffrage: The Emergence of an Independent Women's Movement in America, 1848-1869* (Ithaca, NY: Cornell University Press, 1978); Mary Roth Walsh, *Doctors Wanted: No Women Need Apply: Sexual Barriers in the Medical Profession, 1835-1975* (New Haven: Yale University Press, 1977); Joan D. Hedrick, *Harriet Beecher Stowe* (New York: Oxford University Press, 1994); Brian Harrison, *Separate Spheres: The Opposition to Women's Suffrage in Britain* (New York: Holmes & Meier, 1978); Martha Vicinus, *Independent Women: Work and Community for Single Women, 1850-1920* (Chicago: University of Chicago Press, 1985); Mary Lyndon Shanley, *Feminism, Marriage, and the Law in Victorian England, 1850-1895* (Princeton: Princeton University Press, 1989); Steven C. Hause with Anne R. Kenney, *Women's Suffrage and Social Politics in the French Third*

Republic (Princeton: Princeton University Press, 1984).

18. Gerda Lerner, *The Creation of Patriarchy* (New York: Oxford University Press, 1986) and my review of it in *Journal of the American Academy of Religion* 55, no. 3 (Fall 1987): 608-12.

19. Olwen Hufton, *The Prospect Before Her: A History of Women in Western Europe*, vol. 1, 1500-1800 (New York: Alfred A. Knopf, 1996), esp., 137-76, "On Being a Wife." See also, for example, M. Mitterauer and R. Sieder, *The European Family: From Patriarchy to Partnership from the Middle Ages to the Present* (Oxford: Oxford University Press, 1982); J. Goody, *The Development of the Family and Marriage in Europe* (Cambridge: Cambridge University Press, 1983); Elizabeth Fox-Genovese, "Women and Work," in *French Women and the Age of Enlightenment*, ed. Samia I. Spencer (Bloomington: Indiana University Press, 1984), 111-127; François Lebrun, *La Vie conjugale sous l'ancien régime* (Paris: Armand Colin, 1975); Yves Castan, *Honnêteté et relations sociales en Languedoc (1750-1780)* (Paris: Plon, 1974); Segalen, *Mari et Femme*; Flandrin, *Families in Former Times*.

20. Hufton, *Prospect Before Her*; Olwen Hufton, *The Poor in Eighteenth-Century France* (Oxford: Oxford University Press, 1974); E. A. Wrigley and R. S. Schofield, *The Population History of England 1541-1871* (London: Edward Arnold, 1981); William Goode, *World Revolution and Family Patterns* (New York: Free Press of Glencoe, 1963).

21. Robert P. George and Gerard V. Bradley, "Marriage and the Liberal Imagination," *The Georgetown Law Journal* 84, no. 2 (Dec. 1995): 301-320. See also Robert P. George, "Natural Law and Positive Law," in *The Autonomy of Law*, ed., Robert P. George (Oxford: Clarendon Press, 1996), 321-34 and John Finnis, *Natural Law and Natural Rights* (Oxford: Clarendon Press, 1980).

22. Friederick Engels, *The Origin of the Family, Private Property and the State* (New York: International Publishers, 1972); Karen Sacks, *Mothers and Wives: The Past and Future of Sexual Equality* (Westport, CT: Greenwood Press, 1979).

23. For a fuller discussion of the significance, see Fox-Genovese, *Feminism Is Not the Story of My Life. How the Elite Women's Movement Has Lost Touch with Women's Real Concerns* (New York: Doubleday, 1996) and on some of the implications of the recent sea change, see Richard A. Posner, *Sex and Reason* (Cambridge, Mass: Harvard University Press, 1992), and reviews of Posner by Robert P. George, "Can Sex Be Reasonable," *Columbia Law Review* 93, no. 3 (April 1993): 783-794, and Elizabeth Fox-Genovese, "Beyond Transgression: Toward a Free Market in Morals," *Yale Journal of Law and the Humanities* 5, no. 1 (Winter 1993): 243-64.

24. John Locke, *Two Treatises of Government*, ed. Peter Laslett (Cambridge: Cambridge University Press, 1967 and John Locke, *An Essay Concerning Human Understanding*, 2 vols., ed. Alexander Campbell Fraser (New York: Dover, 1959). See also Elizabeth Fox-Genovese, "Property and Patriarchy in Early Bourgeois Political Culture," *Radical History Review* 4, nos. 2 and 3 (Spring/Summer 1977): 36-59.

25. Notwithstanding some persisting disagreements about timing and effect on the lives of the mass of the population, this view has attained general acceptance, and versions of it pervade most of the vast literature on family and women's history, some of which is cited above.

26. For an elaboration, see Elizabeth Fox-Genovese, *"Feminism Is Not the Story of My Life "*(New York: Doubleday, 1996).

27. Mary Jo Bane, *Here to Stay: American Families in the Twentieth Century* (New York: Basic Books, 1976).

2

The Family Crisis Today

Lawrence Stone

I want to begin with a quotation:

> The more carefully we examine the history of the past, the more reason we shall find to dissent from those who imagine that our age has been fruitful of new social evils. The truth is that these evils are, with scarce an exception, old. That which is new is the intelligence which discerns and the humanity which remedies them.

This was written in 1848 by the great historian Macaulay.[1] Note that Macaulay was certain that the moral and social system was not in fact getting worse. It was getting better, and men of intelligence and good will were ready to make it better still. Today we have lost that sense of optimism.

The Western world is now engulfed in a struggle to preserve the family as the key functioning unit for reproduction, using education, discipline and cooperation to instill in the next generation the moral values of the society. In America, the proportion of illegitimate births to legitimate ones has reached over 60 percent and premarital cohabitation is the norm for all classes and races. Reproduction has declined dramatically as an objective, so that the Italians—of all people—now have the lowest birthrate in Europe. At the same time the educational system is producing more and more semiliterate dropouts; drug abuse is common; and violence from gangs makes the streets of urban ghettoes unsafe. Unemployment, crumbling housing, and deep poverty have become permanent features of ghetto life, where the family has virtually collapsed. Finally, whatever the causes may be, the number of single-parent households is growing rapidly, especially in America. On these facts we can, I hope, all agree.

It is often claimed that the chief cause of this complex of social disorders is the single-parent family. But the statistical evidence for this argument is thin, and the demographic history of the past one hundred and fifty years strongly suggests an alternative model. Forty years ago, Philippe Ariès stunned European and American scholars by claiming that modern attitudes toward children were a development specific to the early modern period. He associated it with the growth of affective individualism as the prime motive for marriage; the rise of the nuclear family to replace the extended one, marriage for affection not property, maternal breast-feeding not wet nursing, and the acceptance of mother love. Many have contested this hypothesis, but it seems to have stood the test of time fairly well. It is paradoxical that, just a few years after the affection-bonded nuclear family was discovered by historians, it is today patently falling apart before our eyes, to be replaced by a sex-driven system of serial concubinage.

It seems incontrovertible that, somehow or other, we need to strike back at this tangle of pathogenic behavior. But where do we start? In practice, we have been terrified by crime, and have mistaken all crime (which has remained fairly stable since 1960) with violent crime, which has escalated in a way that makes the inner city so very dangerous. We have adopted a policy of putting more and more mostly nonviolent criminals in jail, first for drug offenses, and then under the rule of three strikes and you are out. The predictable result is more prisons, more prisoners, but not necessarily less violent crime.

In fact, crime in America fell in the early 1980s, rose in the late 1980s, and fell again in the early 1990s. At the same time, the number of all prisoners rose from 200,000 to over a million, so that today we have relatively more of our population in jail than any other society on earth—even seven times more than in Europe.

What are the causes of these changes? One at least is partly correlated with the demographic: The more teenagers there are on the streets, the greater are the number of crimes, and the larger the number of prisoners. Add to this the lethal gang wars over the control of crack, and you have some explanation of the outbreak of violence in the 1980s. Since we cannot improve the behavior of these intermittent floods of teenagers, we put them in jail instead. If we look at the situation among blacks, we find that no fewer than a third of all black males in their twenties are on probation, or parole or in prison, where today they are treated significantly more harshly than whites. Today, over two-thirds of all blacks are born out of wedlock. Another indicator of social decay is the amount of domestic sexual abuse, on a scale apparently unheard of before the nineteenth century. We can all agree that it is an ugly world out there, and it would be foolish to think otherwise.

A key cause for the trouble is widely believed to be the growth of the single-parent family, the product of families shattered by divorce, the failure of ex-husbands to pay for child support, and the startling growth of unprotected pre-marital sex and of illegitimate children born into a fatherless world. To add to the confusion and despair, more and more mothers are forced to take full-time jobs, thus leaving their children to look after themselves—the latchkey children of our time. By the late 1990s, one-half of all marriages will end in divorce, and a quarter of all children will be the illegitimate products of careless sexual habits. Meanwhile, one in five of all divorced fathers have not seen or spoken to their children over the past year. On all points, the inhabitants of the urban black ghettoes are far more deeply affected by these many catastrophes than are the whites. They are peculiarly exposed to a short life of poverty, school dropout, violent crime, unemployment, drugs, disease, casual cohabitation, and illegitimate children.

There are only a few points on which I disagree with Professor Fox-Genovese. One is over the debilitating affect of the single-parent family, since historically the argument does not stand up very well. In the 1840s, premature adult deaths had created as high a proportion of single-parent households as there were more than a century later in the 1960s. In the century in between, adult mortality had declined substantially. Then after about 1960 the contraceptive revolution dramatically reduced the number of children born, while divorce rocketed, leaving behind it large numbers of children with only a single parent. Looked at objectively, all that had happened between 1840 and 1960 is that divorce had replaced death as the prime cause of the single-parent household. It is not yet clear whether the loss of a parent by death is as traumatic to a child as is loss by a divorce. If this is the case, then the single-parent household cannot be blamed for all the other undeniable woes of society. This makes it uncertain whether a vigorous attempt to strengthen the family would work, even if anyone knew for certain how to do it. A few hundred schools with gifted and dedicated teachers do seem to work—but only as substitutes for the family rather than as buttresses of a new social order. And anyway, who is going to pay for the wide spread of such very expensive institutions? The sad answer is that nobody is.

Another puzzling development has been the marked drop in violent urban crime over the past five or six years. Even the police were at a loss to anticipate this drop or to explain it afterwards. At the same time, another wholly independent indicator of social pathology, that is, the very high level of divorce, has actually declined over the past few years instead of pursuing its previous remorseless rise through the 1960s to the 1980s. Observers warn us that in the next few years, the demographics indicate that a new wave of violence, unemployment, illiteracy, and drug abuse is about to break over American cities as the number of teenagers on the streets rises. If so, the hard-won gains of the last few years are merely a temporary product of a demographic decline.

A final point is that historically the English bastardy rate peaked in 1840 when urban prenuptial agreements were also very common; two out of five of all first conceptions were illegitimate. Premarital sex and illegitimate children were common features of the early Victorian culture.[2] Why should this be? The answer is that we do not really know, except that contraception was almost unknown among the poor, and moral controls over premarital sex seem to have been slight.

U.S. crime is remarkable not for its scale so much as for its extreme violence and brutality. The astonishing level of murder, of ten per 10,000, is far above that of our neighbor Canada, and indeed far above that of any other developed nation. This is why the enforcement of strict gun controls offers such huge potential benefits for society. Unfortunately, however, legislation to this effect is stalled in Congress by the powerful lobbying of the NRA, as well as Prison Guard Unions, who like having more prisoners since they provide more security jobs, and building contractors who like more prisons since they provide more construction jobs. But the indiscriminate incarceration of large numbers of mostly nonviolent petty drug dealers is patently no way to control and suppress the supply of drugs in our society. By focusing on the amount of crime rather than on the violence of crime as the pathogen of late-twentieth-century America, we are throwing the baby out with the bathwater. And by not taking more active measures to reinforce the family, we are opening ourselves to a fresh outbreak of divorce, and therefore of single-parent households, illegitimacy, and marital violence. One obvious suggestion is to revamp the laws governing divorce, to make it more restrictive if there are children involved, and likely to get hurt.

It would be foolish of me—as a mere man—to venture too close to very dangerous waters. But I must say that, though I have some reservations about the wilder side of the feminist movement, I think it is very hard to blame feminists for even some of the all too obvious evils in our society. For one thing there are just not enough of them to make much difference on the street.

I remain, therefore, a pessimist. First, we do not know how to get out of the mess we are in. And second, even if we did know, we are unlikely to be willing to pay the high cost of putting it right. Third, a large new generation of children are now growing up who will soon enter that most dangerous age of fourteen to twenty-five. The future therefore seems to me rather bleak.

The family is collapsing, the civil society is shrinking, and nobody has much confidence in the state any more. The boundless optimism of Macaulay in 1848, that anything can be fixed by men of goodwill, is over.

Notes

1. T. B. Macaulay, *The History of England from the Accession of James II*, 1848, [Everyman Edition] I, pp. 32-33.

2. P. Laslett et al., *Bastardy and Its Comparative History* (Cambridge, Mass: Harvard University Press, 1980), 63, 50-54.

3

The Family *in Extremis*

Gertrude Himmelfarb

Professor Fox-Genovese has so adequately identified the discontinuities and continuities in the history of the family, the variations on the idea of family and the enduring essence of it, that I can add nothing to it. All I shall do is illustrate her remarks.

Let me go abroad for my illustrations. Two years ago, on the death of François Mitterand, the former president of France, we were treated to some titillating revelations about him—revelations in this country, at least; in France many journalists had known about it but either did not think it sufficiently newsworthy to report or were being uncommonly discreet. It appears that Mitterand, for a great many years, had been living a double life, with two families, each complete with spouse and children, with each of whom he spent a specified period of time, and each of whom knew about the other. At his deathbed, both appeared to mourn him and to console each other.

The story itself is interesting, but even more interesting is the way it was reported in this country. It came on the heels of another story about Mitterand—this about his collaboration with the Vichy government during the war and his great and lasting admiration for Pétain. This story, about his political misconduct, was handled rather delicately, as if his belated candor about that event somehow mitigated his unfortunate conduct. And the more recent story about his domestic peccadillo (as it was described) was treated even more sympathetically, as if the civility with which everyone behaved—the wife offering her condolences to his (what does one call her?) "paramour," "mistress"—somehow made that affair more honorable, more estimable, than any conventional monogamous marriage. Candor in the first case, civility in the second—both trumped morality.

There is a common denominator in these stories that is pertinent to our subject today. If we (or at least those reporting on them) can no longer get exercised about collaboration with the Nazis—and this at a time when we are learning more and more about the murderous activities of the French collaborators—it is because we are becoming inured to such atrocities. We are inured partly by habituation; there are so many such stories that we lose our capacity for indignation and outrage. And inured also by conviction; we are so committed to a relativist view of life that we cannot bring ourselves to judge and condemn. How do we know, we ask ourselves, that *we* would have behaved differently under those circumstances? For both reasons, then—out of habit and out of principle—we have become morally insensitive and obtuse. Indeed, it has come to seem almost immoral to pass moral judgments, upon oneself or anyone else.

And so it is with the other Mitterand story, the story of his unconventional (to put it mildly) family life—bigamy, to put it crudely. Now, I am not at all equating the two episodes; there is no moral equivalence for Nazism. But the two cases do have something in common, and that is the pervasive moral relativism that affects our thinking about the most divergent subjects. Even in this congenial group, I sense that it is rather *outré* of me to raise the issue of domestic morality. There I go, I can almost hear it said, being Victorian again. I will probably be told that bigamy was not unknown among the Victorians, and that among the French especially, mistresses have long been a staple of family life. And so they have been—but with a very large difference.

That difference may be illustrated by yet another story about France that appeared in the *Washington Post* only a few weeks after the Mitterand obituary. This story was wittily entitled, "In a Singularly Family Way." The lead paragraph reported on the birth of a child in another of the first families of France—indeed, the very first family, that of President Jacques Chirac. Chirac had just been presented with his first grandchild, and after proudly toasting the event at a ceremony he happened to be attending at the Elysée Palace, he dashed to the hospital to see his heir and congratulate his daughter—his unmarried daughter. Her husband, we are told, had committed suicide some time earlier and she had deliberately set about to have a child; the father, whom she evidently had no intention of marrying, was a former judo champion. (It is not clear, from the *Post* story, whether she was even having an affair with him—a "relationship," as we say.)

From that lead paragraph, the story went on to explain that this was an altogether common experience in France (not the judo champion father, but the unmarried mother)—and, for that matter, elsewhere in Europe. In the past three decades, single-parent families in France have grown five times as fast as two-parent families, and out-of-wedlock births now constitute 36 percent of all births. The article quotes single mothers who praise the state for making it possible for them to have these children by providing generous social services and an $800-a-month stipend for each child; one mother calls it a "tribal support system" reflecting a patriotic desire to have a strong and growing population. Public officials are more wary. "We are not passing any value judgments," says the vice-president of the National Assembly, "but rather evaluating what may be serious risks to society"—risks measured by the higher delinquency, school dropout, and unemployment rates among the two million children living in single-parent families.

It is these statistics that make for a crucial difference between the occasional mistresses of old and the single mothers today. Two million French children living with single parents, a 36 percent illegitimacy rate (the preferred terms in this country are "nonmarital childbearing" and "alternative mode of parenting")—this is quantity transmuted into quality. An entire society is being transformed—not, as was thought for so long in this country, a single class, an underclass, with a distinctive "culture of poverty." When we in this country were confronted with an illegitimacy rate of 32 percent (somewhat lower than France's), we immediately "disaggregated" it, as the sociologists say; we broke it down into a 68 percent black illegitimacy rate and 22 percent white. But France is a much more homogeneous country, and their 36 percent comes not from an underclass but from the working and middle classes. It is they, and the middle classes in particular, who are making illegitimacy and single-parenthood respectable. The Murphy Browns of France are not fictional TV characters, but the real-life mistress of the former president of France and the daughter of the present president. These are formidable role models. In fact, the reality is by now so commonplace that there is no longer any need for role models. The Chirac story attracted little attention in the French press; it was notable only because of the former judo champion who was the father.

Moreover, it is not only France where this is happening. In Britain the illegitimacy rate is much like ours, about 32 percent; in Denmark it is 46 percent; in Sweden almost 50 percent. Even Ireland, where the Catholic Church is stronger than elsewhere in Europe (apart from Italy), the illegitimacy rate is 20 percent. Only in Italy is it relatively low, a little over 7 percent. That last figure is interesting, for it reminds us of a time, not so long ago, when the United States as well as most of Western Europe had illegitimacy rates at that level or lower: In 1960 the rate was 7 percent in France, 5 percent in Britain and the United States, about 2 percent in Italy; even Sweden had only 10 percent. All of those figures are now, only a few decades later, many times higher—as much as five times higher in almost all of these countries.

These figures are interesting for another reason. They tell us that the trend is universal in the West, at least. In this respect, the United States is not the "exceptional" country we sometimes think it is. Everywhere, the decisive starting point for this rapid rise was 1960. Before that, the United States and Europe survived two world wars, a major depression, and momentous technological and social changes, without experiencing any rise in the illegitimacy rate. Nineteen sixty was the magical date when the figures took off. And not only the figures that bear upon the family most immediately—the statistics of illegitimacy, divorce, single-parent families, and "non-marital cohabitation" (as we now call it; "living in sin," our fathers would have said)—but also those revealing the "social pathology" of crime, violence, drug addiction, school dropouts, and welfare dependency.

For a long time we attributed the cultural revolution of the 1960s to the two dramatic events that dominated our own history in that decade: The Civil Rights movement and the Vietnam War, both of which were profoundly subversive of moral and social conventions as well as political authorities. But Europe did not experience those particular events and nevertheless went through the same cultural revolution. We need other explanations to account for it—and perhaps another conference devoted to it. But whatever the reasons for that cultural revolution, it has to be seen in its larger aspect: Not as a cultural revolution but as a moral revolution, and not as a local one but as an international one.

Two final sets of statistics make my point. In 1965, 69 percent of American women and 65 percent of men under the age of thirty (these were not old fogies) said that premarital sex was always or almost always wrong; in 1972, those figures plummeted to 24 percent and 21 percent—69 to 24, 65 to 21—this in seven short years. A more recent set of figures: In 1994, 48 percent of English men and women under the age of thirty-five said they did not believe that there were definite rights and wrongs in life; and 41 percent said that morality always depended on circumstances. The revolution is evidently not only a revolution in behavior; it is a revolution in sensibility affecting every aspect of society.

Everywhere, the same question is raised: Is the condition of the family a consequence of particular social policies—of the generous allowances and services provided in France for single mothers, the tax structure in Sweden that discourages marriage, or the welfare system in this country that encourages illegitimacy? Or is it, as one French official put it, "the natural evolution of morals"?

"The natural evolution of morals"—what a wonderfully reassuring phrase. "Evolution"—how benign that sounds; and "natural"—how can one quarrel with something natural, therefore inevitable? In fact what we are witnessing is not an evolution of morals, natural or otherwise, but a revolution. And not only a cultural and social revolution, not even only a moral revolution, but nothing less than a spiritual revolution. Nietzsche took the measure of that revolution a century ago when he sneered at the "English flatheads," as he called them—John Stuart Mill and George Eliot—who thought it possible to have morality without religion. "They are rid of the Christian God," he said, "and now believe all the more firmly that they must cling to Christian morality." For the moment, Nietzsche granted, "morality is not yet a problem," but it would become a problem, he predicted, when the people discovered that without religion there is no morality. "When one gives up the Christian faith, one pulls the right to Christian morality out from under one's feet."

The "flatheads" of our own day are not people like Mill and Eliot, who seriously tried to substitute a secular morality for a religious one, but churchmen who are so relativistic as to subvert secular morality itself. The bishops of the Church of England were recently surveyed about their priorities. An overwhelming majority of them put adultery, abortion, euthanasia, and homosexuality at the bottom of their list; and the Third World, unemployment, the environment, and politics at the top. I know of no similar survey of religious leaders in this country, but I would not be at all surprised to find the same priorities among our Episcopalian bishops, Unitarian ministers, and Reform rabbis.

A cultural revolution such as we are experiencing can be reversed, or at least abated, by a countercultural revolution. And there are symptoms of the beginnings of such a reversal or abatement in conferences like this sponsored by organizations like this, fortified by the large body of recent literature and social science data demonstrating conclusively the disastrous effects of the breakdown of the family. But if I am right in thinking that what we are experiencing is nothing less than a spiritual revolution, then something more is called for, something like a spiritual counterrevolution. And this too we are beginning to witness, in such events as the mass meetings of "Promise Keepers"—half-a-million men in Washington and fifty thousand or more in city after city, assembled for an entire day of prayer, pledging themselves to familial responsibility and marital fidelity—and paying for the privilege of doing this.

The religious revival in this country is still very much a minority affair. But minorities can be influential far beyond their numbers—all the more so when they are not just religious revivals but, like the current one, moral revivals as well. Until recently I would have said that this was yet another symptom of American "exceptionalism," that there was no evidence of anything like it in Europe. But that may be changing—in England at least, although not yet in France or elsewhere on the Continent.

England has been slower than we have been in coming to terms with what I have called the "de-moralization of society"—a loss not so much of morale as of moral principle and conviction. And there is now talk there, as there is here, of the need for a "re-moralization of society." Margaret Thatcher started the discussion by introducing the idea of "Victorian values," and her successor John Major picked up on that theme by calling for a "return to basics"—basic, traditional values. But it remained for Tony Blair, the leader of the Labour Party—a religious, churchgoing man who sends his children to a Catholic school—to put religion at the heart of those values, and to suggest that Christianity, rather than Marxism, is the proper ideological basis of the Labour credo. He has even been so bold as to resurrect the idea of sin. Sin, he recently said, may seem old-fashioned, but it is a simple and important concept: "In theological terms it is alienation from God. In everyday terms, it is the acknowledgment of right and wrong. It is the rejection of a purely libertarian ethos." (Which prompted one Tory to protest, "What makes Blair think his party has a monopoly on Christianity?")

The British statistics of single-parents, illegitimacy, and the like are appalling, as are ours. But this new ideological turn, suggesting a reversal or diminution of the relativism that has been so pervasive and destructive in our culture, gives some promise for change. One cannot yet speak of a religious-*cum*-moral revival in Britain on the order we are witnessing here, but at least their leaders are not displaying the kind of elegant, urbane cynicism flaunted by Mitterand and Chirac. To a congenital pessimist like myself, that is some small cause for optimism.

4

Delegitimating the Family:
The Classical Liberal Roots

David Wagner

I begin with an anecdotal judgment. If you think about it for a moment, you will probably find—as I most certainly have—that it is rather common to find stories about atrocious parents in the media. Some with whom I have shared this impression have confirmed my suspicion that many late-night television news broadcasts, many tabloids, and even some respectable broadsheets seem to have a Bad Parents Desk, charged with producing at least three stories per week about parents who have murdered, mutilated, or starved their children.

I trust that before a sophisticated audience such as this, there is no need to refute the fallacy that such complaints as I have just made are an unjust attempt to "blame the messenger." When the messenger has enormous discretion as to what messages he brings and what messages he leaves out, as the media do in our country, it would be foolish indeed not to bring a hermeneutic of suspicion to bear on the content of the reportage that they serve up.

But on one point, at least, the media can be defended: They did not start the campaign of which they are a part. Behind them stands a cadre of academics and opinion journalists who attack the family as such, and are ever alert for covert attempts to rehabilitate it.

Thus, for instance, Columbia historian Eric Foner, criticizing Michael Sandel's latest work, *Democracy's Discontent*, in *The Nation*: "Lurking behind these prescriptions one detects nostalgia not only for ordered communities but for the families that once served as their centers."[1] And poor Sandel, who is after all no galloping reactionary, gets blamed for failing to explain "how some notion of justice can be injected into family relationships without reliance on the notion of individual rights."[2]

Columnist and social critic Barbara Ehrenreich devoted one of her *Time* magazine columns two years ago to a sustained attack on the family. While allowing that it can indeed be a "haven in a heartless world," she proceeded to discuss domestic violence for several paragraphs—lumping together nonmarital domestic violence with spouse abuse, properly so-called—and then went on to make clear that a family need not harbor violence to come under her ban. "Even in the ostensibly 'functional,' non-violent family, where no one is killed or maimed, feelings are routinely bruised and twisted out of shape."[3] And lest anyone think Ms. Ehrenreich is merely observing a regrettable reality, rather than threatening all families that fall short of her standards of sensitivity, she winds up her essay as follows:

> We may be stuck with the family—at least until someone invents a sustainable alternative—but the family, with its deep, impacted tensions and longings, can hardly be expected to be the moral foundation of everything else. In fact, many families could use a lot more outside interference in the form of counseling and policing, and some are so dangerously dysfunctional that they ought to be encouraged to disband right away. Even healthy families need outside sources of moral guidance to keep the internal tensions from imploding—and this means, at the very least, a public philosophy of gender equality and concern for child welfare.[4]

Meanwhile, over in Britain, an MP of the party that went on to form the most recent British government called for "a comprehensive approach to integrate education and care into a seamless service for children under five," which approach she deems necessary because "for too long, the early years of a child's life have been seen as the private concern of the parents." This particular MP was said to be personally close to Mr. Tony Blair, Labour leader and now prime minister.[5]

Stepping back from my rogues file, let's take a broader look at where the family stands today. It would be overly alarmist to say that the family has been destroyed in the modern world, or that there are no positive signs of the times for the family as an institution. But the negative signs of the times must be acknowledged. We have, for example:

- A child-protection system that is in many cases trigger-happy about removing children from their parents; provides parents with none of the procedural rights enshrined in the Fourth, Fifth, and Sixth Amendments; and treats all parents as clinical cases, whether removal of children is deemed "indicated" or not.[6]

- Apparently annual United Nations conferences at which, whatever the nominal subject matter may be, a monotonously familiar agenda is urged for pursuit at the world-government level, consisting of universal therapeutic intervention in the lives of children and teens so as to provide them with the "services" deemed necessary in order for them to lead comprehensive sex lives. The documents produced by these conferences envision the relationship between the child and the state-funded therapeutic professionals as absolutely bilateral and free of tiresome intermediaries.[7] Wresting even the most tepid and qualified endorsement of the family from these conferences requires a major expenditure of political capital by the dwindling number of delegations interested in doing so.

- A Supreme Court that has recently held that traditional moral judgments on sexual issues—judgments that were part of the very moral air that Americans breathed as recently as the childhoods of all present members of the Court—are now presumptively unconstitutional when made the basis of legislation.[8]

- Media that saddle defenders of the family with a double marginalization: as "the religious right"—where the word "religious" implies that those so designated have no views that could possibly interest anyone outside their particular sects—and as the "right," which implies a brooding partisanship that is hostile to democracy and probably prone to blowing up buildings.

What is the intellectual pedigree of this highly illiberal situation—and could it have anything to do with historic liberalism? I suspect that the elitist brats at the Bad Parents Desk are sitting on the shoulders of men who were much more intelligent than they, and no less aware of what they were doing.

The Family in Hobbes

Just what the status of the family was in the ancient view is beyond my subject today. Suffice it to say that the famous proposal for spousal communism in Plato's *Republic* was not the majority view of the ancients, or even of Plato, or even—in any practical, party-platform sense—of Socrates in the *Republic*.[9] When Machiavelli, Hobbes, and Locke consulted premodern legal and philosophical sources, they found the family firmly entrenched, when discussed at all.[10] So let us start with Hobbes.

As part of his rejection of the traditional political philosophy, both biblical and classical, Hobbes maintained that the family, like civil society, is a creature of contract rather than of nature. It does not exist in the state of nature, and arises only by a covenant that is itself preceded by force. As Professor Nathan Tarcov observes:

> The fundamental fact about paternal dominion in Hobbes's thought is that it is an instance of acquisition of dominion by force. As such, it is paired with the rule of masters over servants whom they have conquered and then trusted with their liberty in return for an expressed or presumed covenant of obedience.[11]

The closest approximation to a natural foundation for the family in the *Leviathan* is the "natural attraction" of men and women for each other and toward their children:

> But the question lyeth now in the state of meer nature; where there are supposed no lawes of Matrimony; no lawes for the Education of Children; but the Law of Nature, and the naturall inclination of the Sexes, one to another, and to their children.[12]

But these inclinations are only appetites, and life is only a series of appetite fulfillments, each leading to nothing but the next one, as Hobbes declares in certain of the passages in *Leviathan* where he heaps scorn on Christian teleology:

> For there is no such thing as perpetuall Tranquillity of mind, while we live here; because Life it selfe is but Motion, and can never be without Desire, nor without Feare, no more than without Sense. What kind of felicity God hath ordained to them that devoutly honour Him, a man shall no sooner know, than enjoy; being joyes, that now are as incomprehensible, as the word of School-men *Beatificall Vision* is unintelligible.[13]

> For there is no such *Finis ultimus*, (utmost ayme,) nor *Summum Bonum*, (greatest Good,) as is spoken of in the Books of the old Morall Philosophers. Nor can a man any more live, whose Desires are at an end, than he, whose Senses and Imaginations are at a stand. Felicity is a continuall progresse of the desire, from one object to another; the attaining of the former, being still but the way to the later.[14]

In the Hobbesian state of nature, parental rights arise only by contract, though Hobbes concedes, as he must, that in the case of children, contract formation is inferred rather than explicit:

> Dominion is acquired in two wayes; By Generation, and by Conquest. The right of Dominion by Generation, is that, which the Parent hath over his Children; and it is called PATERNALL. And it is not so derived from the Generation, as if therefore the Parent had Dominion over his Child because he begat him; but from the Child's Consent, either expresse, or by sufficient arguments declared. For as to the generation, God hath ordained to man a helper; and there be alwayes two that are equally Parents: The Dominion therefore over the Child, should belong equally to both; and he is equally subject to both, which is impossible; for no man can obey two Masters.[15]

For a pro-family advocate of today, it is no derogation from the family to point out that parental authority is shared by both parents. But perhaps in Hobbes's day, when primogeniture was the rule and the family was more purely patriarchal than today, Hobbes's nod toward gender equality in parenting had a subversive quality that we today are apt to miss.

In any event, Hobbes's scriptural allusion in the above-cited passage—citing "No man can serve two masters"[16] as somehow militating against the joint authority of two parents—cannot be taken seriously. It takes a fool—which Hobbes was very far from being—to think that "no man can serve two masters" is the Scripture text most on point for the relationship of children to parents, when the same Scriptures also say "Honor thy father and mother."[17] As so often when he deals with religion, Hobbes seems here to be patronizing the Christian reader while giggling surreptitiously with his fellow atheists.

There is something else that is sinister in Hobbes's approach, beyond the denial of the natural status of the family (but stemming from it). Hobbes admits that children's consent to the contract must be inferred rather than explicit. But that is not the end of the problem of grounding parental rights in the child's consent. In the common law tradition with which Hobbes was familiar, children who consent to contracts retained an inalienable right to "disaffirm" their contracts, which meant in practice that they generally could not really contract at all.[18] By allowing that they can indeed contract, even if only implicitly, Hobbes is laying the groundwork for the present-day "children's rights" ideology that would adopt a presumption of full consent-giving capacity on the part of children, independent of their parents, up to and including the capacity to sue to "divorce" their parents.[19]

In this context, note must also be taken of Hobbes's teaching that in the state of nature, dominion over children—including the power of life and death over them—belong to the mother:

> If there be no Contract, the Dominion is in the Mother. For in the condition of meer Nature, where there are no Matrimoniall lawes, it cannot be known who is the Father, unlesse it be declared by the Mother: And therefore the right of Dominion over the Child dependeth on her will, and is consequently hers. Again, seeing the Infant is first in the power of the Mother, so she may either nourish it, or expose it; if she nourish it, it oweth its life to the Mother; and is therefore obliged to obey her, rather than any other; and by consequence the Dominion over it is hers.[20]

It cannot escape remark that the Supreme Court's decisions in *Roe v. Wade*[21] and *Planned Parenthood v. Danforth*[22] have essentially held that this state of affairs—which, in fairness to Hobbes, is considered by him as part of pre-civil barbarity—is required by the U.S. Constitution and foundational to our civil order. Of course, in the Hobbesian state of nature, there are no courts to enforce rights. But that is the only consideration that prevents us from maintaining that the children's rights movement and the abortion rights movement, to the extent that they succeed in the courts, are moving us into the Hobbesian state of nature. Perhaps what Hobbes took to be the state of nature is not that at all, but a state of legally enforced barbarism into which civilization falls when its rebellion against nature reaches an advanced stage.

At all events, I tentatively conclude that Hobbes's doctrine relieves Leviathan of a major competitor by making the family a creature of government, and driving between family members the wedge of self-interested contractualism.

The Family in Locke

John Locke makes a different move with the family. To begin with, he chooses to launch his core political works, the *Two Treatises on Government*, as replies to the hyperpatriarchal theories of Sir Robert Filmer's *Patriarcha*. Filmer, defending a doctrine of absolute monarchy beyond what any imperial ideologist of the High Middle Ages would have dared, based all political authority on the paternal authority of Adam. His theory was not that paternal and royal power are analogous, but that they are identical. Notes Tarcov: "For Filmer, however [in contrast to Aristotle], paternal and political power are not merely similar or analogous or related in chronological development; they are simply one and the same."[23]

I see no reason to challenge the consensus that finding fault with Filmer is like shooting fish in a barrel. (For instance, if royal authority and paternal authority are the same, and if one accepts the view that sovereignty is indivisible, then Filmer's theory, far from supporting paternal authority, wipes it out by vesting it all in the sovereign.) One suspects that Locke is after bigger game, such as the patriarchal family, which he means to replace with the democratic family.

Should Locke be considered "anti-family"? There are a number of reasons to answer no. For instance, in contrast to both Hobbes and Filmer, Locke maintains that education is the province of the family, not of the state,[24] which should make him a hero to today's home-school movement. This depoliticization of education is part of Locke's depoliticization of the family. It can be argued that Locke is trying to create a protected zone for the family by creating a radical distinction between the political and the familial, or, to give these spheres their more usual names, the public and the private. In fact, Professor Tarcov, on whom I have relied heavily in this discussion, concludes just that.[25]

One must still ask, however, whether this approach to protecting the family remains tenable at a time when political theorists attack the public-private distinction[26] and political activists declare that "the personal is the political." And one must even ask whether some of the germs of the collapse of the privacy-based protection of the family are to be found in the work of its architect.

Locke grounded the family in the parent's natural desire for "continuing themselves in their posterity,"[27] and in the child's right to self-preservation. These cause the family to be present, at least rudimentarily, even in the state of nature. The first divinely implanted desire in man is self-preservation:

> But next to this, God planted in Men a strong desire also of propagating their Kind, and continuing themselves in their Posterity, and this gives Children a Title, to share in the *Property* of their Parents, and a Right to Inherit their Possessions.[28]

The quantum of parental power that exists in the state of nature passes undiminished into civil society, as Locke makes clear in a key passage in the chapter on paternal power in the *Second Treatise* (chapter 6). In the same passage he also asserts the separateness of "political" and "paternal" power, which is the basis for the separation of public and private:

> *Parents in Societies*, where they themselves are Subjects, retain a *power over their Children*, and have as much right to their Subjection, as those who are in the state of Nature, which could not possibly be, if all Politicall Power were only paternal, and that in truth they were one and the same thing: For then, all Paternal Power being in the Prince, the Subject could naturally have none of it. But these two *Powers, Political and Paternal, are so perfectly distinct* and separate; are built upon so different Foundations, and given to so different Ends, that every Subject that is a Father, has as much Paternal Power over his Children, as the Prince has over his; And every Prince that has Parents owes them as much filial Duty and Obedience as the meanest of his Subjects do to theirs; and can therefore contain not any part or degree of that kind of Dominion, which a Prince, or Magistrate has over his Subject.[29]

This distinction between the political and paternal realms sounds like a fairly air-tight guarantee of the independence of the latter. But—from, say, an Aristotelian viewpoint—are there any screws loose? What about that part about the political and the paternal having different ends? It would be one thing to assert that they are separate and nonfungible means to attain the *same* end, namely, the leading of the good life. But *different ends?*

How long can the family retain any social importance if its *telos* is different from those of the political community? Won't the family eventually come to seem anti-social and anticommunitarian? Is that not exactly what *is* being asserted, for instance, by our British friend Margaret Hodge, with her complaint that "for too long, the early years of a child's life have been seen as the private concern of the parents,"[30] and by our friend in *Time* Magazine, Barbara Ehrenreich, who would like to see families subject to more "outside interference in the form of counseling and policing"?[31]

The difference between political power and the power of parents over their children is that parental power, unlike political, is temporary and, in any event, does not extend to power over their children's lives or property.[32] That it does not extend to children's lives is of course not something I would care to dispute (though I believe it has been disputed within the past decade by parents seeking to withhold routine medical care from their handicapped newborns); and an investigation of what is implied by the notion of children's property would take us too far afield. But let us look more closely at Locke's treatment of the temporary nature of this power.

The power is temporary, because it is based on the children's needs, not the parents' rights.[33] If it is temporary, how long does it last? This would seem a very obvious question, yet Locke avoids it from the point where he first mentions the time limitation on parental power, in § 55, all the way to the end in § 61—and even then he evades it: "If any body should ask me, When my Son is *of Age to be free?* I shall answer, Just when his Monarch is of Age to govern."[34] He then takes refuge in a quotation from "the judicious Hooker"—a favorite device of his for giving his more radical ideas an artificial pedigree. Yet even that quotation evades the issue, declaring merely that attainment of the age of reason is *"a great deal more easie for sense to discern, than for anyone by Skill or Learning to determine."* So we get to the end of § 61 without an answer to the question, and then comes the very short § 62, which still does not tell us what the magic age is, but does, at last, tell us who decides:

> Common-wealths themselves take notice of, and allow that there is a *time when Men* are to *begin to act like Free Men*, and therefore till that time require not Oaths of Fealty, or Allegiance, or other publick owning of, or Submission to the Government of their Countreys.[35]

It is with a certain amount of surprise and alarm that we suspect that for Locke, the great defender of limited government, the decision as to when parental authority over children ceases is assigned to "commonwealths themselves."

Although Locke maintains a limited but real parental jurisdiction over children prior to their reaching the age of reason, and a continuing right of the parents to be honored by their children even after that, and a public/private distinction that seems to insulate paternal power from political power, he nonetheless pokes a hole in that insulation by bringing the principle of equality into the family. In § 54 he reaffirms "the *Equality*, which all Men are in, in respect of Jurisdiction or Dominion one over another." This statement is made as part of the chapter on paternal power: What is it doing there, if not affirming that parental authority is a creature of convenience (or perhaps of children's rights, as he suggests in § 67), rather than of nature or natural law?

At the beginning of § 54 Locke declares that when he said "That all Men are equal by Nature, I cannot be supposed to understand all sorts of *Equality*." He *cannot be supposed* to understand that equality reigns within as well as outside the family—but maybe he *does*. Maybe Professor Mary Walsh is right when she argues that "[w]hile feminists correctly point out some disturbingly patriarchal features of Locke's thought, some also neglect its deeper potential for a radical transformation of patriarchal marriage."[36]

Professor Walsh goes on to maintain that Locke holds all contracts, marital as well as political, to natural law standards, notably the rule against selling oneself into slavery. Given radical feminism's identification of traditional marriage with slavery, Walsh claims a point of contact between them and Locke:

> Locke implicitly recognizes the steps civil government can take to discourage, even outlaw, authoritarian, patriarchal marriages. Liberal politics can actively attack patriarchal marriages which violate this principle of liberty, which violate natural law (the principle of justice in families). Politics, in its legitimate role as a caretaker of these inalienable rights, can and should step into the family to support these rights and to subvert illegitimate marriage contracts.[37]

Since the only concrete example Professor Walsh gives of an intramarital violation of natural law is marital rape, one risks extremely bad visuals by criticizing either her reading of Locke, or Locke himself based on that reading. But hopefully one can ask how far Professor Walsh would take her argument. It is not clear whether the only marriage contracts that would be invalid under a Locke/Walsh analysis are those that allow for marital rape—in which case, why write an entire article trying to sell Locke to feminists?—or whether a marriage based on Ephesians 5:21-33 would also suffice to bring in the Lockean contract-constables to say "What's all this, then?" and arrest the earnest young Christian husband on a natural law rap.

My point here is only that I have not gone nearly as far as others in suggesting that Locke has introduced termites into the foundations of the family.

Tocqueville on the Democratic Family

On the other hand, perhaps Locke has undermined, not the family as such, but only the aristocratic family, as opposed to the democratic family. This would probably be Tocqueville's reading. At any rate, on visiting America, Tocqueville found the aristocratic family gone, but the democratic family thriving, and he seems to believe this is on the whole a good development for the family as such.

Tocqueville notes:

> In America the family, in its Roman and aristocratic signification, does not exist. All that remains of it are a few vestiges in the first years of childhood, when the father exercises, without opposition, that absolute domestic authority which the feebleness of his children renders necessary, and which their interest, as well as his own incontestable superiority, warrants.[38]

So we have the family reduced to Lockean proportions, for Lockean reasons. Tocqueville more or less welcomes this development. For one thing, relations between siblings are now based on common experience and affection, rather than issues of inheritance and feudal relationships:

> It is not, then, by interest, but by common associations and by the free sympathy of opinion that democracies unites brothers to each other. It divides their inheritance, but it allows their hearts and minds to unite.[39]

The position of the father is similarly affected, mostly to the good, by this change:

> In a democratic family the father exercises no other power than that which is granted to the affection and the experience of age; his orders would perhaps be disobeyed, but his advice is for the most part authoritative. Though he is not hedged in with ceremonial respect, his sons at least accost him with confidence; they have no settled form of addressing him, but they speak to him constantly and are ready to consult him every day. The master and the constituted ruler have vanished; the father remains.[40]

Yes, but for how long?

Conclusion

We have come over a half a millennium from a *status quo ante* in which the family had a place in public life—a situation that could indeed lead to injustices, but which gave the family as such real protection—to a situation in which the family is regarded by key policymakers and opinionmakers as an anachronism that continues to exist only because government social services are not yet adequately funded, and in which the legal protections that it still enjoys are either criticized as outmoded or explained away as protection for the "privacy" rights of the family's individual members.

Along the way, we made a transition, which I have tried here to document, to viewing the family as a conventional and legal rather than a natural institution, and as a mere instrumentality for childrearing, implicitly replaceable by others. The family was thus delegitimized, opening the way for its enemies of today.

If we want to be seriously "pro-family," we need to ask some hard questions about liberalism and what it took away from us. Perhaps we cannot restore the patriarchies of republican Rome or medieval Europe, but we can examine them for alternatives to the postmodern therapeutic tyranny that is threatening the family—and human dignity—today.

Notes

1. Eric Foner, "Liberalism's Discontents," *The Nation*, (May 6, 1996): 37.

2. Ibid., p. 38

3. Barbara Ehrenreich, "Oh, Those Family Values," *Time*, (July 18, 1994): 62.

4. Ibid.

5. Minette Marrin, "Don't Let Labour Steal our Babies," *The Sunday Telegraph*, (May 5, 1996): 30.

6. Douglas Besharov, "'Doing Something' About Child Abuse: The Need to Narrow the Grounds for State Intervention," *Harvard Journal of Law and Public Policy* 8, (1985): 539; Richard Wexler, *Wounded Innocents: The Real Victims of the War Against Child Abuse*, (Buffalo: Prometheus Books, 1990); David Wagner, "Defining Deviancy Up: How the Child Protection System Often Harms Families," *Family Policy* monograph (Family Research Council, Washington D.C., 1994).

7. Programme of Action of the United Nations International Conference on Population and Development (Cairo, 1994); Report of the Fourth World Conference on Women (Beijing, 1995).

8. *Romer v. Evans*, 134 L.Ed.2d 855 (1996).

9. Leo Strauss, "Plato," in *History of Political Philosophy*, Leo Strauss and Joseph Cropsey, eds. (Chicago: University of Chicago Press, 1987), 51-52; Leo Strauss, *The City and Man*, (Chicago: University of Chicago Press, 1964), 121-22.

10. On the family in ancient political philosophy, see Judith Swanson, *The Public and the Private in Aristotle's Political Philosophy* (Ithaca: Cornell University Press, 1992).

11. Nathan Tarcov, *Locke's Education for Liberty* (Chicago: University of Chicago Press, 1984), 35.

12. Thomas Hobbes, *Leviathan*, ed. C. B. McPherson, (New York: Penguin, 1985) (orig. 1651) (hereinafter *Leviathan*), 253 (chap. 20).

13. Ibid., p. 130 (chap. 6). Notice the anti-Christian laugh-line here, beyond the obvious dig at the "School-men": If Hobbes is affirming that the Beatific Vision will be "enjoyed" as soon as it is "known," and also that this vision is "unintelligible" and therefore unknowable, he is actually affirming that it will never be enjoyed.

14. Ibid., p. 160 (chap. 11). As it happens, similar views are expressed by Puccini's (and perhaps opera's) greatest villain, Baron Scarpia, in his soliloquy near the beginning of Act II of *Tosca*.

15. Ibid., p. 253 (chap. 20).

16. Matthew 6:24.

17. Exodus 20:12.

18. Allan Farnsworth, *Contracts* (Boston: Little, Brown & Co., 1982), 214-220.

19. Bruce C. Hafen and Jonathan O. Hafen, "Abandoning Children to Their Rights," *First Things*, (August/September 1995): 18.

20. *Leviathan*, p. 254 (chap. 30).

21. 410 U.S. 113 (1973).

22. 428 U.S. 52 (1976).

23. Tarcov, supra n. 4, p. 12.

24. Ibid., chs. 1-2 passim

25. Ibid., p. 210.

26. For example, Susan Moller Okin, *Justice, Gender and Family* (New York: Basis Books, 1988).

27. Locke, *First Treatise of Government* (hereinafter *First Treatise*), § 88, in John Locke, *Two Treatises of Government*, ed. Peter Laslett, (New York: Mentor Books, 1963) (orig. 1698), 244.

28. Ibid.

29. Locke, *Second Treatise of Government* (hereinafter *Second Treatise*), § 71, in John Locke, *Two Treatises of Government*, ed. Peter Laslett, (New York: Mentor Books, 1963) (orig. 1698), 357.

30. Supra n. 5 and accompanying text.

31. Supra ns. 3-4 and accompanying text.

32. *Second Treatise*, § 64, p. 353.

33. Ibid., § 58, p. 348.

34. Ibid., § 61, p. 351.

35. Ibid., § 62, pp. 351-2.

36. Mary B. Walsh, "Locke and Feminism of Public and Private Realms of Activities," *The Review of Politics* 57 no. 2 (Spring 1995): 264.

37. Ibid., pp. 267-8.

38. Alexis de Tocqueville, *Democracy in America*, tr. Henry Reeve/Francis Bowen, ed. Phillips Bradley, (New York: Vintage Books, 1945) (orig. 1835) (hereinafter *Democracy in America*), Vol. II, Bk. III, ch. VIII, 202.

39. Ibid., p. 207.

40. Ibid., pp. 205-6.

5

The State's Assault on the Family

Allan Carlson

No task is more important, these days, than finding a way to clarify the authentic issues behind today's confusing phrase, "family values." On the one hand, in her new book, *It Takes a Village*, Hillary Clinton claims to stand for "family values" and, according to a recent Congressional floor speech, so does Congressman Barney Frank. On the other hand, the Republican authors of the "Contract for America" also stand foursquare behind "family values" and so, we are told, does General Colin Powell. We can only be sure that they cannot all mean the same thing.

So it is important, I believe, for any analyst to begin with a clear statement of what he or she means by "family." I firmly reject, at the outset, the standard contemporary view that the family is "changing" or "evolving" into new forms better suited to modern life. My own study and experience tell me that family structure of a certain kind is rooted in human nature: in our genetic inheritance; in our instincts; in our hormones. The human family is no more subject to rapid change than is the instinctual blink of the eye, or the shiver down the spine. The so-called "changes" we observe in family living are either *deterioration* from a natural order, or *restoration* toward that order: decay or renewal. Holy Scripture affirms these truths, and so do the modern sciences of sociology and psychology, sociobiology and paleoanthropology.

This means that in all corners of the globe, and in every historical age, the human family can be defined as a man and a woman in a socially approved covenant called marriage, for the purposes of mutual care and protection, for sexual intimacy, for the begetting and rearing of children, for the construction of a small home economy of shared production and consumption, and for assuring the continuity of the generations: those coming before, those here now, and those to come. The scientific and historical records tell us that the primary free cultural choice is between monogamy and polygamy; that is, a society can choose between a system of one husband bonded to one wife, or one husband bound to multiple wives. Within the civilization known as Christendom, monogamy has been the rule.

Over the last 150 years, it is true that the natural family has faced extraordinary pressures from two sources: first, from the so-called "permanent revolution" of modern industrial capitalism; and second, from the exponential growth of the modern state. My purpose today is to explore the latter challenge—that of the Leviathan state to the family—through several episodes in American history: two in the nineteenth century, and two in the twentieth.

We need to begin, though, by appreciating the central place of the natural family in our nation's past. Some writers have claimed that the family has always been weak in America—that, in contrast to Europe, we Americans have been individualists from the beginning, without strong ties to kin or community. Yet more systematic investigations of our social history over the last few decades have revealed a very different picture of the American nation in its formative years, 1775 to 1825:

A primary quality of life in this time was the dominance of the family economy. Most Americans organized their economic lives around the family in the home. It is important to note that about 90 percent of Americans in 1800 lived on self-sufficient farms. Even those Americans found in towns and villages made most of their own goods, from candles to clothes, and raised and preserved most of their own food. Fathers enjoyed the legal possession of property and counted their own children as part of the family enterprise. In turn, adults were dependent on the children for support in old age. In this home-centered economy, men and women performed different, although mutually necessary tasks focused on survival of the household as both a biological and economic unit.[1]

The second quality of American social life was the power of religious communities and kin over individuals. Loyalties to extended families—to grandparents, to aunts and uncles, to cousins—remained strong, as did the sense of community given by churches.[2]

The third quality of American social life was the importance of land and the desire to pass family property onto the next generation. In a study of eastern Pennsylvania, for example, one historian found a population committed to the creation of families and the rearing of children as "tender plants growing in the Truth." Land ownership was the central family project, not as a speculative venture, but as the necessary foundation for the Godly home, and for the preservation of one's prosperity.[3]

The fourth quality of American social life was the abundance of children. America, in 1800, was a land swarming with children. One-half of the whole population, at that time, was age fifteen or under, a situation seen today only in a few high-fertility lands such as Kenya. The average American women of that time bore more than seven live children (today, by way of contrast, the average number is under two).[4]

The fifth quality of traditional American social life was the power of intergenerational bonds. As one historian has explained, parents of this era raised children to "succeed them," not merely to "succeed." Duties and rights criss-crossed the generations and the sexes, as the family unit strove to perpetuate itself into the future. Its members understood the family as setting constraints on their individual desires, and as binding them both to the past, and to the future.[5]

The sixth quality of traditional American life was the family's role as the chief educator of children: morally and practically. Home-centered learning included Bible studies and moral instruction, commonly in the hands of fathers; the transmission of intellectual skills necessary to self-sufficient living; and craft apprenticeships structured *within* the family context. When specialists were needed, tutors might be called in, a private scholar retained by several families, or larger schools founded and controlled by the families themselves.[6]

This was an era, I might note, when divorce was almost unknown, when basic literacy was at a peak, when a jealous defense of liberty was strong, and when the state was shackled and modest in its claims.

Appropriately enough, the first major challenge by the state to this family-centered American world came in the field of education. A majority of us, I suspect, are public school graduates, and absorbed along the way the historical myth behind state education—that the public schools sprang up as a valued adjunct to the new American republic, spreading enlightenment, unity, and virtue across the land, while protecting the interests of families and immediate communities by vesting control in local school boards.

In fact, from the very beginning, public school advocates aimed—as they had to—at undermining and displacing the family as the center of children's lives. The so-called "grandfather" of state education in America was Benjamin Rush, a Philadelphia physician, signer of the Declaration of Independence, and philosophical zealot and dreamer. In a 1786 essay, "Thoughts Upon the Mode of Education proper in a Republic," Rush parted company from the education theories of Thomas Jefferson and described a different vision of learning. He began by removing the family from its central role, to be replaced by government:

> Our country includes family, friends, and property, and the state should be preferred to them all. Let our pupil be taught to love his family, but let him be taught at the same time that he must forsake even forget them when the welfare of his country requires it.

Rush was also unusually candid about the kind of taxpayer that this new system would need: "[the young person] must be taught to amass wealth, but it must be *only* to increase his power of contributing to the wants and demands of the state." Adopting an industrial metaphor, Rush called for public schools that would "convert men into republican machines" who might "perform their parts properly in the great machine of the government of the state."[7]

The "father" of modern public schooling, Horace Mann of Massachusetts, held the same attitudes. Citing the "neglect," ignorance, and inefficiencies of families in his state, he emphasized the brutality of what he labeled "monster families." Mann was equally direct in proposing the solution. "Our common schools," he wrote in 1845, "are a system of unsurpassable grandeur and efficiency. Their influences . . . reach all the children belonging to the State,—children who are soon to be the State. They act upon these children at the most impressible period of their existence." A year later, 1846, Mann linked the "common school" system to a vision of the total welfare state, where government simply assumed the *role of parent*, for all citizens. As he wrote: "Massachusetts is *parental* in her government. More and more, as year after year rolls by, she seeks to substitute prevention for remedy, and rewards for penalties."[8]

The *Common School Journal*, founded by Mann and friends in 1838, featured the denigration of family life as one of its regular themes. Contemplate these passages, chosen at random:

— "the little interests or conveniences of the family" must be subordinate to "the paramount subject" of the school [1841];[9]

— the public schools succeed because "parents, although the most sunken in depravity themselves, welcome the proposals and receive with gratitude the services of . . . moral philanthropy in behalf of their families" [1841];[10]

— "there are many worthless parents" [1841];[11]

— "[T]hese are . . . illustrations of the folly of a parent, who interferes with and perplexes a teacher while instructing or training his child" [1846];[12]

— "Worse still,—there are parents, who, with an obstinacy unaccountable, set themselves against the efforts made to recall them to integrity . . . [who] have declaimed against the right of the trustees to compel their children to attend [the state] school, and against the competency of the teachers, have protested at thus being dragooned out of their liberties—with more of such lamentable infatuation" [1841];[13]

— and finally, "Parents must cease to regard wealth as the best inheritance they can leave to their children" [1849]; better that this family wealth be used to expand the common schools.[14]

These twisted sentiments spread with public education across the country over the middle decades of the nineteenth century. John Swett, superintendent of the California state schools from 1863 to 1869, was firm and open in his opinion that the state must replace the family. As he wrote: "Children arrived at the age of maturity belong, not to the parents, but to the State, to society, to the country."[15] Swett maintained that this gave the state the right to reach back into the early home as well, to tend and guide its *future* property. In his 1864 report to the California state legislature, Swett explained that "the child should be taught to consider his instructor, in many respects, superior to the parent in point of authority. . . . The vulgar impression that parents have a legal right to dictate to teachers is entirely erroneous. . . . Parents have no remedy as against the teacher."[16]

F. W. Parker, the so-called "father of progressive education" and inspiration for John Dewey, told the National Education Association that "the child is not in school for knowledge. He is there to live, and to put his life, nurtured in the school, into the community."[17] Understand his meaning: The state schools were not for training in intellectual and practical skills, but were quasi-religious, political vehicles for the restructuring of man and society, at the expense of the family. As Parker explained: "Every school in the land should be *a home and haven* for children."

It is tempting to dismiss such words as the overblown rhetoric of professors and bureaucrats, unrelated to what schools were actually doing. But there is direct evidence linking the spread of public education to family decay. Fertility levels, or the readiness of couples to bear children, is a particularly sensitive measure of family health and stress. Researchers had long been puzzled by the sharp decline in the U.S. birthrate between 1850 and 1900. Throughout this period, the United States remained predominately rural and absorbed masses of new immigrants, situations normally tied to many babies. But in 1983, two sociologists showed that the spread of *mass state education* in these years was the cause of declining family numbers.[18] Data from between 1871 and 1900 revealed a remarkably strong negative relationship between fertility and an index of public school growth. The more average number of days that children attended public school and the higher the percentage of children enrolled, the *lower* the family size in those districts. Even in rural areas, where children retained some economic value as farm workers, the researchers found that *each additional month* that children attended public school *reduced family size* by .23 children. In a very real sense, then, state control of primary education consumed children and weakened families.

Norman Ryder, the chief demographer at Princeton University, explains why, in an essay for *The Population Bulletin of the United Nations.*[19] Reviewing the experience of dozens of nations with mass state education systems, he writes: "Education of the junior generation is a subversive influence. . . . Boys who go to [state] schools distinguish between what they learn there and what their fathers teach them. The reinforcement of the [family] control structure is undermined when the young are trained outside the family for specialized roles in which the father has no competence." As Ryder explains: "Political organizations, like economic organizations, demand loyalty and attempt to neutralize family particularism. There is a struggle between the family and the state for the minds of the young." In this contest, the government school serves as "the [state's] chief instrument for teaching citizenship, in a direct appeal to the children over the heads of their parents." The school communicates a "state morality" and a "state mythology" that intentionally subvert families.

A second and related episode in the American past that I wish to explore is the emergence of the doctrine of "parens patriae."

A disturbing aspect of U.S. educational history is the close linkage between early public schooling and the first juvenile reformatories. The advocates of these institutions and their lobbying organizations were commonly one and the same. Both the New York Free School Society and the Boston House of Refuge claimed to see hordes of children "reared up by parents who . . . are indifferent to the best interests of their offspring" or "unable to exercise any moral government." The so-called "charity schools" they proposed would be the first major effort to "socialize" the children of the poor into a new way of life.[20]

Toward this end, New York City adopted the Lancasterian model of reform schooling, named after its creator, the English schoolmaster Joseph Lancaster. These schools collected up to one thousand children from poor families, placed them in one vast room, and regimented them in military formation. A *single* teacher would instruct monitors in reading, simple sums, or spelling, and these monitors would in turn fan out and transfer the information to the pupils in their charge. Strict discipline, including the suspension of noisy students in bags on a flagpole, kept order. By the late 1820s, over a dozen U.S. cities or states operated Lancaster schools. DeWitt Clinton, the Governor of New York, was effusive in his praise: "I recognize in Lancaster the benefactor of the human race. I consider his system . . . a blessing sent down from heaven to redeem the poor and distressed of this world." Ellwood P. Cubberley, the great conventional historian of public education, declared the Lancaster schools to be the direct inspiration for the public school campaign.[21]

But the dark side of the reform school movement grew increasingly apparent. With mounting frequency, the children of the poor were taken from homes against the will of parents and without any evidence of wrongdoing, for incarceration in reform schools, to "prevent" them from entering a life of crime. Immigrant children, particularly from the new wave of Irish Catholics arriving on American shores, became the favorite targets, as Yankee elites sought to retain social control. In 1839, the Pennsylvania Supreme Court broke with the liberties embodied in English common law, and declared such actions constitutional. Twisting an ancient concept of English chancery law designed to protect the estates of orphaned minors, the court established a new doctrine in American jurisprudence: *parens patriae*, literally "the parenthood of the state." In supporting the termination of parental rights, the justices stated: "May not the natural parents, when unequal to the task of education or unworthy of it, be supplanted by the *parens patriae*, or common guardianship of the community?"[22] This elevation of the state over the family rapidly expanded into a sweeping usurpation of American liberties. As the Illinois Supreme Court ruled in 1882:

It is the unquestioned right and imperative duty of every enlightened government, in its character of *parens patriae*, to protect and provide for the comfort and well-being of such of its citizens, as, by reason of infancy, defective understanding, or other misfortune or infirmity, are unable to take care of themselves. The performance of this duty is justly regarded as one of the most important governmental functions, and all constitutional limitations must be so understood and construed so as not to interfere with its proper and legitimate exercise.[23]

Roughly translated: The family in America no longer enjoyed constitutional protection.

From this fundamental usurpation of parental rights would grow a series of assaults on family integrity, including the juvenile justice system of the 1890s and the child abuse and neglect enforcement machinery of the 1990s. But the evidence, ably summarized by Anthony Platt in his book *The Child Savers*, shows that these programs not only disrupted families, smashed authentic cultural diversity, and diminished constitutional liberties but also aggravated the very problems of delinquency and urban disorder that they were supposed to solve.[24]

For the third episode in state-family relations, I want to jump ahead to our century, the twentieth, and examine the influence of the state on relations between women and men.

The paleoanthropologists offer mounting evidence that human males and females have a "natural affinity" toward each other, a desire to be together that goes beyond the sexual act. They argue that monogamous pair-bonding, intensified parenting relationships, and specialized sexual and reproductive roles are behavioral traits *defining* the human species for over one million years.[25] This seems to be an evolutionist's way of understanding the biblical language of "two becoming one flesh."

The modern state, though, shall put asunder what nature and nature's God have joined together. This might be seen most concretely in modern employment patterns, which have a peculiar relationship to the modern welfare state.

The best data here come from outside the United States, specifically from Denmark, a small laboratory-like nation where the welfare state is more complete. There, the number of female homemakers declined by 579,000 between 1960 and 1981. Over the same years, the number of female employees in the Danish public sector climbed by 532,000, with most of the growth in just four areas: day care, elder care, hospitals, and schools. Roll these numbers together, and the process emerges primarily as one of women moving from tasks of family-centered "home production" to the same tasks performed now for the government. But there are obvious differences. First, the women do these tasks less efficiently because the objects of their attention are nonfamily members in whom they have no stake. And, second, their labor has now been transferred from the private family to the state, and must be paid for by taxation.

Recently, feminist analysts in America have abandoned their once fashionable "New Left," antistate pretensions and have become brutally blunt in their embrace of the welfare state as the *only* possible vehicle for their ideological success. Carole Pateman, for example, now argues that women's *dependence on the state* is preferable to dependence on individual men, since women need not "live with the state" or sleep with the state, as they must do if bonded to the male creature.[26]

Francis Fox Piven is equally frank in her stated preference for what she calls *public patriarchy*, instead of *private patriarchy*. Public patriarchy, she argues, offers a better venue for the exercise of female power. She adds: "Women have also developed a large and important relationship to the welfare state as employees of these programs. By 1980, fully 70 percent of the 17.3 million [American] social service jobs on all levels of government were held by women, accounting . . . for the larger part of female job gains since 1960."[27] So while it seems true that women living under a system of *public patriarchy* will not have to cohabit with the state, they *will* have to work for it.

The stark lesson here resembles the title of sociologist Steven Goldberg's infamous book: The inevitability of patriarchy. Steely-eyed feminist analysis makes the only choice plain and clear: Will that patriarchy be private? Or public?

The fourth, and final, episode I wish to examine involves the bonds between generations of a family—specifically, the effect of Social Security on family structure.

Analysts from the United States, Australia, and New Zealand have identified a common pattern to our nations' recent histories—what might be called "the two welfare states."[28] The first welfare state emerged after World War II, in the late 1940s, and was designed to help young couples and their children. Payroll tax rates for such families were low, while child tax deductions or allowances were generous. Young families, in America as in Australia, also had access to government subsidized mortgages and housing, which encouraged family formation and fertility.

Yet this "Youth State" of the 1945-1970 era gave way to the second welfare state, or the "Elder State," of the post-1970 period. The welfare system now became a vehicle for aiding the relatively old: large and generously indexed state pensions unrelated to earlier and low social security "contributions," fully subsidized health care, favored tax treatment, and an array of other special programs for those over age sixty.

The critical fact to know about the "two welfare states" is that one generation has been the principle beneficiary of both: persons born in the period 1915 to 1935. They gained dramatically from the benefit package available under the "Youth State," 1945-1970; and they have gained dramatically under the "Elder State" of the last twenty five years. The losers in these transfers were the generations born before 1915, who founded the "Youth State," and generations born in the 1950s and after, who are now funding the "Elder State," with little hope of its continuation. One researcher calculates that couples from the second losing age group (such as young people today) will have to work at least fifteen more years than couples born in the favored 1920s, to enjoy comparable real incomes. Converting this disparity between generations into dollars per average household, the generation born in the 1920s will enjoy a gain of $500,000 or more over their lifetimes from state transfers, while the poor souls born in the 1960s and 1970s will suffer an average half-million-dollar loss per household.

On top of this, married households composed of adults born in the 1950s and 1960s are expected to support, through taxes and welfare, single mothers and their children. The so-called "single-parent family" will enjoy a net average gain of $100,000, or more, under current law.

With the old cosseted by the "Elder State," and with the Unmarried-with-Children cohabiting with the Provider State, only younger married couples are left to pay the bills. In the calculations that Alan Tapper has done for Australia, the annual average cost for the "Elder and Illegitimacy States" is between $10,000 and $15,000 per intact household. The figure for Americans is at least as high. To meet these costs, younger couples are driven to deeper immersion in the industrial economy (that is, toward the "two-career family") and they are likely to forego additional, or any, children. The state has successfully driven a deep wedge of interest and security between the generations.

By way of contrast, under a truly free order, the economic incentives bind the generations of a family tightly together. Each generation has a vested interest in the success of those going before, and those coming after. This takes form in the communal nature of family wealth, in security centered on family relations, and in retention by the family of the talents of progeny.

But the cynic responds that such principles are no longer possible, given the complexities of the modern world. It is true, he says, that the state has displaced the family as an educational, security, and welfare unit. But this was inevitable in an age of advanced capitalism.

To which I always reply with my favorite countercultural example: The Old Order Amish.

The Amish community violates every modern rule. Relative to the industrial economy, they use true horsepower rather than tractors in their fields. They rely on horse and buggy for transport, rather than auto and truck. They make their own clothes and furniture. They avoid credit. They resist most uses of electricity and electronic devices. And they build and sell products using considerable hand labor, dedicated to craftsmanship.

Relative to the state, self-employed Amish are, at their request, exempt from Social Security and Medicare. The Amish refuse welfare, relying instead on family savings or help from their neighbors and relatives in time of crisis. They keep their children out of state schools, operating their own schools through the eighth grade, after which the children learn trades from their parents. Indeed the Amish shamelessly exploit child labor from age three on, and they maintain segregated gender roles in all aspects of labor and life.

Living by such rules in twentieth century America, the Amish should have disappeared long ago. Instead, the Amish population has grown from 5,000 in 1900, found primarily in Pennsylvania and Ohio, to 150,000 today, found in colonies in a dozen American states. To place this growth in context, it is important to remember that the overall U.S. farm population *fell* from 35 million to 2.5 million over these same years. Using even the modern scientific measure of success—numbers—I ask: Who succeeded here? And who failed?

Someone, though, will surely ask in shocked tones: Do you mean to imply that we should all become Amish?

Well, I can imagine worse fates for the world, but that is not my message.

This is the lesson I draw from the Amish example: *We do not have to live as we do*, in a regime of mounting family and social disorder and continuous state growth. The modern economy does not make inevitable only one pattern of life. That determinist belief was among the great errors of the Marxists.

The natural family can thrive in our age, *if the oppressive centralization* of the state can be resisted or reversed. The Amish show one way. The burgeoning "home schooling" movement shows another, as families reclaim the educational function after 150 years of retreat before the aggressor state. In every case, the key actions are for families:

— To unmask the myths surrounding the growth of the state;
— to understand that true liberty means resisting the state's siren song of "we're here to help" and rejecting the subsidies that constitute dependence;
— and to take hold, with confidence, those responsibilities that do belong within the natural family.

Notes

1. See James A. Henretta, "Families and Farms: *Mentalité* in Pre-Industrial America," *William and Mary Quarterly* 35 (Jan. 1978): 20-21; Daniel Blake Smith, "The Study of the Family in Early America: Trends, Problems, and Prospects," *William and Mary Quarterly* 39 (Jan. 1982): 15,24; and Christopher Clark, "Household Economy, Market Exchange and the Rise of Capitalism in the Connecticut Valley, 1800-1860," *Journal of Social History* 13 (1979): 169-90.

2. John Demos, *A Little Commonwealth: Family Life in Plymouth Colony* (New York: Oxford University Press, 1970): 77-78; and Daniel Snydacker, "Kinship and Community in Rural Pennsylvania," *Journal of Interdisciplinary History* 13 (Summer 1982): 41-61.

3. Barry Levy, "'Tender Plants': Quaker Farmers and Children in the Delaware Valley, 1681-1735," *Journal of Family History* 3 (Summer 1978): 116-29; Philip J. Greven, Jr., *Four Generations: Population, Land, and Family in Colonial Andover, Massachusetts*, (Ithaca, NY: Cornell University Press, 1970); and Henretta, "Families and Farms," 9, 12-15, 18-19, 28-29.

4. Daniel Scott Smith, "The Demographic History of Colonial New England," *Journal of Economic History* 32 (1972): 165, 179-82; Ansley J. Coale and Melvin Zelnick, *New Estimates of Fertility and Population in the United States* (Princeton, NJ: Princeton University Press, 1963); and Maris Vinovskis, *Fertility in Massachusetts from the Revolution to the Civil War* (New York: Academic Press, 1981).

5. See: Henretta, "Families and Farms," 26, 30; Greven, *Four Generations*, 221, 253-58; and John E. Crowley, "The Importance of Kinship: Testamentary Evidence from South Carolina," *Journal of Interdisciplinary History* 16 (1986): 576-77.

6. Joel Spring, *The American School, 1642-1985: Varieties of Historical Interpretation of the Foundations and Development of American Education* (New York and London: Longman, 1986): 23-24; and Ian M. G. Quimby, *Apprenticeship in Colonial Philadelphia* (New York: Garland, 1985).

7. Benjamin Rush, "Plan for the Establishment of Public Schools [1786]," reprinted in Frederick Rudolph, ed., *Essays on Education in the Early Republic* (Cambridge, MA: The Belknap Press of Harvard University, 1965): 14, 17.

8. Horace Mann, "Challenges to a New Age [1845]," in Lewis Filler, ed., *Horace Mann on the Crisis of Education* (Yellow Springs, OH: The Antioch Press, 1965): 86; and Horace Mann, "The Ground of the Free School System [1846]," in *Old South Leaflets*, No. 109 (Boston, MA: Old South Meeting House, 1902): 12-14, 17-18.

9. Horace Mann, "Fourth Annual Report of the Secretary of the Board of Education," *The Common School Journal* 3 (December 1, 1841): 359.

10. Dr. Chalmers, "The Power of Education," *The Common School Journal* 3 (September 1, 1841): 269.

11. "Extract from the Christian Review for March, 1841," *The Common School Journal* 3 (May 1, 1841): 143.

12. "Duty of Parents to Cooperate with Teachers," *The Common School Journal 8* (August 1, 1846): 226.

13. "Extracts from the Report of the Charleston School Committee," *The Common School Journal* 11 (June 15, 1841): 187.

14. William G. Crosby, "Duty of Parents to See That the Appropriations for Education are Liberal," *The Common School Journal* 11 (November 15, 1849): 349-50.

15. John Swett, *History of the Public School System of California* (San Francisco: Bancroft, 1876): 115; from Rousas John Rushdoony, *The Messianic Character of American Education* (Philadelphia: Presbyterian and Reformed Publishing Company, 1963): 79.

16. In Rushdoony, *Messianic Character,* 80-81.

17. Francis Wayland Parker, "Response," *N.E.A. Journal* (1895): 62; in Rushdoony, *Messianic Character,* p. 104.

18. Avery M. Guest and Steward E. Tolnay, "Children's Roles and Fertility: Late Nineteenth Century United States," *Social Science History* 7 (1983): 355-80.

19. Norman Ryder, "Fertility and Family Structure," *Population Bulletin of the United Nations* 15 (1983): 18-32.

20. Spring, *The American School,* 50-55.

21. Ellwood P. Cubberley, *Public Education in the United States: A Study and Interpretation of American Educational History* (Boston: Houghton Mifflin, 1919): 90-95.

22. *Ex Parte Crouse,* 4 Wharton, Pa. 9 (1838).

23. *County of McLean v. Humphreys,* 104, Ill. 383 (1882).

24. Anthony Platt, *The Child Savers: The Invention of Delinquency* (Chicago: University of Chicago Press, 1969).

25. C. Owen Lovejoy, "The Origin of Man," *Science* 211 (23 January 1981): 348.

26. Carole Pateman, "The Patriarchal Welfare State," in A. Gutmann, ed., *Democracy in the Welfare State* (Princeton, NJ: Princeton University Press, 1988): 231-60.

27. Francis Fox Piven, "Ideology and the State: Women, Power, and the Welfare State," in Linda Gordon, ed., *Women, the State, and Welfare* (Madison: University of Wisconsin Press, 1990).

28. For a good summary of this work, see Alan Tapper, "Family Changes in a Transformed Welfare State," *The Family in America* 9 (Jan. 1995).

6

Rawlsian and Feminist Critiques of the Traditional Family

Celia Wolf-Devine

The future of the family has become an increasingly important issue recently. The rate of family breakdown has been skyrocketing, and many people are worried about the damaging effects this change is having on children. A bitter debate is raging over what we ought to do about the increasing fragility and instability of the family; some regard the family as an oppressive, patriarchal institution (and therefore welcome evidence pointing to its demise), while others regard it as our main bulwark against social chaos and advocate measures to shore up families. Among social and political philosophers also, the family is coming in for more attention than it has for a long time. On the whole, critics of the traditional family among philosophers appear to be more numerous, or at least more vocal, than its defenders. What I propose to do here is to sketch briefly some of the most common objections to the traditional family and see what answers can be offered to them. In general, I conclude that although critics do make some legitimate criticisms, they fail to establish that there is something morally defective about the traditional family as such. In order to show this, I will in each case try to uncover and criticize problematic assumptions underlying their arguments.

First, however, it is necessary to clarify what is meant by the "traditional family" in the context of the current debate. Certainly in its most central sense a family arises when a heterosexual couple produces a child who is the genetic offspring of both of them. The concept has been extended to include childless married couples, and couples who have adopted children or obtained them through the use of a sperm donor or surrogate mother (although in each of these cases dispute is possible). A variety of other morally important relationships develop out of this core, such as those between siblings, between aunts and uncles and their nieces and nephews, between grandparents and grandchildren, and between cousins of various degrees of closeness. Traditionalists wish to retain this core concept of family and reject suggestions by cultural radicals that homosexual couples or group marriages, for example, be recognized as "families."

Furthermore, a great many of those who defend the "traditional family" would add the provision that a traditional family is one in which the mother has the primary, although not the sole, responsibility for homemaking and for care of the children, while the father is the primary breadwinner (although he is also expected to spend as much time with his children as his job allows). A smaller number of them would also include in their definition of the traditional family the idea that the husband is, in some sense, the "head of the family," and rightly exercises (at least nominal) authority over his wife and children, but I will not discuss this aspect of the family.

Criticisms of the Traditional Family

Criticisms of the traditional family fall into two broad categories: those made by feminists who argue that it is damaging to *women* in particular, and those made by people who argue that it is morally defective for other reasons. Feminist criticisms, in turn, fall into three groups: (1) the claim that it is bad for women because it prevents them from realizing their full humanity as free, self-creating beings (the existentialist critique); (2) the claim that it maintains male dominance and female subordination (the radical feminist critique); and (3) the claim that it is unjust to women (the liberal feminist critique).

Criticisms of the family that do not focus on its effect on women in particular have taken many forms, but the only one I will consider here is the claim that the family is unjust because it makes it impossible for society to provide all citizens with genuinely equal opportunity to succeed (a claim which is suggested by Rawls in his influential *Theory of Justice*, although he himself does not go so far as to recommend the abolition of the family). Considerable common ground exists between liberal feminists and the Rawlsians, so I will discuss them together. I begin with a quick discussion of the existentialist feminists and the radical feminists, indicating briefly why I believe their criticisms of the family are not persuasive, and then move on to a more detailed examination of the Rawlsian critique of the family and the way it has been developed in a feminist direction by Susan Moller Okin.

Feminist Existentialist Criticism

Simone de Beauvoir, one of the founding mothers of contemporary feminism, was extremely critical of the institution of marriage and believed that traditional sex roles dehumanize women. In order to understand why she thought that they do so, we need to look at her metaphysical assumptions. Underlying her criticism of the traditional family is her commitment to existentialism, a philosophy that values above all the ability human beings have to transcend our merely biological nature and be autonomous, free, self-creating beings. She believes that women are less able to develop and exercise their autonomy than men, and are thus condemned to be second-class citizens, unable to fully realize their humanity in the way men are. The problem according to her is both biological and social. Pregnancy is particularly degrading; the pregnant woman is "ensnared by nature," and feels "the immanence of her body." This stands in contrast with "the transcendence of the artisan, of the man of action."[1] De Beauvoir hopes that new medical technologies will at last free women from the burden of pregnancy. Being a woman is more than biology, however, and De Beauvoir also argues that the bourgeois institutions of marriage and family restrict women's potential for being free, creative and autonomous. Since her argument is at bottom a metaphysical one, the preferences of women themselves have no weight, and those who enjoy childrearing and homemaking are to be censured for having abdicated their full humanity.

My response to this criticism is twofold. (1) Why should we accept the existentialist ideal at all? Why should being autonomous, free, self-creating beings who are able to radically transcend their bodies be regarded as the highest realization of our humanity? Why not instead affirm the importance and value of the body, celebrate our interconnectedness with others, and regard our capacity for relationships of love and friendship as especially (or at least equally) central to our fulfillment as human beings? (2) If one looks at the life of most human beings instead of concentrating on a narrow intellectual elite, it is clear that the kinds of things most men do are really no more creative than what the average "housewife" does. Indeed, childrearing affords more possibilities for creativity than most people's jobs. This is not, of course, to say that there are not many sources of fulfillment for women other than childrearing and homemaking, or that those who want to pursue them should not be encouraged to do so. My point is merely that traditional women's work does not necessarily afford less opportunity for creativity and self-expression than the kinds of work most men do.

Radical Feminist Criticisms

What is distinctive about radical feminists' criticisms of the traditional family is that, unlike liberals who think in terms of justice, their central focus is on power. They seek to expose the ways in which the traditional family maintains male dominance and female subordination. In doing this, they analyze not only economic or political institutions but also the intimate emotional and sexual dimensions of male-female relationships in terms of how they distribute power. Thus Sandra Lee Bartky,[2] for example, explores the way in which women are disempowered through their emotional caregiving in marriage. Women provide emotional sustenance to men (feeding egos and tending wounds) in a way men do not provide it to women, she argues, and this pattern contributes in an important way to the construction of women as inferior in the gender hierarchy. Other radical feminists find the source of women's subordination in the act of heterosexual intercourse itself (Andrea Dworkin,[3] for example), and most of these women advocate female separatism. Regardless of exactly how they understand the specific mechanisms through which women are subordinated, they all agree that their goal is promoting the power and autonomy of women.

Their criticisms of the traditional family can be addressed on a number of different levels. To the extent that autonomy and independence from men are central to them, the same objection I raised against existentialist feminists holds—namely, that there is no reason to accord autonomy and independence quite such a dominant place in one's vision of the good life. There are goods that can be attained in relationships of interdependence, and even in ones that involve one-sided dependence, such as caring for infants or those who are seriously ill. In addition, radical feminists all too often interpret autonomy in a shallow materialistic way. Women, like men, must form their own consciences and take responsibility for the principles on which they act (this sort of autonomy is important for every human being), but this is quite a different thing from merely having one's own paycheck and doing whatever one feels like doing.

Another important problem with radical feminist analysis of the family is that it analyzes all human relationships exclusively in terms of dominance and subordination—in a word, power. The vast majority of radical feminists, thus, subscribe to an essentially Nietzschean vision of the world. Whereas classical liberal feminists believed in justice, reason, truth, and a common human nature, radical feminists think in terms of a struggle of wills to power in which the victor gets to impose his or her vision of reality on others. All talk of truth, reason, or justice is, on this view, merely a mask for the will to power. I find it hard to understand why adopting this sort of theoretical framework could be thought to be beneficial to women, since it undercuts any attempt to criticize existing institutions as unjust. To the extent that radical feminism is viewed as simply promoting the power of women as such, it seems highly unlikely that many men will be persuaded to support it (as many men did and do support the liberal feminist demands for fairness and justice). And in a situation of naked struggle of wills to power there is no reason to suppose that *women* would emerge victorious (children, of course, stand to lose most).

In fact, I believe that traditional marriage (in America—I am not talking about Iran or Uganda) does not usually involve the kind of domination and subordination of women that radical feminists claim to discover in it. It is a good idea when reading social philosophy to occasionally do a kind of reality check and see if what is being said fits one's experience. I, at least, find that when I reflect about the married couples I know, I find that in some relationships the husband appears to be dominant, in some the wife is more dominant, and in others the power is about equal, depending on the personalities involved. Often it is hard to tell who is dominant since apparent subordinates sometimes dominate those who appear to be in power, and often the two share power in such a way that one of them controls one area of their common life while the other controls another area.

This point leads to a deeper question—namely, what is meant by "power?" Like Nietzsche before them, radical feminists have not given this question enough thought. Once one stops thinking in simple terms like having an army at your command, it is far from clear that women are disempowered by entering into traditional marriages. For one thing, they may exercise considerable power through their influence upon their husbands (Nancy Reagan, for example), who may also provide them with considerable wealth. Men have more income, but women control almost as much wealth as men do (and by some measures, more). Many have exercised strong moral leadership both in local communities and nationally (many of the leading abolitionists were women, for example). Every mother has considerable influence over the next generation through the way she raises her children. And if getting one's own way is what is meant by power, many women in traditional families seem to be fairly successful at this. (Consider the cartoon in which the man says that in his marriage he makes all the big decisions while his wife makes the little ones. He then explains that the big decisions are things like whether the U.S. should remain in the U.N., what legislation Congress should pass, etc., while his wife decides how we spend our money, where we should live, whether I should change my job, etc.[4]) I do not mean to advocate any one definition of power here. I am merely pointing out that power is not one homogeneous thing and that once we recognize this it is not clear that women in traditional families lack power.

Rawlsian Liberal Criticisms of the Traditional Family

The Family in Rawls's *Theory of Justice*

The term "liberal" is one that has gone through a lot of changes since its appearance in the nineteenth century. For our purposes here I will concentrate on the sort of liberalism developed by John Rawls in his influential book *A Theory of Justice*, published in 1971.[5] In it, Rawls argues that just institutions are those that would be agreed upon by rational self-interested agents, who had to decide what sort of institutions to adopt under what he calls a "veil of ignorance." Specifically, the contractors in the original position would be ignorant of their own place in society, their physical characteristics, their intellectual abilities, and their own moral and religious convictions (they would not know, for example, whether they are atheists or religious believers). One of the things he thinks they would agree about is that those offices and positions that carry with them important social and economic benefits must be open to all under the conditions of fair equality of opportunity.

Rawls says very little about the family, but observes that

> the principle of fair opportunity can be only imperfectly carried out, at least as long as the institution of the family exists. The extent to which natural capacities develop and reach fruition is affected by all kinds of social conditions and class attitudes. Even the willingness to make an effort, to try, and so to be deserving in the ordinary sense is itself dependent upon happy family and social circumstances.[6]

In other words, children with equal native endowments will not have equal chances of success so long as they are raised by their natural families. The family thus perpetuates inequality. Rawls does not go so far as to recommend the abolition of the family, and refrains from applying his theory of justice within the family itself (maintaining, as liberals do, a dichotomy between the public and private spheres, and regarding the contractors in the original position as "heads of households"). He says that "Taken by itself and given a certain primacy, the idea of equal opportunity inclines in this direction [the abolition of the family]. But within the context of the theory of justice as a whole, there is much less urgency to take this course."[7]

Philosophers who have followed Rawls, however, have not found his treatment of the family satisfactory. There are two questions Rawls needs to address. (1) What good reason can be given for exempting the family itself from the kind of scrutiny he accords other important social institutions? Might it not be the case that some family structures are just and others unjust? (2) Why, after all, shouldn't we abolish the family on his premises?

The critics are, I think, right to point out that there is no good reason on Rawlsian principles for neglecting to evaluate family structures as just or unjust. And Rawls does not seem to have an adequate response to the second question either. It is true that there is a conflict between preserving the family and providing all citizens with fully equal opportunity, since children with good families (who of course did nothing to deserve the families they were born into) will be unfairly advantaged over those with bad families. This conflict cannot be made to disappear so long as we believe both that all citizens ought to have an equal opportunity to become successful, *and* that parents are obligated to work hard to give their children every possible advantage in life. Perhaps Rawls can argue that retaining the family as an institution leaves the worst off better off than they would be otherwise, but the argument is never developed.

One Rawlsian, Jeffrey Blustein, has tried to develop a defense of the family on Rawlsian principles, arguing that society should assign at least the bulk of the nurturing of children to their biological parents because only in this way can children develop the capacity to form intimate relationships. In adding this, of course, he is going beyond Rawls by promoting "the capacity to establish deep personal relations" to the status of a basic good[8] that must be justly distributed (in addition to things like liberty, wealth, income, and health). Blustein's theory is continuous with Rawls's in that he argues that the capacity for establishing intimate relationships is essential to genuine "self-respect"—a primary good acknowledged by Rawls.[9] In extending Rawls's theory in this way, however, Blustein is building upon one of the more problematic aspects of Rawls's system. Thinking of "self-respect" as a primary good that we can distribute justly or unjustly makes very little sense, and Rawls himself quickly retreated from talking in this way to speaking instead of distributing "the social bases of self-respect."[10] But just what "the social bases of self-respect" are remains obscure.

The difficulties Rawlsians encounter when trying to reason about the family point, I believe, to some deep inadequacies in Rawls's theory of justice, at least in its pure form. Liberal social theory has always had some difficulty in accommodating children, since they are not yet autonomous or capable of agreeing to the social contract. And the requirement added by Rawls that contractors in the original position come to an agreement about social institutions under a "veil of ignorance" raises especially intractable problems in the case of family structures.

(1) It is impossible to reason about just social institutions under a veil of ignorance about whether or not one might be an infant or prerational child. By the very fact that one is able to engage in this sort of highly theoretical speculation, one is assured that one is not a child.[11]

(2) It is impossible to reason about family structures under a veil of ignorance for another reason. Our choices about how the family should be structured are deeply connected with our conception of the good life. Persons ignorant of their own view of the good life could have no basis for deciding between alternative family structures, since family structures have an important role in shaping what the next generation of human beings will be like. Blustein, for example, assumes that the capacity to form intimate personal relationships is an essential aspect of the good life. But this is not uncontroversial. Many people have argued for communal childrearing precisely because it would produce a generation of children whose emotional energy is diffused more widely.[12] Such children would develop into adults who bond more equally with all others in their community rather than forming emotionally intense and exclusive bonds with only a few others. Since children are not yet autonomous they will, in one way or another, be shaped by the guidance and example of other people. There is no way to get around this. Therefore, those institutions that govern the way children are reared cannot be neutral between different visions of the good life.

In short, then, Rawlsians can neither avoid extending their analysis to evaluate family structures, nor deal satisfactorily with it when they do confront the issue. At the deepest level I think the reason for this is their underlying conception of society as a race in which each individual is in competition with each other individual to attain wealth, status, and power. Certainly, this is one aspect of modern society, but it leaves out very important dimensions of the good life. Specifically, it leaves out the whole communal side of human beings, as should be clear when we think about the fact that friendship is not listed as one of the primary goods for Rawls. (Aristotle, by contrast with Rawls, ranks friendship very highly, saying that "No one would choose to live without friends, even if he had all other goods."[13]) Thus Rawls's theory is pervasively individualistic in ways that make it unable to accommodate the kinds of goods attainable within families and communal structures—goods that are important components of a good life. Liberalism of the Rawlsian variety has been coming under increasing criticism of late for these sorts of reasons.[14]

Okin's Rawlsian Feminist Critique of the Family

We turn, finally, to the way in which Rawlsian principles have been employed to develop a distinctively feminist critique of the family—namely, that the traditional family is unjust to *women*. Among the things Rawls believes we are ignorant of under the "veil of ignorance" is our sex. Susan Moller Okin therefore invites us to reflect about what a just family structure would look like under a veil of ignorance about whether we are male or female.

She begins by arguing (persuasively, I think) that the family itself should be evaluated in terms of justice. Although I don't believe that justice is the only, or perhaps even the most important virtue of families, still family structures ought to be evaluated in terms of justice. To structure the family in such a way that the youngest child is required to forgo marriage or career and serve as an unpaid slave to his or her parents until their death, for example, seems to me unjust. Allowing fathers the right to execute unruly adolescents is likewise unjust (in spite of the fact some people these days claim to find this sanctioned by the Bible).

But is the traditional family inherently unjust? Okin argues that indeed yes, the "gender-structured" family (by which she means a family in which the husband is the primary breadwinner and the wife has primary responsibility for maintaining the home and caring for the children) is unjust specifically to women. The customary expectation that women will assume primary responsibility for housework and child care systematically disadvantages women in a wide variety of ways, and therefore the gender-structured family would not be chosen under a veil of ignorance about whether one is a man or a woman.

As a kind of background to her argument Okin cites statistics on the dearth of women in positions of political and economic influence in our society, on the skyrocketing rate of divorce and the impoverishment of women and children in its wake, and on the rapidly rising participation of women in the work force and especially the increasing number of mothers of small children who now work outside the home. Those women who do not work outside the home are, she argues, rendered dependent on their husbands which undermines their sense of self-respect and renders them vulnerable to various forms of abuse and domination. Those who try to combine family and full-time work outside the home find themselves exhausted by trying to do two jobs at once, and the extra burden they carry disadvantages them in their careers. In the wake of divorce, stay-at-home wives are most severely penalized since they have not developed the skills that would enable them to compete in the labor market successfully, but even working wives will suffer in the wake of divorce since they also have (although to a lesser degree) failed to develop their highest earning potential due to the double burden they bear. In fact, all women are disadvantaged by the traditional division of labor within the family even before they marry, since they make their career choices in accord with their expectations about their future, and often pursue occupations that will harmonize most easily with their family commitments.

In order to provide real justice for women, Okin recommends that we ought, so far as possible, to eliminate all gender role expectations and to seek to encourage marriages in which males and females share equally in all burdens and benefits. We should, thus, discourage the gender-structured family (and indeed all customary gender role differences), but should stop short of actually forbidding the traditional division of labor within the family, since some people in fact prefer the traditional pattern. She does, however, advocate extensive state-sponsored attempts to facilitate and encourage equally shared responsibility for childrearing and homemaking. These measures include not only changes in the workplace relating to flexible hours and parental leave but also require schools to promote the minimization of gender—including educating children about "the present inequalities, ambiguities, and uncertainties of marriage, the facts of workplace discrimination and segregation, and the likely consequences of making life choices based on assumptions about gender."[15] In addition, she believes it should be legally mandated that in the event that couples do choose the traditional division of labor (something that must be tolerated, at least for the time being, although it will be regarded as "socially problematic"[16]) the wage earner's paycheck will be divided in half with "the partner who provided most or all of his or her unpaid domestic services"[17] receiving half of it. And in the event of divorce both households must be guaranteed the same standard of living.

Certainly Okin is right that women who staked their lives on the stability of their marriages only to see their husbands go off with a younger woman when their charms began to fade have gotten a rotten deal, and something should be done about this problem. It is also true that working mothers of small children, especially in cases where both parents work full time, are in a very difficult position. To the extent that mothers also assume all the responsibility for housework and care for the children (during the few hours when they are at home) they will be driven to desperation and worn to a frazzle. If both parents have been working all day, it is not fair for the husband to come home, put up his feet and read the paper or watch TV, while expecting his wife to cook, shop, clean up, and care for the children.

But Okin's proposed solutions offer a cure that is worse than the disease. First, they are likely to further destabilize the family, and this in turn will have damaging effects on children. The interests of children are conspicuously absent from her analysis, except insofar as they are impoverished along with their mothers in the wake of divorce. But children are also harmed by divorce in nonmonetary ways that she does not consider. Stable families in which both parents spend significant time with the children are better for children, and the father's money in the wake of divorce is a poor substitute for his loving presence. Mandatory education of children in the politics of gender geared to make them aware of the uncertainties of marriage and discourage them from adopting traditional sex roles is likely to destabilize the family further. Her entire analysis of the family is conducted with divorce in mind, and expectations are often self-fulfilling. Her proposals for sharing all household and child care work equally may also turn out to be destabilizing. Interestingly, studies have shown that the more housework men do the more it becomes something the couple quarrel about, and insisting on strict justice and sharing every task fifty-fifty is likely to be inefficient and to lead to constant bickering.

Second, although Okin's proposals appear to allow those who wish to retain traditional sex roles to do so, they would actually make life increasingly difficult for such people. That, indeed, is her intention. Since several of her proposals would discourage men from entering into traditional marriages, the biggest losers will be women who feel their primary vocation is to be wives and mothers. Consider, for example, her proposal that both postdivorce households must enjoy the same standard of living. This sounds fair enough initially, but when one looks closely at what she proposes it appears more problematic. For she says that this level of support (the same standard of living for both households) must continue

> for at least as long as the traditional division of labor in the marriage did and, in the case of short-term marriages that produced children, until the youngest child enters first grade and the custodial parent has a real chance of making his or her own living. After that point, child support should continue at a level that enables the children to enjoy a standard of living equal to that of the noncustodial parent.[18]

The provision for keeping the children at the same standard of living as the noncustodial parent virtually indefinitely seems to imply keeping the former wife also at that level, regardless of who initiated the divorce and why. Thus, in a case of a short-lived marriage that produced a child, a man could be liable to lose half his income for a potentially unlimited period of time, even if the cause of the divorce was that the wife was sleeping with every man in sight.[19] Laws of this sort would arguably place an unfairly heavy burden on men and therefore discourage them from entering into gender-structured marriages. (I am not arguing that former wives and their children should be cut loose financially in the event of a divorce, or that divorce law is not in need of reform, but merely that Okin's proposals are unacceptable as they stand.)

Even her less radical-sounding proposal that wage-earning men with stay-at-home wives should have half their paychecks automatically sent to their wives might discourage men from entering into traditional marriages—both because of the instant drop in their pay and because of the attitude of distrust conveyed by such a policy. (It could, of course, work out that the woman would work and the man be a househusband, but the reverse is likely to be much more common.).

It is disingenuous of Okin to claim that "this proposal does not constitute unwarranted invasion of privacy or any more state intervention into the life of families than currently exists. . . . it seems like intervention in families only because it would alter the existing relations of power within them."[20] But how is this not intervention? Since her proposals would in fact make it considerably more difficult for those who prefer traditional gender-structured marriages to choose them and to pass on their own values to their children (something I think everyone wants), they would not be chosen by contractors under a veil of ignorance about whether they favor traditional gender structured marriages or a non-gender-structured conception of marriage.

Third, I am troubled by the illiberal and antidemocratic implications of her proposals. It is important to distinguish between informal social expectations (however deeply ingrained) and legal restrictions. It is one thing to argue that traditional sex roles ought not to be enforced legally (something I think almost everyone would agree to in late-twentieth-century America), and another to use state power to deliberately put pressure on people to make their private decisions in some particular way. Those who conform to traditional sex role expectations do so voluntarily, and most people enjoy at least *some* aspects of these roles. State power may have to be employed to constrain "private" choices when these are clearly damaging to the public welfare—for example when manufacturers pollute the environment with dangerous chemicals or when those who frequent bathhouses spread a devastating epidemic disease; the private/public distinction is not completely hard and fast. But how couples arrange the distribution of domestic chores between them seems to me to fall clearly on the private side of the line.

Like many feminists, Okin holds that "the personal is the political," and hence she regards the use of state power to "minimize gender" as entirely legitimate. But, I would argue, this quickly leads to bureaucratic encroachment into people's personal lives of a very dangerous sort. The antidemocratic tendencies of such policies are also troubling because of the implicit condescending attitude toward other women. Not all women feel their self-respect requires financial independence or a successful career. She seems to presume that she knows what is in the real interests of other women better than they do themselves, and this implies contempt for their capacity to understand and intelligently pursue their own self-chosen ends.

There is a variety of policies that might significantly improve the lot of women while preserving the freedom of couples to make their own decisions (Okin advocates at least some of these, but my list goes beyond hers in significant ways). We might begin by making divorce more difficult to obtain, particularly where there are children. And there are all sorts of changes in the workplace that would facilitate the task of working parents—generous paid maternity leaves, the possibility of paid or unpaid leave time for fathers as well as mothers of small children, flexible hours, job-sharing, mommy-track jobs that could also be taken by fathers, part-time work with benefits during the years when the children are small, on-site child care at workplaces so that parents can see their children on breaks and lunch, and career sequencing so that women will not have to abandon their careers entirely during their childbearing years. Significant tax breaks, or perhaps even outright money grants to those performing the socially valuable task of childrearing might be in order.[21] All of these sorts of policies are in effect in some other industrialized democracies, virtually all of them have far more such policies than we do.

Ultimately it is not possible to assess the justice of differing ways of arranging sex roles within marriage from a standpoint that is neutral or impartial between differing worldviews any more than it is possible to be neutral between various conceptions of the good life when choosing childrearing practices under a "veil of ignorance." The theorist who claims that certain social institutions would be chosen under a veil of ignorance is like a magician pulling rabbits out of a hat. He or she can only find the rabbits previously hidden there. Okin, for example, permits the contractors under the veil of ignorance to know that "women have been and continue to be the less advantaged sex in a great number of respects"[22] (considering this one of the general facts about human society that Rawls allows them to know), but does not permit them to know "their beliefs about the characteristics of men and women."[23] If, for example, she allowed them to know that women, on average, are far more likely than men to want to stay home with small children, then her theory would look quite different. I fail to see any principled way in which she can justify allowing them to know about the disadvantaged position of women and exclude any beliefs about the differences between men and women.

Therefore, Okin's claims to be simply articulating the requirements of justice in a way that is genuinely impartial between differing views about gender roles and family structures turn out to be disingenuous. Although she has directed our attention to important problems besetting women, I believe we should pursue instead remedies that are less invasive of people's private lives—ones that both provide significant social supports for the parents of young children *and* maximize the freedom of couples to arrange their domestic lives as they see fit.

Finally, her theory, like that of Rawls, is pervasively individualistic in ways that make it impossible for her to accommodate the kinds of goods attainable within families and communal structures—goods that are important components of a good life. Her acceptance of a highly individualistic model of society as a race for wealth, status, and power keeps her from recognizing and valuing the whole communal sphere of life. While such a philosophy is not fully adequate for analyzing even our major public institutions (as Rawls attempts to do), it is disastrous when applied to the family, since it is blind to precisely those values that can be uniquely realized through familial life.

Rawls's Response to Okin

Rawls, in his 1997 article,[24] clarifies his position on the family on a few points, but his attempts to placate his critics and paper over the difficulties in his theory are, I believe, ultimately unsuccessful.

The family is, he says, a part of the basic structure of society, and its central role in nurturing and forming future citizens makes it an essential part of that structure. There is therefore no question of eliminating the family, and he admits that this fact creates a constraint on our efforts to achieve equality of opportunity. He tries, however, to minimize the severity of the constraints by saying that the family constrains the *ways in which this goal* (equality of opportunity) *can be achieved,* rather than admitting that it will place limits on how much equality of opportunity can be achieved.

Rawls also says that political principles of justice do not apply directly to the family, but still constrain the family, since it must guarantee the basic rights, liberties, and freedom of opportunity of its members (what "freedom of opportunity" means here is unclear). The family, like other associations that people may enter into freely (churches, for example), does have various norms embedded within itself, including conceptions of justice internal to it, but these are not political conceptions. We will not apply principles of distributive justice, for example, to the family. But he says very little about what internal principles are permissible in the case of the family. The sticking point, of course, is just how we are to relate the broader political conceptions of justice to those internal to the family.

Rawls appears to concede more to his feminist critics than he actually does,[25] and when he does come close to making genuine concessions, he does so in a way that leads him into inconsistencies. He also does not, I think, realize quite how radical Okin's proposals are, or at least fails to confront her on this issue.

His most important discussion of Okin is in the following passage:

> A long and historic injustice to women is that they have borne and continue to bear an unjust share of the task of raising, nurturing, and caring for their children. When they are even further disadvantaged by the laws regulating divorce, this burden makes them highly vulnerable. These injustices bear harshly not only on women but also on their children; and they tend to undermine children's capacity to acquire the political virtues required of future citizens in a viable democratic society. Mill held that the family in his day was a school for male despotism; it inculcated habits of thought and ways of feeling and conduct incompatible with democracy. *If* so, the principles of justice enjoining a reasonable constitutional democratic society can plainly be invoked to reform the family. . . *If* a basic, if not the main, cause of women's inequality is their greater share in the bearing, nurturing and caring for children in the traditional division of labor within the family, steps need to be taken either to equalize their share or to compensate them for it.[26]

Apart from the tentativeness of his concessions, signaled by his use of "if" at key points, two issues require discussion.

First, in speaking of women's greater share in the burden of caring for children as "unjust" Rawls run up against the difficulty mentioned above—namely, how private and public life connect with one other. Since political conceptions of justice do not apply within the family, it cannot be "unjust" in *that* sense for women to do more child care. But, then, by what internal principle of justice is it "unjust" for women to do a larger share of the child care? He hasn't told us what the relevant principle internal to the family *is*. Clearly, none of the parties to the discussion believe that the family should sanction predation by the strong upon the weak, but this does not get us very far in terms of articulating just what limits are to be placed on the internal norms and principles permissible within voluntary associations.

Second, when it comes down to what they recommend, what Rawls favors is deeply different from what Okin is advocating. He, like Okin, speaks of the gendered division of labor in families as a possible cause of women's vulnerability, but believes that the freedom to divide their labor on the basis of gender is guaranteed by freedom of religion, provided that it is fully voluntary and "does not result from or lead to injustice." (Explicating just how to tell when it is fully voluntary is, he admits, a difficult task.) He really does want to protect the private sphere from public intrusion. He says "It is a mistake to say that political liberalism is an individualistic political conception, since its aim is the protection of the various interests in liberty, both associational and individual."[27] Okin, by contrast, has strong tendencies toward what might be called "hegemonic liberalism."[28] For, as I have shown above, her proposals involve using state power to actively discourage the gender-structured family.

The difference between their positions emerges particularly clearly on the issue of divorce. Okin's proposals, as argued above, amount to a very heavy, and arguably unjust burden on the husband (since even in the case of a short-lived marriage that ended through no fault of his own, a man could be required to support the former wife and their children at the same standard of living he enjoys for a possibly unlimited period of time), and this cannot but discourage men from choosing traditional gender-structured marriage. Rawls simply ignores Okin's proposal that in the postdivorce family, both households should have the *same standard of living*. Instead, he cites with apparent approval a proposal that the wife's work in raising the children entitles her to an equal share of the husband's income during the marriage, and "an equal share in the increased value of the family's assets during that time [the duration of the marriage]."[29] In fact, this would leave former wives with less than they now receive, since the most important common asset for most families is their house, and the house is usually awarded to the wife in divorce cases. He does not call attention to his divergence from Okin on this point and provides no reason in support of his alternative proposal.

This is not fair to Okin, who is entitled to a more careful hearing and a less evasive and timid response that sets out clearly his reasons for his disagreements with her. Nor is it fair to readers, who are likely to go away with the misleading impression that Rawls has endorsed Okin's views when he has not. Furthermore, Rawls is allowing a good opportunity for clarifying and developing his views to pass him by, which is both his loss and ours.

Conclusion

In the end it is not surprising that liberal political theory (especially Rawlsian liberalism) has trouble accommodating the family. Reasoning about family structure under a veil of ignorance about our understanding of the good life is impossible, since one's choice of family structure is inextricably bound up with what sort of people we want the next generation to be. Parental authority cannot be grounded in a social contract, even an implicit one, since infants and small children are incapable of understanding and assenting to it. Family relationships are unchosen, and internal to us in the sense that who we are cannot be separated neatly from our relationships to our family of origin, and this severely limits our autonomy to be only what we choose ourselves to be. Liberals, therefore, either must force liberal principles upon the family, thereby crippling its ability to perform its task, withdraw from familial questions altogether, thereby creating a sphere of legitimate predation, or have recourse to an endless series of *ad hoc* accommodations.

Notes

1. Simone de Beauvoir, *The Second Sex* (New York: Alfred A. Knopf, 1983), 495.
2. Sandra Lee Bartky, *Femininity and Domination* (New York: Routlege, 1990).

3. See, e.g., Andrea Dworkin, *Intercourse* (New York: Free Press, 1987).

4. I haven't seen the original cartoon, but it is cited by Phyllis Schlafly in *The Power of the Positive Woman* (New Rochelle, N.Y.: Arlington House, 1977).

5. In his 1993 book *Political Liberalism* (Columbia University Press), Rawls has substantially revised the theory propounded in the *Theory of Justice*. But a thorough consideration of the changes made in his second book and the even more radical changes made in the preface to the paperback edition (1996), would take us too far afield. However, since it includes a response to some of Okin's arguments that the traditional family is unjust to women, I have included a brief discussion of his 1997 *University of Chicago Law Review* article in the final section of this paper.

6. John Rawls, *A Theory of Justice* (Cambridge: Harvard University Press, 1971), 74.

7. Rawls, op. cit., 511-12.

8. Jeffrey Blustein, *Parents and Children: The Ethics of the Family* (New York: Oxford University Press, 1982), 219.

9. Ibid.

10. John Rawls, "Social Unity and the Primary Goods," in Amartya Sen and Bernard Williams, eds., *Utilitarianism and Beyond* (Cambridge: Cambridge University Press, 1982), 166.

11. I am indebted to Jacob Joshua Ross for pointing out this problem with accomodating children in Rawls's theory. Jacob Joshua Ross, *The Virtues of the Family* (New York: Free Press, 1994), 149.

12. B.F. Skinner in *Walden Two* thinks in this sort of way.

13. *Nichomachean Ethics*, Book VIII, 1155a 5-6, trans. Martin Ostwald, (Indianapolis: Bobbs-Merrill, 1962), 214.

14. See, e.g., Michael Sandel's *Liberalism and the Limits of Justice* (New York: Cambridge University Press, 19882); Mary Ann Glendon, *Rights Talk* (New York: Maxwell Macmillan, 1991); and Amitai Etzioni, *The Spirit of Community* (New York: Crown Publishers, 1993).

15. Okin, *Justice, Gender and the Family* (New York: Basic Books, 1989), 177.

16. Okin, op. cit., 180.

17. Okin, op. cit., 181.

18. Okin, op. cit., 183.

19. This sort of thing does happen. The father of a friend of mine, while in the military, married a woman who then slept with virtually all the men on the base, and demanded exorbitant alimony, which he agreed to out of embarrassment. As a result, all his children by his second wife were seriously disadvantaged economically. Under the system proposed by Okin, if she had had a child (as in the case she did not) he would have been required by law to maintain her and her child at the same standard of living he enjoyed virtually indefinitely.

20. Okin, op. cit., 182.

21. Some valuable suggestions for ways in which businesses and government could help ease the burden on parents of small children, and make it easier for them to spend more time with their children, are found in Sylvia Hewlett's *When the Bough Breaks* (New York: Basic Books, 1991).

22. Okin, op. cit., 101-2.

23. Okin, op. cit., 174.

24. "The Idea of Public Reason Revisited," *University of Chicago Law Review* 64 (1997), 765, 787-94.

25. The same is true of his concessions to those advocating same sex marriages (p. 788n.30). He says that gay and lesbian marriages do not necessarily violate justice as fairness "so long as the family is arranged to fulfill these tasks [nurturing the next generation of citizens] *effectively and doesn't run afoul of other political values*" (p. 788, Italics added). But what exactly does the italicized phrase exclude? In addition to this unexplicated qualification, he employs *ifs* and *ceteris paribus* clauses so freely that he ends up saying very little.

26. "The Idea of Public Reason Revisited," 790 ff. (italics mine).

27. Rawls, op. cit., 795.

28. I am indebted to my husband Phil Devine for this phrase.

29. Rawls, op. cit., 793.

Part Two

Men, Women, and Children in the Family Today

7

A Demographic Picture
of the American Family Today—
and What It Means

David Popenoe

One of the greatest tragedies of modern times is the worsening situation of children. Who would ever have thought that, once we achieved high levels of affluence, longevity, medical sophistication, technological achievement, and mass education, the situation of children would worsen? But that is exactly what has happened. The decline of child well-being is one of the most striking trends of recent decades. During this period, 1960-1990, juvenile violent crime increased sixfold; teen suicide tripled; reports of child neglect and abuse quintupled; SAT scores declined nearly eighty points; and, after decreasing for a long period, child poverty rates increased from 15 percent in 1970 to 22 percent in 1990. Today, 38 percent of the nation's poor are children.[1] The deteriorating condition of children has become a regular feature of the daily news. One *New York Times* article, for example, was headlined "Study Confirms Worst Fears on U.S. Children."[2] Another begins, "the dissolute picture of youth portrayed by Beavis and Butthead is growing alarmingly close to the truth, a new study suggests."[3]

One can think of many reasons for such declining child well-being, including the pervasive influence of television and the mass media, the decline of religion, the widespread availability of guns and addictive drugs, the decay of community relationships and social order in neighborhoods, and the growth of commercialism and consumerism. None of these reasons should be dismissed. But the evidence is now strong that the changing American family, as discussed in this paper, is the most prominent reason of all. This is because the single, most consequential element in the lives of children is the close relationships they have with others, and by far the most important of these relationships are with their parents and other intimate caretakers.

The Changing American Household

A good place to start our discussion is with a portentous, long-term social trend that is seldom noted. In the middle of the last century, about 75 percent of all American households included children.[4] This means that most adults of that era interacted with children on a day-to-day basis. Today, some 150 years later, the percentage of households containing children is a mere 35 percent.[5] Most adults do not now interact with children on a daily basis. Why is this such an important shift? Because children depend completely on adults for their well-being. Take the distribution of personal income. Such income is shared within, but not between, households. Most of the nation's personal income in the earlier era was filtering down to children; today it is not.

The picture grows even darker when we look at the households today that still do have children. Far more households with children than ever before, some 28 percent, now involve just a single parent, an increase from only 9 percent in 1960. Most of these single parents, of course, are mothers, which brings us to what is—in my mind—the most problematic family statistic of our time. In a little over three decades, from the early 1960s to today, the percentage of children living apart from their natural fathers has jumped from 17 percent to about 38 percent. Thus, if present trends continue, we are rapidly approaching a society in which a majority of children will not be living with the father who biologically sired them. Of all the family changes that have helped to generate deteriorating child well-being, the evidence is now strong that the loss of fathers from the lives of children may be the most consequential change of all. It is heavily implicated in such growing social problems as child poverty, juvenile delinquency, and unwed pregnancy.

Parental Time

A sine qua non of good childrearing is the parental investment of time in children. Yet with other adults already out of the home, and so many children now living with but a single parent, parental time investments in children have fallen. Precise data on the decline of parental time in recent decades are notoriously hard to ascertain. They have even become the focus of controversy.[6] The most reliable estimate, based on a 1992 study by two Stanford University economists, is that the time parents have available to spend with children declined ten hours per week for whites and twelve hours for blacks between 1960 and 1986.[7]

Another reason for the parental time-investment decline is that most married mothers used to be home full-time with their children; today many are not. In 1960, only 19 percent of married mothers with preschool-age children were in the labor force, but by 1990 this figure jumped to 59 percent (73 percent for mothers of school-age children).[8] These figures include part-time as well as full-time workers, but still the increase is one of the most remarkable social trends of our era. According to the 1990 National Child Care Survey, 47.5 percent of children under three (infants and toddlers) are not being cared for by either parent during the day, with about two-thirds of these children being looked after by nonrelatives, including the staff of institutional day care and family day care centers.[9]

The Decline of Marriage

What lies behind the momentous family shift of the past few decades? Two rates of family breakup have gone into orbit. The first is divorce. The divorce rate has doubled or tripled, depending upon how it is calculated. Only 14 percent of white women who married in the early 1940s eventually divorced, whereas almost half of white women who married in the late 1960s and early 1970s have already been divorced! For blacks the figures are 18 percent and nearly 60 percent.[10] If present rates hold, some 50 percent of all marriages entered into today will end in the divorce court.

It used to be the case that a high percentage of children were left in broken homes because of a high parental death rate. Parental death rates have been steadily declining for generations, and death was surpassed by divorce as a marriage terminator in 1974. Today, only 4 percent of children in single-parent families live with a widowed parent. This has led some analysts to proclaim about today's high divorce rate: What's the problem?—children are merely losing their parents in a way different from the one they used to. But surprising new social science evidence shows that view to be based on unfounded optimism. The children of divorced parents are less successful in life by almost every measure than are the children of widowed parents. The replacement of death by divorce, it turns out, is a monumental setback in the history of childhood.[11]

The second highly consequential rate of family breakup is out-of-wedlock births, which have climbed from a minuscule 5 percent of all births in 1960 to a staggering one out of three in 1994 (32.6 percent). Think about it—one out of every three births to women who are not married! The current rate breaks down to nearly 70 percent of all black births and 25 percent of all white births. Since only about a quarter of all unwed births involve a cohabiting male, who may or may not be the child's father, we are witnessing a massive increase in the number of children who are fatherless from birth on.[12]

The timing and trajectory of the two key rates of family breakup are somewhat different. While the divorce rate began its steep ascent in the 1960s, the out-of-wedlock birth-rate didn't pick up steam until the 1970s. At the present time, both the divorce and the out-of-wedlock birth-rates have plateaued at the high levels. Yet as recently as between 1993 and 1994, the out-of-wedlock birth-rate recorded its largest one-year increase since national figures have been kept.[13]

Both of these changing rates are symptomatic of a family trend that is the focus of much too little attention in America today: The institution of marriage has been steadily weakening. We are reluctant to talk about it. Despite an extensive discussion of family change and family problems in his 1996 State of the Union Message, for example, President Clinton did not even once utter the "M" word. No national commissions have been established to investigate marriage decline. Fewer than 50 percent of all Americans even think that "being married" is an important part of family values.[14] Yet, as the eminent demographer Kingsley Davis has noted, "at no time in history, with the possible exception of Imperial Rome, has the institution of marriage been more problematic than it is today."[15]

The decline of marriage is a very recent phenomenon. In 1994, 91 percent of all Americans had married at least once by age forty-five, a figure which is little different from the high of 94 percent in 1960. But for the younger generation, the picture is entirely different. Thirty-three percent of women in their late twenties are unmarried today, compared to just 11 percent in 1960. To be sure, this to some extent represents a delay rather than the abandonment of marriage, yet the strong presumption is that many in the younger generation will end up skipping the institution altogether.[16] This is not to say that people have become reluctant to couple as sexual partners; there has been a steep increase in nonmarital cohabitation. By recent estimates, about a quarter of unmarried adults between the ages of twenty-five and thirty-four are currently cohabiting.[17] Indeed, if both marital and nonmarital cohabitation are considered, the amount and average age of union formation in recent decades have remained relatively unchanged.[18]

The Causes of Marriage Decline

Probably the single, most important social change that has affected marriage is the movement of married women into the labor force. The arrangement worked out in the "modern nuclear family" of the industrial era, of a male breadwinner with a full-time housewife, increasingly proved untenable as young women went into the labor market at nearly the same rate as young men. These women expected men, in turn, to take on more domestic responsibilities. This dramatic gender-role shift is still an unfinished revolution, and a new set of marital gender roles is by no means clear.[19]

The traditional economic basis of marriage has eroded. Women's economic gains have left them with an independence from men that they never previously have had, and a consequent unwillingness to put up with a less than satisfactory mate. And men's commensurate economic losses have perhaps put them into a position where they are less eager to marry. In place of economic considerations, marriage has become an institution largely rooted in interpersonal intimacy, friendship, and sexual gratification. If the needs for personal fulfillment of either marital partner in each of these areas are not met, there is a much greater willingness and also cultural acceptance for breaking up than ever before. Moreover, the high level of divorce generates a large supply of potential new partners. Given this situation, there is growing reluctance to enter into marriage in the first place.

Other factors that have helped to generate the decline of marriage are the sexual revolution and changes in the divorce laws. The sexual revolution was brought about in part by the widespread availability of reasonably safe and affordable contraceptives and abortion. It has meant that couples can have sex outside of marriage with little risk of pregnancy and birth. Legal changes, leading to no-fault divorce, have made divorce far easier and more accessible to the masses than ever before.

In short, marriage has become less a well-established and revered *social* institution, one shaped by moral imperatives and in which all people are expected to participate over the course of their adult lives, and more a private relationship based on personal choice and the needs for personal fulfillment. It might be said that "till death do us part" has been replaced by "so long as I am happy." Consider this implicit change in our sense of obligation toward future generations: Despite that fact that almost all Americans believe that "two parents are best," less than a fifth of Americans today believe that couples should stay together for the sake of the children.[20]

The Cultural Shift

Underlying the decline of marriage is an abrupt and extraordinary transformation, occurring largely in the 1960s and 1970s but continuing to this day, of people's cultural values, worldview, and even self-definition. Large segments of the population have come to regard self-fulfillment as their dominant life goal, pushing aside such traditional "Victorian" values as self-sacrifice, commitment to others, and institutional obligation. Pollster Daniel Yankelovich found, for example, that people today place a much lower value on what they owe others as a matter of moral obligation and a much higher value on self-realization and personal choice.[21] Associated with the growing affluence of modern societies, this cultural shift has been signally advanced by advertising and the mass media, with their never-ending emphasis on feeling good, having fun, consuming vigorously, and "being the best you can be"—with or without others.

This unprecedented cultural shift toward a "radical individualism" has generated a suspiciousness of all social institutions that are thought to impair our personal freedom. There have been striking decreases in the trust and confidence we feel toward government, organized religion, and higher education. But marriage and the family have been particularly hard hit. As the authors of a recent history of the American family put it, "What Americans have witnessed since 1960 are fundamental challenges to the forms, ideals and role expectations that have defined the family for the last century and a half.[22] Americans in large numbers still believe in "getting married someday," but the meaning of the institution has radically shifted. The institution is still desired, but only on one's own personal terms.

Social Outcomes

What have these social and cultural changes wrought? One can argue about their significance for adults. Surely we are a more tolerant society today, and the situation for many minorities has improved. For women, the loss of many of the restrictions of the earlier era can only be applauded. The legal, sexual, and financial emancipation of women has become a reality as never before. And who can be against self-fulfillment? Isn't that what we all want?

For children, however, the rise of radical individualism and the associated collapse of the married, two-parent family have been devastating, with many of the conditions of growing up worsening considerably. As Senator Daniel Patrick Moynihan has observed, "the United States [now] may be the first society in history in which children are distinctly worse off than adults."[23] Ten years ago it was commonly believed, especially within the social science community, that if breaking up was better for parents, it could not be all that bad for children. After all, what keeps parents happy should also keep children happy. But the findings of extensive, long-term, empirical research now indicate precisely the opposite.

One review of the research by sociologists Sara McLanahan and Gary Sandefur, who examined six nationally representative data sets containing over twenty-five thousand children from a variety of racial and social class backgrounds, concluded:

> Children who grow up with only one of their biological parents (nearly always the mother) are disadvantaged across a broad array of outcomes . . . they are twice as likely to drop out of high school, 2.5 times as likely to become teen mothers, and 1.4 times as likely to be idle—out of school and out of work—as children who grow up with both parents.[24]

One of the reasons is the much lower incomes of single-parent families. By one estimate, 51 percent of the increase in child poverty observed during the 1980s (65 percent for blacks) can be attributed to changes in family structure.[25] It is no wonder some are now saying that the best antipoverty program of all is marriage.

But is the problem only that single-parent families have lower incomes? No. McLanahan and Sandefur concluded that:

> Loss of economic resources accounts for about 50 percent of the disadvantages associated with single parenthood. Too little parental supervision and involvement and greater residential mobility account for most of the rest.[26]

Many other researchers have reached similar conclusions. Elaine Ciulla Kamark and William A. Galston report, for example, that:

> The relationship [between family structure and crime] is so strong that controlling for family configuration erases the relationship between race and crime and between low income and crime. This conclusion shows up again and again in the literature.[27]

What about stepfamilies? Can't they fill the breach and adequately provide the necessary two parents? While many stepfamilies are successful, a surprisingly high percentage are not. McLanahan and Sandefur present this remarkable finding from their research: "Children of stepfamilies don't do better than children of mothers who never remarry."[28] As the nation shifts toward more and more step-parents, therefore, our family troubles are likely to mount. The new field of evolutionary psychology gives us one reason why: Across the animal kingdom, parenting is fundamentally rooted in biology and is at least partly activated by the "genetically selfish" activity of favoring one's own relatives.[29]

Hope for the Future?

The inescapable conclusion of the many now-completed empirical investigations in the social sciences is that the active presence of biological fathers is indispensable for child development, and that their absence generates a deterioration in child well-being. As a nation, therefore, we must seek to turn around the recent family trends and bring natural fathers back into the homes—and into the lives—of their children. To accomplish this will require reinvigorating the institution of marriage, for it is marriage—in all societies to date—that has been the institution holding men to their wives and their children. With a progressively weaker marriage system, we can look forward to a continuing decline in the lives and opportunities of our nation's children.

We cannot return to the older marriage system based on male dominance and economic dependency; those days are largely gone. What we have to create is a new, modern marriage system based on economic cooperation and equal regard between husbands and wives, but one in which the children still come first. The system will require new marital gender roles, as well as a higher level of commitment to child well-being.

Judging from existing demographic trends, there is not much to be hopeful about. Marriage rates continue to drop, while the out-of-wedlock birth-rate and the divorce rate persevere at very high levels. One reason for the leveling of the divorce rate is the jump in nonmarital cohabitation; if you don't marry, of course, you can't get a divorce. But you can still break up—as do nonmarital relationships, including those with children, in proportions far higher than marital relationships.

There are, however, some admittedly impressionistic signs of a possible cultural shift in the nation toward greater concern for the plight of modern marriage and the family, and such a shift in values and attitudes is a necessary precursor to any behavioral shift. First, that huge and highly influential population cohort known as the baby boomers is aging; the vanguard of the cohort reached the age of fifty in 1996. As people age they become more familistic and conservative. This cohort is pulling the media, the government, and indeed the entire nation in a more conservative direction. Led by the baby boomers, there is now a widespread sense of anxiety in the country about moral and social decline, especially surrounding the raising of children. When people are asked what issues our national leaders should be concerned about, "moral breakdown" now ranks very high on the list. Both political parties now preach "family values."

But a values shift among baby boomers is not nearly so important as one on the part of persons who are now entering the ranks of the marriage-prone. How does the younger generation see the situation? Will they reject their parents' free-wheeling ways? A "cultural dialectic" may come into play; every thirty years or so, some cultural values toggle back and forth between, for example, restrictiveness and permissiveness in social life. One generation comes to place a higher value, because they have less of it, on what their parents' generation rejected. Such may be the case with marriage and family stability. The percentage of high school seniors who say that "having a good marriage and family life is extremely important" has climbed from 75 percent in 1980 to 79 percent in 1993. Yet are these youngsters so emotionally troubled from their own upbringings that they have sharply diminished chances of marital success? Some existing evidence suggests as much, but only time will tell.

Social scientists are not good at making predictions. After all, what social scientist predicted the end of communism—even six months before its fall? No scholar predicted the baby boom, either! The reason is that human beings have the capacity for a sudden "change of heart." Let us hope that such a change of heart regarding marriage and family life lies just below the surface, for one prediction can be made with 100 percent certainty: In the words of an ancient Chinese proverb, "unless we change direction, we're likely to end up where we're headed."

Notes

1. For statistical sources, see D. Popenoe, *Life without Father: Compelling New Evidence That Fatherhood and Marriage Are Indispensable for the Good of Children and Society.* (New York: The Free Press, 1996).

2. April 12, 1994, A1

3. D. Goleman, "New Study Portrays the Young as More and More Troubled," *The New York Times,* Dec. 8, 1993, C-16. The study referred to is T. M. Achenbach and C. T. Howell, "Are American Children's Problems Getting Worse? A 13-Year Comparison," *Journal of the American Academy of Child and Adolescent Psychiatry* (1993): 32-6.

4. J. S. Coleman, *Foundations of Social Theory* (Cambridge: Harvard University Press, 1990), 590.

5. Statistics are from official U.S. Government sources, such as the Census Bureau, unless otherwise indicated.

6. See David Whitman, "The Myth of AWOL Parents," *U.S.News and World Report,* (July 1, 1996): 54-56.

7. Victor R. Fuchs and Diane M. Reklis, "America's Children: Economic Perspectives and Policy Options," *Science* 225 (1992): 41-46.

8. Sara McLanahan and Lynne Casper, "Growing Diversity and Inequality in the American Family." in *State of the Union: America in the 1990s,* Reynolds Farley, ed. (New York: Russell Sage Foundation, 1995), 1-45.

9. Reported in *Starting Points,* (New York: Carnegie Corp. of New York, 1994), 45.

10. T. C. Martin and L. L. Bumpass, "Recent Trends in Marital Disruption," *Demography* 26 (1989): 37-51.

11.This evidence is reviewed in D. Popenoe, *Life Without Father: Compelling New Evidence That Fatherhood and Marriage Are Indispensable for the Good of Children and Society* (New York: The Free Press, 1996), 151-52.

12. L. L. Bumpass and J. A. Sweet, "Children's Experience in Single-Parent Families: Implications of Cohabitation and Marital Transitions," *Family Planning Perspectives* 21, no. 6 (1989): 256.

13. C. Murray, "Bad News about Illegitimacy," *The Weekly Standard*, (Aug. 5, 1996): 24-26.

14. D. Yankelovich, "How Changes in the Economy are Reshaping American Values, in *Values and Public Policy*, H. J. Aaron, T. Mann, and T. Taylor eds. (Washington, DC: Brookings Institution, 1994): 37.

15. K. Davis, "The Meaning and Significance of Marriage in Contemporary Society," in *Contemporary Marriage*, K. Davis, ed. (New York: Russell Sage Foundation, 1985) 21.

16. Data reported in Frank Furstenberg, Jr., "The Future of Marriage," *American Demographics* (June 1996): 34-40.

17. L. J. Waite, "Does Marriage Matter?" *Demography* 32 (1995): 483-507.

18. L. A. Bumpass, A. Cherlin, and J. Sweet, "The Role of Cohabitation in Declining Rates of Marriage," *Journal of Marriage and the Family* 53 (1991): 913-25.

19. See D. Popenoe, "Modern Marriage: Revising the Cultural Script," in *Promises to Keep: Decline and Renewal of Marriage in America*, D. Popenoe, J.B. Elshtain, and D. Blankenhorn, eds. (Lanham, MD: Rowman and Littlefield, 1996), 247-70.

20. A. Thornton, "Changing Attitudes toward Family Issues in the United States," *Journal of Marriage and the Family* 51 (1989): 873-93.

21. op. cit.

22. S. Mintz and S. Kellogg, *Domestic Revolutions: A Social History of American Family Life* (New York: Free Press, 1988), 204.

23. *New York Times*, Sept. 25, 1986, C7.

24. S. S. McLanahan, "The Consequences of Single Motherhood," *The American Prospect* 18 (1994): 48-58. Article is drawn from S. McLanahan and G. Sandefur, *Growing Up with a Single Parent* (Cambridge, MA: Harvard University Press, 1994).

25. David J. Eggebeen and Daniel T. Lichter, "Race, Family Structure, and Changing Poverty among American Children," *American Sociological Review* 56, no. 6 (1991): 801-17.

26. McLanahan, "Consequences," 52

27. E. C. Kamark and W. A. Galston, *Putting Children First* (Washington, DC: Progressive Policy Institute, 1990), 14-15.

28. McLanahan, "Consequences," 51

29. See: Robert Wright, *The Moral Animal* (New York: Vintage Books, 1994).

8

The Indispensable Role
of the Father in the Family

David Blankenhorn

Let me tell you my thesis as simply as possible—we are becoming an increasingly fatherless society:

Tonight, 40 percent of the children in the country are going to sleep in a home where their father does not live. More than half of all American children are going to spend at least a big part of their childhood living apart from their fathers before they reach the age of eighteen.

This is historically unprecedented. We are in uncharted waters. Never before in the history of our nation, never before in the history of *any* human society, have this many men been estranged and separated from their own children and from the mothers of their children. This trend of fatherlessness is the most dangerous social trend of our generation. It is the principal cause of the decline of child well-being today.

The scholars and the blue-ribbon commissions have investigated this question quite carefully in recent years. Time and again, as they examine the question of what is happening to our children, they tell us the same thing; with each passing year it is getting harder to be a child today. A bipartisan commission, the report called "Code Blue," told us several years ago that this generation of children and youth is the first generation in American history to be worse off than their parents were at the same age. Worse off economically, worse off educationally, worse off socially, worse off morally, and worse off spiritually.

We see a kind of interruption of the American dream that says "Things will be better for my children than they have been for me." What is the reason for this historic reversal? The scholarly investigations are very clear on this point. The principal reason for the decline of child well-being today is the unprecedented breakup of the mother/father child-raising unit, the splitting apart of the nucleus of the nuclear family so that millions of our children are growing up without a father to help take care of them. That's not the only reason, but it's the single biggest reason.

This trend of fatherlessness is the engine driving our worst social problems. If you look down the list of things that seem to be spinning out of control and getting bigger every year—crime and juvenile delinquency, teen pregnancy, the growing number of children in poverty, domestic violence against women, child sexual abuse and neglect—these are not merely separate and unconnected problems. The underlying engine, a kind of a propeller that is driving the increase of each of these otherwise separate problems in the central engine, driving the growth of our most urgent social problems, is father absence. Let's just take a look very briefly at a couple of these problems.

The Number One Issue Is Crime

Look at the issue of crime, because we are becoming a nation that's building prisons just as fast as we can. Our number one social program today for young men is prison construction. It doesn't matter whether you are a conservative Republican governor in one state or a liberal Democratic governor in another, we are building prisons as fast as we can build them to incarcerate ever larger numbers of our young men.

Which young men? Some people say it's a race problem. It's the black kids that we're locking up and putting in jail. It's a residue, a legacy of racism.

Other scholars have said no, it's not. It's income. If you're poor, that's the risk factor. If you're not poor, that inoculates you as a young man against the likelihood of getting in trouble with the police and going to jail.

Other scholars have said no, it's not race or income. It's education. If you can get that high school degree, that's going to protect you and send you in the right direction. Whereas if you drop out of school, that's going to send you in the wrong direction.

Other scholars have said perhaps the key risk factor is actually the quality of the neighborhood you live in. If you're in a bad neighborhood with drugs and guns and gangs, that's obviously going to put you at greater risk and more likelihood of getting into trouble hanging out with the wrong crowd. Whereas if you're in a good neighborhood where those problems are less prevalent, that's the protective influence for you. The young man in that kind of neighborhood is much less likely to get into trouble.

Again, the scholars and the criminologists have investigated this question about as carefully as it can be investigated, and here is their conclusion: *Father absence is the single most important predictor of criminal behavior for young men.* The connection between father absence and criminal activity is so strong that it erases any connection between race and crime, between income and crime, and between educational attainment and crime.

So while these other issues are important (and no one would deny the importance of each of these other considerations), there is a central reason why so many of our young guys are going to jail.

Fathers Are Important to Their Sons

Why would it be the father? Why would that risk factor be the most important? We know from the clinical studies that there comes a time in the life of the young boy when he needs to separate a bit psychologically from his mother and figure out what it means to be a man. He needs to figure out the meaning of his maleness. "Why am I embodied as a male? What does it mean to prove and to show that I am a man?"

The fathered boy, the *well-fathered* boy, can get the right answer to that question. In a sense, it's as if he can almost be what psychologist Frank Pittman calls a "knighted man," He can understand that he is man enough because his father can help him understand the right answer to the question, "What does it mean to be a man?" And part of the answer is, "You want to be a big, strong guy? Good! You're my son. I want you to be. Part of being a strong man means treating other people right. It means taking the needs of other people into account. It means treating women right."

But the poorly fathered boy and the unfathered boy still need to find the meaning of their masculinity. They still need to go on that search. I don't mean any disrespect to mothers when I say that the best mother in the world cannot teach her son the answer to this question.

So the boy needs to figure this out, and where does he look? He looks to the street and the peer group, and he looks to the Rambo and Arnold Schwarzenegger movies of male sexual predatory behavior and omnipotent violence, and he develops what the scholars often call "protest masculinity." It's that hyper, almost cartoonish, version of masculinity that says, "I will hurt you if you look at me the wrong way. I will sleep with my girlfriends and some of them will have my babies, and that is how I show that I'm a man."

These young guys with that swagger and that look and the talk of, "I'm a man, treat me like a man," make us afraid on the one hand. But it also should be understood by us as a kind of cry, or even a prayer, for help, because they just don't have a father in their lives. For a lot of them, there are no responsible men in their lives to help them understand the right way to be a strong man.

And so these are the kids we're locking up. *Eighty percent of the young men in long-term juvenile facilities today are kids who grew up without a father in the home.*

Fathers Are Important to Their Daughters

Look at the other side for a moment, at the daughter side. Some people say, "Oh, fathers are important, especially for sons." That's not true. They are important for sons, but we have to think about the daughters just as much. The problems are just as important.

If you look at teen pregnancy, it's an escalating problem in our society. I was in a heartland state earlier this week. It looked like a Norman Rockwell scrapbook:

rural American, upper income. (And for people who think this is a racial problem, this community was entirely white.) The leading baby doctor in that county, the one who invited me, said 40 percent of the babies he delivered last year were to never-married mothers. Of the seventy girls who graduated from the high school this past year, over twenty were either mothers or were pregnant at the time of their graduation.

So we have this remarkable phenomenon of our daughters becoming sexually active and having babies, many of them before they're much more than children themselves. More than 10 percent of all births are born to unmarried teen girls. More than 30 percent of all births in the country are to never-married mothers. Where is this coming from?

The scholars again have tabulated the facts on this and here is what they tell us. *The presence or absence of a father in the life of the daughter is the single most important predictor of whether she will become sexually active early, whether she will have a child outside of marriage, and, if she gets married, whether she's likely to have a divorce.* It's also the most important predictor of her happiness, and her ability to find a satisfying relationship with a spouse.

Now again, why would it be the father? Why would he play such an important role in determining the outcome for his daughter? Well, who's the first man in every girl's life? Who's the first man that she wants to love and be loved by? It's her father.

So we know from studies that the *well-fathered* girl is helped by a loving relationship with her father. She is helped to develop a sense of confidence in her love-worthiness, a sense of esteem about her own femininity, a sense that she is capable of loving a man and being loved by a man because she is loved by this first man in her life. And she sees him love her mother. So she has that essential foundation of understanding what a healthy, loving relationship is with a man. This is the girl who develops a sense of confidence in her love-worthiness.

The poorly fathered or the unfathered girl is at much greater risk for engaging in a kind of anxious search for male approval that says, "I'll sleep with my boyfriend. I'll have his baby because I really [if you translate the psychological content] am looking." She is looking for that comfort from a male and approval from a male that she didn't get from the first man in her life. This is also why so many of our young women get involved with older men.

I won't go down the rest of the list. But whether it's the issue of children in poverty, whether it's the issue of domestic violence, or whether it's the issue of child sexual abuse, the underlying phenomenon that is the predictor—the engine driving the increase of the problem—is this unprecedented estrangement of adult males from their offspring.

So a society with fewer and fewer fathers had better be prepared to become a society that builds more and more prisons, and creates more and more welfare offices, and hires more and more social workers and more and more court-appointed psychologists and child-support enforcement officers, and the whole panoply of well-intentioned people who try to come in after the fact and deal with some of the consequences of this breakdown of this fundamental social relationship between father and child. Doesn't that sound familiar? Because that's the direction we're going in.

Do Children Need Fathers?

That is about half of the problem. The other half is we're not simply losing fathers today in such large numbers—we're losing our *idea* of fatherhood. We're losing our belief that fathers are necessary. In some ways, this cultural loss is the most tragic loss of all.

The basic question is fairly simple. "Do children need fathers?" The answer that we have come up with in our generation is "not necessarily." We don't know; it's all so complicated perhaps. Maybe the single mothers can do okay. Maybe we can find a substitute.

Earlier this week in the beautiful heartland of the American community that I mentioned to you a moment ago, a very attractive, self-confident young woman, sixteen years old, stood up at the high school assembly and said, "You're all wrong." She told me that. "You're all wrong. I'm a mother and my baby gets everything he needs from me." I heard a thunderous applause from her classmates.

So we've changed our minds. We've changed our minds on the basic question, and we adults have changed our minds to some degree. If you really want a surprise, talk to the teenagers today, and you'll see a changed attitude on this basic question. They're very confident that they know the right answer.

Do children need fathers? Not necessarily. This is a basic civilizational question, "Shall males nurture their offspring?" The famous anthropologist Margaret Mead once said that the supreme test of any society is whether it can teach its men to be good fathers. And why would she have said that? An esteemed anthropologist, a woman anthropologist, surely she was not dismissing or ignoring the central importance of mothers.

No, she well understood the central role of mothers. What she was telling us is that compared to the mother-child relationship, the father-child relationship is weaker. We men like to think of ourselves as the strong ones, but in this area we are the weak ones. You will not find human societies in which large numbers of mothers abandon their children. It does not happen. Today, large numbers of men are leaving their children because the father-child relationship is a weaker, a more fragile, a more perishable, a more breakable relationship. That's why Margaret Mead reminded us that we need culture—we need society—to reinforce fatherhood, to teach and encourage and expect and to some degree, to enforce responsible fatherhood from males. It does not happen naturally or automatically. We need a strong cultural story, a strong cultural message that helps men to go into the role of married fatherhood so that we can supplement maternal investment in children with paternal investment in children. That's the trick. Some of the anthropologists say that's *the* trick that distinguishes the rise of successful human societies across culture and across history. It is a fundamental, civilizational matter.

Now what are we going to do about this? Is there anything we can do? Some people say, "Well, this is largely an economic matter. If only we could get more jobs or better jobs, or economic justice, or economic this or economic that, then the fathers would be more responsible." And I think there's a little bit of truth to that argument.

And some people say, "No, it's the government. If only the government would do more of this or less of that . . . or if only we would stop these misguided government policies in the area of welfare or taxes . . . if only we would change the government programs, then the fathers would be more responsible." And I think there's a bit of truth to that.

A Cultural Crisis Needs a Cultural Movement

But the heart of this issue is cultural. It is essentially a cultural crisis, a crisis of belief and attitude about what it means to be a man, what it means to be a husband, a father. Not that we shouldn't fix the economy as best we can. Not that we shouldn't change some of the things the government is doing. But it is largely an illusion to think that we can economically solve the problem or politically solve the problem. This is essentially a cultural matter. And for a cultural crisis, we need a broad-based cultural movement—call it a kind of fatherhood movement.

One analogy I would suggest is that of cigarette smoking. Nobody's smoking cigarettes right now. A few years ago, probably half of us would be smoking cigarettes right now in this room. We've changed our minds on the issue of cigarette smoking. Within one generation cigarette smoking in public has gone from being basically okay to being basically not okay. The scientific research had something to do with it, and yes, government policies had something to do with it. But essentially we changed our minds.

On the issue of drunk driving, Mothers Against Drunk Driving and other important organizations have effected a cultural shift. We have raised our standards on this issue as we have simultaneously lowered our standards on the issue of male responsibility and male accountability for their children.

What's needed to get a grip on this problem is a broad-based cultural movement toward higher standards of male responsibility for children and higher standards of male accountability to mothers of their children. Put in simpler terms, more responsible, married fathers.

A Movement Is Beginning

The good news is that this is not simply something that would be good to happen, or that might happen. This fatherhood movement is something that is already beginning to happen. I've had a chance in the last year to travel around and talk to people, and I honestly believe that something is happening now in our society. A shift is occurring, and it's happening at two levels.

On the one level, there is much greater recognition of the problem, much less of a sense of "Well, only conservatives believe this" or "Liberals believe that." There is a greater recognition by the opinion leaders in the academy, in the media, and in public policy that there is an elephant in the room with us. We've spent a long time just saying "Hello" to one another, "Have a nice day," "Pass the salt." Nobody's said, "There's an elephant in the room! It's not a cuddly little mouse, it's an elephant!" If you open up the newspapers and look around today, there's a little bit of recognition that there's an elephant in the room. And we should say it. Something fundamental is happening here.

There is that beginning of recognition that creates for us the opportunity for social change, a window of opportunity to make headway on this issue in the next few years. The most inspiring thing I've seen, even more important that the elite shift of opinion, is movement at the grass roots. New leaders. New initiatives. New efforts.

I think of men like Charles Ballard and his National Institute for Responsible Fatherhood that started in Cleveland. This year it is spreading to six other cities, working with young guys—in his case African Americans—all with strikes against them, helping them understand and learn what it means to be a responsible father. A terrific effort!

I think of cities like Indianapolis that have started a nineteen-point grassroots community effort called Rebuilding Families. Its central goal is to bring the fathers back. They've gotten together with the churches, the religious leaders, the community groups, and the local television stations, and they've decided to dedicate themselves to reversing this trend.

I had a chance to spend a couple days with Merced, California. They've done the same thing. They're holding community hearings on how to reverse the trend of father absence. They are saying, "We're not going to wait around for it to happen nationally. We're not going to wait for some politician to get elected who'll do it for us. We're going to do it here in Merced right now, and we're going to turn the trend around."

I think of the big movements often coming out of the churches like The Promise Keepers that have involved hundreds of thousands of men committing themselves. It is a spiritual renewal movement that is centrally connected to higher standards of husbandhood and fatherhood.

The Marriage Savers organizations that are springing up in a number of our churches are seeking to create a culture of marriage in the congregation, with less divorce and less out-of-wedlock childbearing. Pastors and religious leaders are working together on a community basis to replace a culture of divorce and out-of-wedlock childbearing in their congregations with one of enduring marriage and fatherhood. It's a very inspiring thing. A number of churches are involved, and it ought to spread a lot further. I think that it will.

In a number of states now, initiatives are being proposed to change no-fault divorce, especially in areas of contested divorce, and to get rid of the right to unilateral divorce. Michigan has done a lot in this area. The governor of Iowa recently proposed a reform of their no-fault divorce laws.

Why is this emerging now in a lot of states? We know that the two engines that are propelling fatherlessness in America are, on the one hand, out-of-wedlock childbearing, and on the other hand, the highest divorce rate in the world. It may be our divorce laws have something to do with our divorce rates, and so legislators in a number of states are beginning to reexamine the no-fault divorce revolution for its impact on marriage. I think we are going to see some significant reform in this area in the next several years.

So whether it's the legislative arena, whether it's the religious community, or whether it's in the civic sector of the society, something is happening. I don't want to exaggerate it. It's not sweeping the country. It's not going to change everything tomorrow. It took us a long time to get into this mess, and it will take us a long time to get out. I don't know if we can get out. But I know that it's given to us now to try, and I know more and more people are involved in this central effort to reconnect fathers to their children. We can begin to speak of a fatherhood movement, or at least we can begin to speak of the *seeds* of a fatherhood movement in the United States. It's something that I've been proud to be a small part of, and it is a terrifically important challenge for us in the days ahead.

9

Is the Economic Emancipation of Women Today Contrary to a Healthy, Functioning Family?

Mary Ann Glendon

Until recently, many voices at meetings to discuss the state of the family could still be heard insisting that families were adapting reasonably well to new circumstances. By contrast, there was virtual unanimity at the 1996 American Public Philosophy Institute conference on "The Family, Civil Society, and the State" that family life and civil society alike are in serious disarray. Naturally, no single cause for such complex phenomena can be identified, but a number of inter-related factors were suggested, and their relative weight was vigorously debated. Among the culprits nominated were: television, the birth control pill, fatherlessness, male fecklessness, feminism, the operation of the market, the expansion of the state, and women's increased economic independence.

Dire predictions regarding this last factor were commonplace in the nineteenth century. Today, the discussion is much more muted, but anxiety regarding the social effects of women's changing roles has never really disappeared. The most unapologetic exposition that I have heard of the idea that the economic emancipation of women is contrary to a healthy, functioning family was by the late Allan Bloom at a meeting of the International Society on Family Law held in Brussels in 1985. Bloom told a flabbergasted audience of law professors and sociologists that women's independence undermines the only "natural" inclination that binds men to families, namely, a weak disposition to be protective.

Such sentiments are not confined to conservatives. A similar assumption seems to be implicit in a major work issuing from the heart of the family studies establishment. In a 1977 Report for the Carnegie Council on Children, Kenneth Keniston stated that economic advances for women had not only made it easier for women to leave marriages but also rendered it psychologically easier for husbands to leave their wives.[1]

Finally, an affirmative answer to the question in my assigned title is at least one plausible interpretation of the March 1996 Gallup poll that finds nearly half of all Americans saying the ideal family structure is one where the husband is the breadwinner and the wife cares for the children at home.[2] (That news merited a headline in the *New York Times*, but the paper's account of the poll unfortunately did not reveal how the responses broke down between men and women.)

Those scattered references are sufficient, I believe, to indicate that the question I have been asked to address deserves to be taken seriously. Nevertheless, as a mother who was continuously in the labor force while raising three daughters, I feel an irresistible impulse to quibble with the word "emancipation." A question closer to real life would be: What is the effect on family life when both parents work outside the home?

On that subject, there is a good deal of testimony from parents themselves. Working parents report serious and growing conflict between the demands of the workplace and their desire for a decent family life. In a 1989 poll, large majorities of both sexes, women more than men (83 percent to 72 percent), said that children and family life were the primary casualties of workplace demands.[3] The women, especially, reported that both their children and their marriages were being shortchanged, and lamented having too little time for themselves. Nearly half the women said they felt they had had to sacrifice too much for their gains. Since that survey was made, the pressures have steadily increased, with parents working harder than ever to counter the drop in family income that occurred in the 1990s.[4]

If the pollsters had probed more deeply, I think they would have found that, for most working parents, women more than men, the fuller picture is that *everything* is being shortchanged. Sometimes it is the marriage, sometimes the children, and just as often it is the job—not to mention civic, social, and cultural activities.

I have always considered myself fortunate that the schedule of a university professor offers a certain flexibility for work-family accommodations. Nevertheless, I experienced the fifteen-year period when my daughters were small as kind of a blur. Like Don Imus, but for different reasons, I passed the late sixties and all of the seventies in a haze. I can recall domestic details from that time reasonably well, and developments in property law (the main subject I was teaching). But where the 1968 Chicago convention, the ending of the Vietnam War, Watergate, and many other events of that era are concerned, I was merely a distant spectator. I might as well have been living abroad.

How much more difficult must it be for parents with rigid work schedules and lower pay. The expression that best captures the feel of day-to-day life for most working mothers, I believe, is "robbing Peter to pay Paul." One lives with the sense of falling continually short of what one hopes to accomplish at work or at home.

Undeniably, women's economic opportunities have increased enormously in recent years, to the point where one can speak of economic emancipation in connection with childless women. But the great majority of women are mothers. Even with falling birthrates, the Census Bureau projects that nearly 84 percent of American women will bear at least one child.[5] The word "emancipation" does not quite fit the increased movement of mothers of young children into the workplace.

As the economic circumstances of child-raising families have worsened in relation to other types of households, more families need two earners just to make ends meet. Somehow it doesn't feel like emancipation when so many working mothers say that their preference would be to spend more time at home when their children are very young.

Leaving the word emancipation aside for the time being, there does seem to be a widespread perception, shared by most women, that work outside the home by mothers of young children is in severe tension with women's own aspirations for a decent family life.

What follows?

The response in some conservative circles has been to charge women themselves with the responsibility for rectifying the problem—presumably by staying home to raise their children (unless they are welfare mothers, in which case off to work they must go.)

The response of 1970s feminism, by contrast, was to insist that women should not feel primary, or even special, responsibility for the care of children. It was up to men and society to change their ways. Organized feminism turned the question around and asked: "Is family life contrary to women's emancipation?" Notwithstanding a certain diversity within feminist circles, the answer was a resounding yes. That is plain from Penelope Dixon's annotated bibliography of feminist works on motherhood: "The major works have a common thread . . . the institution of motherhood is the root cause of oppression for women."[6]

It seems to me that both the archconservative and mainstream feminist positions are nonstarters. Both are out of touch with the actual circumstances of child-raising families, and both are insufficiently respectful of women's own legitimate needs and desires. Having said that, however, it is not easy to imagine an approach to the work-family dilemma that is realistic, respectful of women's freedom and dignity, and conducive to the well-being of children.

The reason that task is so difficult, I suggest, is that no society has yet adjusted to the separation between home and business that took place a century ago in the developed countries. When one reflects on the unprecedented features of our current situation, it is not surprising that we have not yet learned to cope with them.

Every generation believes its problems are unprecedented. But in our case certain facts are striking. It is the *scale* of many phenomena, rather than the phenomena themselves, that is wholly new. Consider that, for most of human history, most men, women, and children have lived together in closely interdependent economic units, toiling together for subsistence. At the time of the American Founding, four-fifths of the nonslave population worked on family farms or were independent artisans.[7] Indeed, it is only now, in the 1990s, that that pattern is shifting world-wide. We are currently passing through a historic watershed equivalent in importance to the transition from hunter-gatherer to settled agricultural societies.[8] The developing countries are currently replicating what occurred in the United States and Western Europe in the nineteenth century when most remunerative work moved outside the home, and, for the first time, the majority of men were working for wages.

That momentous shift was the beginning of the breadwinner-homemaker pattern that some now call "traditional." The new family pattern brought relief for women and children, as well as men, from the hard life of the family farm or shop. But it brought some other things too. (We have here a prime example of what makes problems regarding the family so thorny: Many of our current difficulties are the by-products of genuine advances.) The wage-earning husband and father was no longer so dependent on his wife and children, but their economic welfare depended more than ever on him.[9] Alas, far from stimulating men to be more protective, that asymmetrical dependency seems to have marked the erosion of marriage as a reliable support institution. A change in custody law at the turn of the century is revealing: As children became liabilities rather than assets (in the economic sense), the ancient legal preference for the father gave way to a presumption favoring maternal custody.[10] The modern family, bonded primarily by emotional ties, was less stable—and less secure for women and children—than the old economically interdependent production community.[11]

Even before the 1960s, when already high American divorce rates began the steep climb to their present levels, the message to women was clear: Full-time motherhood is a risky occupation. The demographic indicators reveal that women have hedged their bets in two ways: by having fewer children, and by maintaining at least a foothold in the labor force even when their children are very young. But that strategy still does not protect mothers very well against the four deadly Ds: divorce; disrespect for nonmarket work; disadvantages in the workplace for anyone who takes time out for family responsibilities; and the destitution that afflicts so many female-headed families. To make matters worse, women's work outside the home may even marginally increase the risk of divorce while hedging against its effects!

Under those circumstances, for men (or society as a whole) to ask women to give up their attachment to the labor force for the sake of children and the family is like the story of the pig and the chicken who were trying to think what they could give to Old MacDonald for a nice birthday present. The chicken suggested to the pig that they could collaborate on a hearty breakfast of bacon and eggs: "I'll provide the eggs and you give the bacon." The pig, for obvious reasons, preferred a vegetarian solution.

Two other factors that aggravated this vexing situation in the 1970s were a wave of heedless family law "reforms" and the dominant ideology of the feminism of that period. Family law came to mirror the intensity and instability of relationships held together more by emotional than economic ties. It increasingly treated family members as separate, independent individuals.[12] By holding up self-sufficiency as an ideal, the law reinforces the impression that dependency is somehow degrading. By expecting women to be self-sufficient after divorce, the law rendered the situation of mothers riskier than ever. Given that the majority of divorces involve couples with minor children, it is nothing short of astonishing that divorce law basically treats the dissolution of marriage as though it involved only two adults—with custody and child-support tacked on almost as afterthoughts.[13]

Official feminism acted as cheerleader for many legal changes that burdened the roles of mothers and homemakers. Instead of attending to the actual circumstances, needs, and desires of mothers, and helping women to achieve reasonable accommodations between work and family, old-line feminists concentrated on what they thought women *ought* to want. At the 1995 United Nations women's conference at Beijing, the warhorses of 1970s feminism were still at it—fighting every positive reference to marriage, motherhood, or the family in the conference documents.

It is now beyond dispute, however, that old-style ideological feminism has failed to win the hearts and minds of American women. In a June 1996 *New Yorker* article, feminist founding mother Betty Friedan made a remarkable concession: "As a number of recent polls have made clear, the most urgent concerns of women today are not gender issues but jobs and families."[14] The polls to which Ms. Friedan referred are those that show two-thirds of American women answering "No" to the question "Do you consider yourself a feminist?"[15] Even more striking are the responses of young women. Among college women, fewer than one in five says she considers herself a feminist.[16]

The same women, however, are enthusiastic about increased opportunities for women, especially in the realms of education and employment—and grateful to organized feminism for helping to bring about improvements in those areas. So why are most women alienated from feminism? The main reason, according to Elizabeth Fox-Genovese, is that they perceive the women's movement as indifferent to their deepest concerns. They are put off by old-style feminism's negative attitude toward marriage and motherhood, its antagonistic attitude toward men, and above all by its relative indifference to children.

As women (and men) have begun to be critical of social and economic arrangements that pressure them to give priority to market work over family, women have come to see the women's movement as a significant contributor to that pressure. They resent the refusal of organized feminism to go to bat for women who want to give priority, at least for a few years, to family life. They hold feminism responsible for reinforcing the idea that the only work that counts is work for pay outside the home.

Ironically, feminists from the nineteenth century onward were right on the mark when they criticized our culture for asking women to make all kinds of sacrifices for children and the family, while according little respect, reward, or security to women's unpaid work. But as Fox-Genovese has pointed out, the feminist movement of the 1970s bought right into that disrespect by denigrating marriage and motherhood as obstacles to women's advancement. The model they held up for women was a certain male model for success that many men are currently questioning.[17]

Meanwhile, the family and civil society are drifting ever deeper into a situation that is satisfactory to almost no one, and alarming to many. Never have there been so many families where both parents are working outside the home. Never has such a large proportion of mothers of young children worked outside home. Never before has a majority of our future citizens been spending at least part of childhood in a single-parent household. Never have _women_ had more individual rights—yet the situation of _mothers_ has become precarious in novel and worrisome ways.

From the societal point of view, it is not only the nurture and education of future citizens that is at risk. In a time of intense change, it is always interesting to notice those areas where the demographic needle remains steady. One constant for nearly a century has been the proportion of the dependent population (defined as people needing care) to the rest of the population.[18] (The _composition_ of the dependent group has changed—more elderly people, fewer children—but the _ratio_ has remained stable.) In other words, while the pool of unpaid caretakers has shrunk drastically, society is still trying to figure how to cope with the needs of persons requiring care. No adequate substitute for the loss of unpaid caretakers has been found—nor indeed does any seem to be in sight. Meanwhile, many women find themselves facing "Work-Family Dilemma II": No sooner has the last child left home, than the needs of aging parents start the process of juggling job and family responsibilities all over again.[19]

As if that were not enough cause for concern, the array of institutions that long served as auxiliaries to the family—schools, neighborhoods, churches, temples, voluntary associations of all sorts—are in distress, in part because they too depended on the unpaid labor of women. Just when families need outside help more than ever, the mediating structures of civil society themselves are far from peak condition.

It is beginning to sound as though I am coming perilously close, after all, to the conclusion that women's economic emancipation is not only contrary to a healthy, functioning family, but to a healthy, functioning society!

The fact is, however, that the question in my title is the wrong question. It is a serious question, but wrong nevertheless.

It is wrong, first, because the work of so many mothers of young children outside the home when they would prefer not to do so is not economic emancipation.

It is wrong, secondly, because, by focusing on women and the family, the question leaves out of the picture the structure of the world of work.

A better question might be: Is the emancipation of greed contrary to a healthy, functioning family? Or, less tendentiously, is the free market, especially in its "creative destruction" mode, contrary to a healthy, functioning family?

At one stage in the planning of the conference on which this volume is based, many of the topics were grouped together under the heading: "How the state gobbles up civil society." That is an image we owe to the Polish poet Czeslaw Miloscz, who once likened the state to a cancer destroying everything that lay between itself and the individual.[20] But as another great twentieth century Pole has pointed out, the market too can take a toll on civil society, especially the family.[21] That is why John Paul II, while decisively affirming the market economy, has called for a new "culture of work" in which human values would have priority over economic values, and where the dignity of all legitimate types of work would be respected.[22] "The true advancement of women," he wrote in *Laborem Exercens*, "requires that labor should be structured in such a way that women do not have to pay for their advancement . . . at the expense of the family."[23]

Such a broad principle as the priority of human over economic values is easier to state than apply. But critical appraisal of the effects of economic policy is not foreign to American political thought. As Michael Sandel documents in *Democracy's Discontent*, public deliberation on economic policy in this country regularly included serious consideration of the "civic consequences" of economic decisions until well into the present century.[24]

The devil, of course, would be in the details. Let us stipulate that the free market is the greatest device that human beings have discovered for unleashing economic energy and creativity, for utilizing resources, and for responding to human needs. Let us stipulate, too, that many attempts to establish a normative and juridical framework for the market have been spectacularly counterproductive. Nevertheless, those who do not want to see any interference with market forces in the form of family policy or labor policy need to think again. As Nobel prize winning economist Gary Becker told a conference on the economy and the family in March 1996, healthy families have a direct influence on the creation of capital.[25]

There is more than one way to kill the goose that lays the golden eggs. The market, like our democratic experiment, requires a certain kind of citizen, with certain skills and certain virtues—honesty, work ethic, competence, cooperation. In short, it depends on culture, which in turn depends on nurture and education, which in turn depend on families. Capitalism, like liberalism, long took civil society, the family, and women's roles in nurture and education for granted. Now capitalism, like liberalism, needs to worry about whether it is eroding its own supports in civil society. Again, this is not alien to traditional American ways of thinking. Not so long ago, the duty to conserve capital was regarded as almost an eleventh commandment. Today we need to attend to social capital, to consider how to replenish it, and to reflect on how to keep from destroying it.

If I am close to the mark on this, the really important questions from now on will not involve big theory so much as the art and science of practical politics and economics. We need to find out what works and to build cautiously on successful ideas. Promoting women's exercise of all their talents, rights, and responsibilities without undermining their roles within the family will require calling not only husbands and fathers to their family responsibilities but also governments and private employers to their social duties. That will involve nothing less than a cultural transformation. And as Glenn Loury reminds us, cultural transformation begins with personal conversion, of men and women alike, "one by one, from the inside out."

With that thought in mind, it seems possible to amend and answer the question posed in the title of this essay. True emancipation of women and men (the emancipation that has not yet been seen) is not only not contrary to a healthy functioning family, but is necessary to that end!

Notes

1. Kenneth Keniston and the Carnegie Council on Children, *All Our Children: The American Family under Pressure* (New York: Harcourt Brace Jovanovich, 1977), 22.

2. Tamar Lewin, "Americans Attached to Traditional Roles for Sexes, Poll Finds," *New York Times*, 27 March 1996, A15.

3. Alison Cowan, "Women's Gains on the Job: Not without a Heavy Toll," *New York Times*, 21 August 1989, A1.

4. Robert Trott (Associated Press), "Despite Two Incomes, Family Earnings Drop," *Manchester Union Leader*, 21 January 1996, 1.

5. Amara Bachu, "Fertility of American Women: June 1992," U.S. Bureau of the Census, Current Population Reports, Series P-20, No. 470 (Washington, D.C.: U.S. Government Printing Office, 1993), 1, 29.

6. Penelope Dixon, *Mothers and Mothering: An Annotated Feminist Bibliography* (New York: Garland, 1991), 3.

7. Robert Heilbroner, "Reflections: Boom and Crash," *The New Yorker*, (August 28, 1978): 52, 68.

8. Richard Critchfield, *The Villagers* (New York: Anchor, 1994), 3-39.

9. For cross-national data, and an elegant analysis, see Judith Blake, "The Changing Status of Women in Developed Countries," *Scientific American*, (September 1974): 136.

10. Mary Ann Glendon, *The Transformation of Family Law: State, Law, and Family in the United States and Western Europe* (Chicago: University of Chicago Press, 1989), 198.

11. See, generally, Mary Ann Glendon, *The New Family and the New Property* (Toronto: Butterworths, 1981) 17-20, 28-46.

12. See, for particulars, Glendon, *Transformation of Family Law*, 291-98.

13. A fuller critique of these aspects of divorce law appears in Glendon, *Abortion and Divorce in Western Law* (Cambridge: Harvard University Press, 1987), 81-111.

14. Betty Friedan, "Children's Crusade," *The New Yorker*, (June 3, 1996): 5, 6.

15. Elizabeth Fox-Genovese, "'Feminism Is Not the Story of My Life'" (New York: Doubleday, 1996), 32.

16. Ibid.

17. A recent study finds both male and female workers, women only slightly more than men, making career trade-offs in the effort to balance work and family life. Tamar Lewin, "Workers of Both Sexes Make Trade-Offs for Family, Study Shows," *New York Times*, 29 October 1995, 25.

18. Glendon, *The New Family and the New Property*, 90.

19. "Mothers Bearing a Second Burden," *New York Times*, 14 May 1989, 14.

20. "An Interview with Czeslaw Miloscz," *New York Review of Books*, (February 27, 1986): 34.

21. John Paul II, in *Centesimus Annus*, par. 42, describes as unacceptable a capitalism that operates without "a strong juridical framework which places it at the service of human freedom in its totality and sees it as a particular aspect of that freedom, the core of which is ethical and religious." For a description of how the values of the marketplace can invade the family circle, see, Christopher Lasch, *Haven in a Heartless World: The Family Besieged*

(New York: Basic Books, 1977), 35-36, 147, 166.

22. *Centesimus Annus*, 15; *Laborem Exercens*, 9, 26.

23. *Laborem Exercens*, 19.

24. Michael Sandel, *Democracy's Discontent: America in Search of a Public Philosophy* (Cambridge: Harvard University Press, 1996), 124.

25. William F. Murphy, "The Economy and the Family," *The Pilot*, (March 22, 1996): 10.

Part Three

Law, Divorce, and the Family

10

The Legal Definition and Status of Marriage

Bruce C. Hafen

American society has grown confused during the last twenty years about the definition and meaning of such historically stable terms as "marriage" and "family." In 1980, for example, a session of the White House Conference on the Family came very close to adopting a proposal that would have defined the family as any "two or more persons who share resources, responsibility for decisions, values and goals, and have commitment to one another over time."[1] And for some people, a common family name now creates a sort of psychological claustrophobia, even for children. A cartoon from the 1980s showed a man and woman with two children standing at the door of a neighbor's apartment. The apartment owner had just opened the door. The man standing outside said, "Hi! We're the new family from next door. I'm Bill Jones, this is Sally Smith, and these are our kids, Beth Townsend and Jason Connally."

During the 1970s and 1980s, such wide-open approaches to family definition began to seem more socially acceptable, hastened by geometric increases in the national rates of divorce, births outside marriage, unmarried cohabitation, and society's new tolerance for gay and other sexually open lifestyles. The Supreme Court also extended abortion rights and contraception rights to single as well as married persons. And most states relaxed their regulation of both marriage and divorce, particularly as the no-fault divorce movement expanded in many states to allow divorces whenever one party simply wanted to end a marriage. Ironically, at the same time the states were deregulating the formation and the dissolution of marriages, they clearly increased their regulation of the single-parent families their withdrawal was helping to create. When the government removed some of its fences on the cliff, it had to increase the number of emergency vehicles needed to retrieve crash victims in the valley below. The net effect of these developments was not to reduce total state intervention into family life so much as to change the point and nature of the intervention. In more recent years some states and cities also extended selected spousal and antidiscrimination protections to people living in domestic partnerships, both straight and gay.

Yet by the mid-1990s the personal relationships most protected by U.S. state and federal laws are still limited—at least at the formal level—to those that arise from kinship, adoption, and heterosexual marriage. All states recognize a definition of marriage similar to the one in the Uniform Marriage and Divorce Act, which provides that:

> Marriage is a personal relationship between a man and a woman arising out of a civil contract to which the consent of the parties is essential. A marriage licensed, solemnized, and registered as provided in this Act is valid in this state. A marriage may be contracted, maintained, or dissolved only as provided by law.[2]

Cohabiting and gay couples are still not regarded as marriages or families for most legal purposes, as reflected, for example, in our laws of inheritance, property, and taxation. And the Supreme Court in 1986 refused to recognize a constitutional right of sexual privacy in a noted gay rights case.[3] No court has been willing to adopt the theory urged in the early 1980s by law professor Kenneth Karst, who advocated a constitutional right of intimate association that would protect any intimate relationship on the same basis as the Constitution protects the sanctity of marriage.[4] Even the financial support claims of unmarried partners that some courts have recognized (such as in the Lee Marvin palimony case) were based on contract theories, not on equating cohabitation with marriage. So, for the most part, despite a sizeable shift in public attitudes about marriage and despite changes in the state's legal posture toward the family, our state and federal laws actually have remained quite certain about what a marriage is at the level of formal law.

At the same time, the question of society's right to define and to regulate marriage is today closer to the forefront of national policy debates than it has been in many years. This sudden emergence of the nature of marriage as a high priority issue on the national agenda is due primarily to two divergent recent trends—first, a growing sense that divorce has become too easy to obtain and, second, the movement to recognize same-sex marriage, which has erupted most visibly in Hawaii, a state that also has other active volcanoes. I welcome the opportunity these trends present—indeed what these trends demand—that we reexamine and more clearly articulate the very nature of marriage as both an individual and a social institution. In my view, one simple and general principle would significantly strengthen U.S. legal and social policies toward marriage and the family: Rather than thinking of marriage only as an expression of an individual right or the fulfillment of an individual need, we must reenthrone marriage as a *social* institution that deserves cultural, political, and legal priority—in addition to its major role in individual lives. Properly understood, our legal system's long-standing concept of marriage actually encourages just that understanding.

Consider two current assumptions about the legal meaning of marriage that are not really valid. First, many people today assume that U.S. law defines marriage simply as a private contract between two individuals. Even though this assumption increasingly reflects society's practical understanding, as a matter of legal theory the assumption is wrong. Marriage is actually very public, it involves three parties, and it isn't just a contract. It is, rather, a legal act that creates a status, not just a contract, of marriage. In most marriages, even today, marital status imposes its basic expectations through the force of general laws, not through private, point-by-point negotiating between two contracting parties. These laws now clearly create a marriage of equals, not a marriage of male domination. The three parties are a man, a woman, and society—with society represented by the state.

The sense of status involved in relationships based on marriage and kinship is captured by the words of Jesus, spoken from the cross to Mary, his mother, and to John, his close friend. As he invited these two people to look after one another permanently after his impending death, he said, "Woman, behold thy son!" And to John, "Behold thy mother! And from that hour that disciple took her unto his own home." (John 19:26-27) The words "husband" and "wife" are historically and culturally charged with the same kind of meaning. The parties who accept these titles accept rights and duties toward each other that were not drafted by lawyers or handed down by a court; the meaning of these terms was handed down by the ages.

Consider a second current assumption. Marriage creates distinctive legal benefits under laws dealing with taxes, inheritance, personal injuries, social welfare benefits, concepts of marital privacy, and even the laws of evidence. Many people assume that U.S. law attaches such privileges to marriage simply because marriage is so important to the married individual. This assumption is also wrong. The law obviously recognizes the individual significance of marriage, but it gives marriage extraordinary protections also because marriage as an institution is so important to society. Thus, there are "social interests" as well as "individual interests" in our legal concept of marriage. One example of these social interests is the long-term welfare of children, who would not technically be parties to a simple marriage contract.[5] The state's historic, formal involvement in the formation and dissolution of marriage reflects all of the social interests, including the interests of children.

The individual rights emphasis of constitutional law since the 1960s, however, has confused American society to the point that we are hardly conscious now of the social interests in marriage. Our reduced consciousness of these vital interests is vividly illustrated by the current debates over two major family law issues, divorce reform and same-sex marriage. In these debates, the major but often unspoken premise of those who advocate unilateral, no-fault divorce and those who advocate same-sex marriage is that marriage involves only individual interests, not social ones. Despite our growing recognition that "the abolition of marriage" is destroying American society, as Maggie Gallagher put it, "we have refused to act, taking . . . bizarre comfort in the belief that . . . marriage is ultimately a private matter, and therefore we can do nothing as a society to prevent its collapse."[6]

We must unpack this assumption and examine it. We must ask whether the time has come simply to discard what is left of our theory of social interests, or whether it is time to reassert and rebuild the concept of the social interests in marriage. This is the hinge point on which many specific arguments about divorce and same-sex marriage turn. The direction we swing on this conceptual hinge will help determine both the legal and the cultural meaning of marriage and family relationships in the twenty-first century. Simply put, should marriage merely be a private contract, totally controlled by private contracting parties? Or should it be a major social institution that is also laden with heavy individual interests? These questions frame the issue for my presentation.

Interestingly, despite the confusion generated by individualistic interpretations of constitutional law in the last thirty years, a certain concept of constitutional analysis may help us think more clearly about these questions. This traditional concept is that, in general, constitutional law should reserve its highest protections for individual rights and interests that *also* promote the long-term interests of the larger society. The law promotes these longitudinal social interests when it *endorses*, not just *tolerates*, particular principles, institutions, or behaviors in individual cases. Thus, the distinction between what the law endorses and what it merely tolerates is of crucial importance. Unfortunately, however, some recent legal and political reasoning about individual rights assumes that personal autonomy alone, even when it undermines the social interests, is entitled to the law's highest protections. Under the assumptions of autonomy, the law must *endorse* or promote whatever principle, institution, or behavior the law *tolerates*—because tolerance of autonomous personal choice has become, for some people, the highest constitutional good. I consider this doctrine of unfettered autonomy a wrongheaded and serious threat to the continuity of democratic society. Understanding the difference between legal toleration and legal endorsement can help us put autonomy arguments into proper perspective. I will return to this theme before concluding.

Against this background framework of legal theory, let us consider the examples of divorce and same-sex marriage. I hope these two topics will illustrate my introductory comments enough to give some coherence to my conclusion that we must reestablish the social interests among the first premises in our reasoning about marriage today.

Let us first look at divorce law. Personal attitudes toward marriage and divorce have been profoundly affected by the growing strength of individualism throughout American law and society. In the rights-oriented rhetoric of our day, some now describe the notion of unrestrained personal autonomy as "the right to be let alone," a right Justice Louis Brandeis once called "the right most valued by civilized men."[7] The emphasis on individual rights in family law over the past generation has led the American legal system to take the idea of individual freedom to terminate a marriage further than do the laws of any other Western nation, including Sweden.[8]

This development is but one part of a "transformation" in American family law that Mary Ann Glendon calls "the most fundamental shift [in the state's legal posture toward the family] since the Protestant Reformation."[9] Not surprisingly, a change of such breadth has deep historical roots. One of Western history's oldest and largest themes is what Robert Nisbet calls "the decline of community." As Sir Henry Maine's Status-to-Contract thesis put it, since ancient times, "[t]he movement of the progressive societies has been distinguished by the gradual dissolution of family dependency and the growth of individual obligation in its place."[10] The decline of family dependency within the last century reflects not merely social change, but economic change. Corporate employers and the state have in many cases eclipsed the family as the primary source of economic status and property rights. That is why former judge Randall Heckman, who currently advocates the reform of Michigan's no-fault divorce laws, recently said, "Right now it is easier for [people] to divorce their spouse, even if they were married for 25 years, than to fire someone they hired last week."[11] Fifty years ago, by contrast, divorce was difficult to obtain, and an employer could terminate an employee at will.

Family law professor Janet Dolgin recently summarized the emergence of individualistic autonomy in U.S. family law. She wrote that our society has recently moved from an outdated world in which attitudes about women and children were "founded in a hierarchical ideology that manifest[ed] natural differences in the actual relationships between people to . . . an egalitarian ideology that presumes the autonomy of the individual in a world of contract."[12] Professor Dolgin moderates her enthusiasm for this new vision by realizing that it leaves family members "without a sense of ultimate responsibility within, and toward, any social group."[13] She also senses that the new spirit of individual autonomy is unable to "anchor people in a social order that encourages responsible connection."[14] But in the world she describes, the presumption of personal autonomy remains, eroding our interdependence within families and leaving us unsure whether the natural bonds between spouses, parents, and children are valuable ties that bind, or are sheer bondage.

Increasingly, legal autonomy has meant the right to be left alone, even within the family structure. Thus, while earlier Supreme Court cases dealing with marriage "turned on the importance of marriage to society," its more recent marriage cases "turn on the importance of the [marital] relationship to individuals."[15] This individualistic perspective also shows up in empirical studies of personal attitudes toward marriage. In *Habits of the Heart*, Robert Bellah and his colleagues reported their finding, based on hundreds of interviews, that many Americans have shifted their view of marriage from that of a relatively permanent social institution to a temporary source of personal fulfillment. As a result, when marriage commitments intrude on people's preferences and convenience, they tend to walk away. Yet, ironically and significantly, Bellah's group also found that despite Americans' preoccupation with self-interest, most of the people they interviewed still cling, perhaps in a hopelessly dreamy sense, to the nostalgic notion of marriage and family life based upon loving and *permanent* commitments as "the dominant American ideal."[16]

During the late 1970s and early 1980s, many scholars and policy analysts discussed the emerging priority of individualism and personal autonomy in both family law and family life. Most recognized that we were essentially deregulating marriage. The legal system retained a basic definition of marriage; but increasingly, it left the matter of creating and terminating marriages largely to individual choice.

The no-fault divorce reforms of the 1960s originally intended to leave some responsibility for evaluating society's interests in each marriage in the hands of family court judges, but in practice the judges deferred to the wishes of the parties. And family courts deferred to the choice of partners who wanted a divorce more than to the choice of partners who wanted to stay together. The judges intuitively valued the right to be let alone more than the right to be together, perhaps because togetherness is harder for a court to enforce than separateness. Law is inherently better at pulling things apart than it is at keeping them together. The unwillingness of one party to continue the marriage also communicated to most judges that the marriage itself was irretrievably broken down.

Meanwhile, other social and legal changes combined with the effects of higher divorce rates to produce more single-parent families, more births outside wedlock, and greater tolerance of personal lifestyle choices. Predictions among both experts and the public varied widely about the likely consequences of these changes in both personal experience and in society. But the growing preeminence of individual autonomy as a social and constitutional value made most people feel it was not their business to worry about the effects of these changes on adults, on children, or on the larger society.

Now, however, the evidence has become undeniable that the deregulation of personal decisions about marriage and children has inflicted serious harm on the nation's children. The negative effects of growing up in a single-parent family, compared with growing up in a two-parent family, have recently been very well documented.[17] In addition to the emotional trauma suffered by members of broken families, we are witnessing considerable strain on our collective efforts to ameliorate the financial and social difficulties these people face. Many of these problems (though clearly not all of them) are attributable to the divorce revolution and to a national disengagement by the state, at both local and federal levels, from supporting marriage as a primary social institution. As social scientists Jean Elshtain and David Popenoe concluded, "the most important causal factor of declining child well-being is the remarkable collapse of marriage, leading to growing family instability and decreasing parental investment in children."[18] Such are the results of an orientation toward family law and social policy that values leaving adults alone to the point that they are relieved of "a sense of ultimate responsibility within, and toward, any social group," including their children.[19]

A century ago, the U.S. Supreme Court declared that while "other contracts may be released upon the consent of the parties," it is "not so with marriage. The relation once formed, the law steps in and holds the parties to [their] obligation." Why was the state a conscious party to each marriage? Because, said the Court, marriage "is the foundation of the family and society without which there would be neither civilization nor progress."[20] Yet in the last quarter century we have seemed to change our national view of marriage, as if divorce and childbearing were victimless private choice for consenting adults only. Today's evidence forces us to face the truth in G. K. Chesterton's remark that we should "regard a system that produces many divorces as we do a system that drives men to drown or shoot themselves."[21]

Within the last two or three years, increasing numbers of scholars, policy analysts, and now legislators have begun to realize that this mounting body of evidence calls for a reexamination of the laws and attitudes that have governed public policy during the last two or three decades. A central concern driving this reform movement is the harm obviously inflicted on children—and thereby on society—by all causes of single-parent environments, including divorce. Legislatures in twelve states are now considering bills intended to discourage divorce.[22] The introduction of such legislation has predictably triggered emotional debates about the actual causes and the actual effects of divorce on children, comparing the harm of divorce with the harm of staying within a family suffering from emotional terminal illness. Other issues include whether law actually has the power to keep together a family that has already broken down socially and economically, and whether no-fault divorce laws have actually contributed to higher divorce rates.

What interests me most today about these recent policy debates is the virtual absence of attention to the issue of society's interest in marriage as a fundamental social institution. Many of the arguments against proposals to reform no-fault divorce laws proceed from the sometimes unspoken premise that marriage is a matter of individual choice, like any other private contract. For that reason alone, many people simply assume that the state's role in reforming divorce laws is extremely limited. Consider three illustrations of the way this assumption expresses itself in the national dialogue about divorce laws.

A recent report by a committee of the American Bar Association on the legal needs of children begins with a vivid parable about two fishermen watching babies floating down a stream. After pulling several children from the water, one fisherman finally runs upstream to see who is throwing the babies into the river in the first place. The report thus urges lawyers to look upstream beyond the legal issues in particular cases involving children who confront the legal system. Nowhere, however, does the report engage the crucial headwaters issue of the state's legal posture toward family formation and dissolution.[23]

Second, the 1994 Report on "The State of the World's Children" authored by the United Nations Children's Fund reviews the harms children suffer in today's world as a result of childhood disease, malnutrition, poverty, illiteracy, and unmanageable population growth in less developed nations.[24] This report acknowledges, as does much contemporary research, that children in single-parent families suffer disproportionately compared to children in two-parent families. However, on this point the UNICEF report offers only the aloof observation that "some of the changes affecting American children—such as the sharp rise in single parenthood—are beyond the immediate reach of government."[25]

Third, soon after publishing recent media reports on proposed legislation that would alter no-fault divorce laws, a Salt Lake City newspaper editorialized that, "Most Americans would agree that two-parent families are best for children. But far fewer would support government coercion as a way of fostering traditional families." The editorial then acknowledged the data showing that children in single-parent homes are far more likely to be disadvantaged than children in two-parent homes. But the editorial expressed doubt that altering no-fault laws or other "government policy reform" would improve children's circumstances, not because of evidence derived from experience with other divorce policies, but primarily because "it is not government's place to dictate marital relations, the most personal of decisions."[26]

I attribute these three responses in significant part to the ideological assumption that personal lifestyle choices, including choices about divorce and decisions to bear children, are just not the business of society or government. This is but another way of saying that the legal system should not seriously weigh social interests in its approach to divorce law. I will return to this topic after commenting on the second trend that is provoking us to reexamine our assumptions about the nature and meaning of marriage; namely, same-sex marriage.

The Supreme Court of Hawaii recently held that the equal rights clause of its state constitution requires the state to grant marriage licenses to same-sex couples who seek marriage, unless the state can demonstrate a compelling interest to the contrary. The lower court has not yet ruled on the state's attempts to prove its case, but it may be only a matter of time until same-sex marriage becomes legal in Hawaii—unless the citizens of Hawaii amend their constitution to prohibit that result. If same-sex marriage is legalized in that state, the full faith and credit clause of the U.S. Constitution will probably require other states to recognize Hawaiian marriages in other states. Some states have already passed laws refusing to recognize such marriages, and a federal law having a similar effect is pending before Congress.[27] The constitutionality of laws forbidding recognition of same-sex Hawaiian marriages in other states may ultimately require a Supreme Court determination.

The proponents of same-sex marriage in Hawaii argue that they are merely seeking vindication of their obvious civil rights. If that is true, it is curious that during the past three decades of intense development of civil rights and anti-discrimination laws, no other state or federal court has recognized a constitutional right to gay marriage. The past cases that have considered the matter generally found that marriage is by definition reserved for a man and a woman. One cannot reasonably claim that this approach to marriage discriminates on the basis of gender, because it treats male and female homosexuals the same way. And no court has otherwise recognized sexual orientation as a category of special protection under the U.S. Constitution. Indeed, the Supreme Court specifically rejected such an argument in 1986.[28]

Earlier this year the Supreme Court did strike down an amendment to the Colorado constitution that prohibited cities and other entities from granting preferred civil rights to gay and lesbian persons. However, the Court carefully avoided holding that sexual orientation is a protected constitutional classification; rather, it reasoned that Colorado's approach had no rational basis at all, given the broad way in which it was drafted. The Court specifically found that the state's claim that the "measure does no more than deny homosexuals special rights" was simply an implausible interpretation of the amendment.[29]

This most recent Court decision is still likely to accelerate a recent trend in which state and local governments, as well as business entities, have begun to recognize homosexual couples as domestic partners entitled to some of the same spousal benefits as married couples. Because this trend is bringing long-awaited victories to gay rights advocates who have claimed they only want equal treatment, it is reasonable to wonder why those advocates also insist on changing existing marriage laws so that same-sex couples can be legally married. Walter Berns's exploration of that question led him to conclude that gay and lesbian leaders "are obviously after bigger game" than equal treatment alone. Rather, said Berns, "they want to change the marriage laws because they want to change the culture. . . . [T]hey view themselves as part of the broader countercultural movement," whose purpose "is to undermine the traditional idea of the family: The family as the building block of society, the family of fathers and mothers who naturally care for their children," and who "care for the society in which those children will have to live."[30] Some of these advocates question whether it is natural or healthy for economic and health benefits to be entangled with love or marriage.[31] Essentially they want the individual, not the family, to be the social unit that engages with the state.

The subject of same-sex marriage raises a host of questions, but taking my cue from Walter Berns's comment, I will focus only on the general issue I raised regarding divorce law reforms—the social interest in marriage. Addressing the controversy surrounding same-sex marriage in his state, Hawaii Governor Ben Cayetano recently stated that Hawaii's legal quandary over same-sex marriages could be resolved if the state simply removed itself from issuing marriage licenses altogether. Said he, "[t]he institution of marriage should be left to the church . . . . The government should not be in the role of sanctifying marriages."[32] In other words, if the state is not in the business of giving its official imprimatur to any marriages, no one could criticize the state for now endorsing and fostering same-sex marriages. Governor Cayetano evidently believes that the state has no business endorsing or fostering any kind of relationship, presumably because he regards all personal relationships as strictly private—which is the same point made by those who say the state should not regulate divorce. Applying that assumption to the same-sex marriage issue can place traditional marriage and same-sex marriage on an equal footing; but is that because same-sex marriage now shares with traditional marriage a preferred status, or is it because traditional marriage has been removed from a preferred status? Equality in the status of the two relationships can be achieved either way.

The case law outside Hawaii shows that the biggest obstacle to legal recognition of same-sex marriage is the statutory definition of marriage, which has always been expressed in terms of a union between a man and a woman. One advocate of gay and lesbian marriages recently argued that the traditional definition is inherently flawed, because it derives historically from scripture and canon law—hence continued use of that definition inappropriately mixes church and state.[33] Mary Ann Glendon's historical research shows that the Christian doctrine of marriage as a sacrament did provide "the theoretical basis for the assertion of ecclesiastical authority" over marriage in the latter half of the Middle Ages.[34] And the Protestant reformers, while rejecting the idea that marriage is a sacrament, simply assumed that secular marriage should reflect the Christian concept of marriage. But beginning with the Enlightenment of the eighteenth century, consciously secular legal systems throughout Europe and the United States established marriage as a significant expression of formal legal status, symbolized especially in France by a civil ceremony and a secular registration. During the nineteenth century, the secular legal concept of marriage emerged as a primary illustration of robust Western legal systems in which "legal norms and concepts" were being "formalized and expressed" in a "conceptualistic way" in rules thought to be both "logical" and "necessary." "The notion of *legitimacy* was increasingly coming to be identified with *legality*," understood as formally correct.[35]

Reflecting this conceptual development, the Supreme Court in 1888 described marriage in clearly secular terms as "the most important relation in life" and "the foundation of the family and of society, without which there would be neither civilization nor progress."[36] And while recent ideas about marriage have focused on individual rather than social interests, the Supreme Court as recently as 1971 underscored society's interest in the formation and dissolution of marriages:

> [M]arriage involves interests of basic importance to our society. . . . It is not surprising, then, that the States have seen fit to oversee many aspects of that institution. Without a prior judicial imprimatur, individuals may freely enter into and rescind commercial contracts, for example, but we are unaware of any jurisdiction where private citizens may covenant for or dissolve marriages without state approval.[37]

To this observation by the majority of the Court, Justice Black added:

> It is not by accident that marriage and divorce have always been considered to be under state control. The institution of marriage is of peculiar importance to the people of the States. It is within the states that they live and vote and rear their children. . . . The States provide for the stability of their social order, for the good morals of all their citizens, and for the needs of children from broken homes. The States, therefore, have particular interests in the kinds of laws regulating their citizens when they enter into, maintain, and dissolve marriages.[38]

This brief historical sketch suggests that marriage as a legal concept has embodied a substantial component of secular social interests, quite apart from—and in addition to—its meaning as a religious doctrine. Thus, the rationale urged by Governor Cayetano and other proponents of same-sex marriage would change not only the definition of marriage, but the very concept of marriage as both a legal and a social construct. These advocates recognize that the biggest issue in considering the legal merits of same-sex marriage is whether the state has an interest in defining and maintaining marriage as a social institution. If one decides that marriage is essentially a private contract between consenting adults, it is difficult to exclude same-sex couples from marriage for the same reason that we would have difficulty prohibiting a gay person, on the basis of his gayness alone, from buying insurance or taking out a loan.

By the same token, however, the notion of marriage as a private contract would have difficulty preventing any other personal relationships from calling themselves marriage. As William Bennett observed, once we rearrange the traditional definition of marriage enough to accommodate homosexual partners, "On what *principled* ground can [we then] exclude others who . . . want legal recognition and social acceptance" for their relationship?" The possibilities range from "a bisexual who wants to marry two other people" to "two sisters" and beyond. The use of "sexual relativism" in defining marriage causes society to lose "the capacity to draw any lines and make moral distinctions."

Recent polls show that a majority of the American people have grown more tolerant of gay lifestyles, just as they have grown more tolerant of personal choices on most lifestyle issues. In other words most people would not criminally punish homosexual behavior. But the polls also show that only one-third favor same-sex marriage. The American public draws a clear distinction between *tolerating* gay lifestyles and *promoting* them by such socially legitimizing endorsements as marriage.[39] Thus, public attitudes draw a clear line between "passive toleration" and "active support" of homosexual conduct.[40] It could be argued that these results reveal the public's schizophrenia, or at least its inconsistency; however, the difference between tolerance and promotion is both legally and sociologically significant. Indeed, the public intuitively shows more sophistication than does the Hawaii Supreme Court about the difference between these two concepts.

For example, research on "Changing Attitudes toward Family Issues in the United States" from the University of Michigan's Institute for Social Research found that most Americans today are much more "tolerant" than the past generation toward the choices they believe others should be free to make regarding sex roles, divorce, premarital sex, unmarried cohabitation, and decisions to marry. At the same time, the researchers reporting these data also found that:

> [T]he normative and attitudinal shifts toward tolerance of a broad range of behavior does not mean that there has been an increased endorsement of remaining single, getting divorced, remaining childless, or reversing the roles of women and men. That is, while there were marked shifts toward permitting previously proscribed behavior, there were no significant shifts toward believing that remaining single, getting divorced, not having children, or reversing gender roles were positive goals to be achieved. The data clearly suggest that the vast majority of Americans still value marriage, parenthood, and family life. . . . [W]hat has changed in these areas of family life has been an increased tolerance for behavior not previously accepted, but not an increase in the active embracement of such behavior.[41]

Thus the distinction between passive tolerance and active promotion revealed in the polls on homosexual behavior is consistent with a similar distinction most

Americans draw across the board on family lifestyle issues.

The legal system has generally reflected this distinction by maintaining three broad categories of human conduct: conduct that is "prohibited," such as robbery; conduct that is "permitted," such as making a contract; and conduct that is especially "protected," such as giving a political speech. Constitutional law has been especially concerned with the protected category, because the Bill of Rights gives extraordinary preferences to such conduct as speech or the free exercise of religion. The state may not regulate protected conduct except under very compelling circumstances.

The civil rights movements of the past generation were concerned primarily with moving the choices and needs of women and racial minorities from being merely "permitted" to being legally "protected" by potent antidiscrimination laws. During most of this same era, gays and lesbians sought to move their choices and needs from being "prohibited" to being "permitted" by securing decriminalization of their private conduct. Thus, some states have, for example, repealed statutes against sodomy. When a legislature repeals criminal laws, it moves the subject behavior from the prohibited to the permitted category.

I would draw the line of "tolerance" between prohibited and permitted, and I would draw the line of "endorsement" between permitted and protected, as follows:

PROHIBITED [tolerance] PERMITTED [endorsement] PROTECTED

In a variety of cases over many years, the Supreme Court has held that such family and kinship-based interests as the right to marry, the parental right in one's own offspring, and the right to direct the upbringing of one's own children are constitutionally "protected" rights. The Constitution not only "tolerates" personal choices in these areas of behavior, it affirmatively endorses and protects those choices against most forms of state intrusion. We have now reached the point in society when public attitudes and governmental actions reflect a greater tolerance for homosexual behavior than in the past. Does that mean that same-sex marriage should fall within the "permitted" range or the "protected" range? The question is not whether the legal system should *tolerate* homosexual lifestyles by not penalizing gays and lesbians—that, to a large extent has already occurred. Beyond that, the question in the same-sex marriage debate is whether the legal system should *endorse* and *promote* homosexual lifestyle choices by giving them its highest legal preferences.

I think it significant that both the universally accepted legal definition of marriage in American law and the broadly held attitudes of the American public would answer this question negatively. That is why the only way the state of Hawaii can equalize the treatment of male/female marriage and same-sex marriage is to change its historic definition of marriage in order to place same-sex marriage in the protected category, or, alternatively, to remove any state interest (and, hence, state protection) for traditional marriage and leave it as a private act of contract within the permitted sphere.

Consider laws regulating divorce within this analytical framework. One of the consequences of the state's having placed marriage within the protected legal category is that the state is essentially a party to the marriage—both in its formation and in its dissolution. Thus, a state license and ceremony are required to create a legal marriage, and a state court judgment is required to dissolve a marriage. These formalities are not required to create or dissolve a typical legal contract, because—for reasons such as those cited by the Supreme Court in its cases on marriage—society actually has a greater stake in the survival of each marriage than it does in the survival of each business agreement, even though stable business is obviously important for a healthy economy.

In this context, to argue that the state should withdraw from the regulation of divorce is to move the entire concept of marriage back from the protected category into the permitted category. Interestingly, just as the contemporary American public is more willing to *tolerate* gay behavior than it is to *endorse* that behavior by authorizing same-sex marriage, the public is also more willing to tolerate the behavior of those who are divorced than it is to endorse and encourage divorce.

The two issues of divorce and same-sex marriage both raise the same underlying question of legal and social policy: Does our society have a fundamental interest in marriage as a social institution? Those who favor unilateral, no-fault divorce argue that society has only negligible interests in personal divorce decisions. Those advocating same-sex marriage argue that the state should withdraw from any official role that expresses a social interest in marriage.

My central point is that American society should more clearly, consistently and forcefully articulate a position that reenthrones heterosexual marriage as a crucial and highly preferred element in perpetuating both personal liberty and social stability. This fundamental premise for all of our policy reasoning should find newly clarified expression throughout our legal system and in all the other places where society expresses its political, economic, and cultural incentives and values. Whatever the particular point that might be made about same-sex marriage or the specific merits of a given legislative approach to divorce, my argument is a general one: Our discussion should proceed from a renewed understanding of what it means to say that marriage is a highly protected legal and social institution.

Having placed the institution of marriage within this conceptual framework, consider a final perspective on the social interests in marriage, interests that have fallen into relative obscurity during the last three decades of emphasis on individual rights and liberties.

Of course the individual has a crucial interest in the freedom to marry. When the Supreme Court used that phrase, "the freedom to marry," in *Loving v. Virginia* in 1976, the Court reinforced its own precedents about the protected place of marriage in the constitutional scheme. However, that decision addressed the specific problem of interracial marriage. And in wisely overturning a state law against such marriages, the Court's language emphasized the individual interests in marriage without also reinforcing the social interests. Thus, the language of the opinion in *Loving*—the very phrase "the freedom to marry"—conveyed to some the erroneous impression that the Constitution protects marriage only for personal reasons, not for social ones.

I turn to a venerable legal scholar named Roscoe Pound for perspective on the relationship between individual and social interests in family law. In an article that has been called "perhaps the best known essay in the history of family law,"[42] Pound wrote in 1916: "It is important to distinguish the *individual* interests in domestic relations from the *social* interest in the family and marriage as social institutions."[43] He defined "social interest" as:

> [O]n the one hand a social interest in the maintenance of the family as a social institution and on the other hand a social interest in the protection of dependent persons, in securing to all individuals a moral and social life and in the rearing and training of sound . . . citizens for the future.[44]

For Pound, it was elementary that individual and social interests must be analytically compared "on the same plane," lest the very decision to categorize one claim as "individual" and the other as "social" cause us to "decide the question in advance in our very way of putting it."[45] Moreover, from Pound's viewpoint:

> When the legal system recognizes certain individual rights, it does so because it has been decided that society as a whole will benefit by satisfying the individual claim in question; for example, when the legal system guarantees the individual freedom of speech, it advances society's interest in facilitating social, political, and cultural progress. This interest . . . is more important than society's interest in preserving existing institutions.[46]

Thus, when the Supreme Court excluded obscenity from the free speech guarantees of the first amendment, the Court stated that obscene expression is not entitled to constitutional protection—not because it isn't "speech," but because it is speech that utterly lacks "social value."[47] So a primary reason for placing some personal relationships (such as marriage) within the "protected" constitutional category while placing other relationships (such as a business partnership) in the "permitted" constitutional category is that the relationships in the protected category more fully promote society's fundamental interests over the long term.

For example, ever since the 1920s, the Supreme Court has included within the "protected" constitutional category the relational interests of marriage and kinship and the right of parents to direct the upbringing of their children.[48] Yet the Court has refused to include other personal relationships or the sexual privacy of unmarried persons (straight or gay) within the protected sphere.[49] The constitutional distinction between married and unmarried persons springs primarily from the Court's recognition that the obligations of parenthood, marriage, and biological kinship are fundamental to preserving a civilized order. Thus, those obligations are worthy of being constitutionally protected, not merely tolerated or permitted, by the law.

Similarly, the right of children to receive an education deserves protection because education serves not only children's individual interests, but also the long-term social interests of democratic societies, which utterly depend on having a well-educated and stable citizenry.

In these illustrations, both individual interests and social interests play some role in defining the contours and the purposes of the most protected constitutional categories. The emphasis on personal autonomy and individual rights during the last twenty-five years, however, inherently takes a nonnegotiable stance that seeks to override the social interests, as Pound predicted, in the very way of putting its question. Autonomy arguments not only typically fail to establish high social value but they also often thrive on challenging the existing order of social stability. That is why some gay rights advocates are willing to remove the state entirely from expressing the social interest in marriage and family life in the name of equal civil rights in order to justify their desired legal conclusion that intimate personal relationships are purely private matters.

Indeed, in the most forceful available statement of support by a Supreme Court Justice for the notion that sexual orientation is a fundamental right, Justice Harry Blackmun wrote in 1986 in a dissenting opinion that he would protect homosexual behavior not because it furthers any social interests but precisely because it dissents from the established social order: "We protect these rights not because they contribute . . . to the general public welfare, but because they form so central a part of an individual's life." Further, stated Justice Blackmun, the ultimate test of a constitutional freedom is whether it protects the personal "right to differ as to things that touch the heart of the existing order."[50] It is difficult to find any social interest that would justify a preferred position for this view, except the arguable hypothesis that protecting personal autonomy in any form always has social value.

But the power of the protected sphere to communicate society's endorsement and sponsorship tells us that our system does not, and should not, protect everything it tolerates. When we merge tolerance with protection, we ultimately reduce every relational interest to the permitted category, because this conceptual merger by definition denies the possibility that some relationships are more significant in our scheme of constitutional values than others. This approach illustrates what happens when one confuses the distinction between what the law merely permits and what it protects.

Wendell Berry was describing the social interest in marriage when he wrote, "Marriage [is] not just a bond between two people but a bond between those two people and their forebears, their children, and their neighbors." When "you depreciate the sanctity and solemnity of marriage" so understood, "you have prepared the way for an epidemic of divorce, child neglect, community ruin, and loneliness." Thus,

> [L]overs must not, like usurers, live for themselves alone. They must finally turn from their gaze at one another back toward the community. If they had only themselves to consider, lovers would not need to marry, but they must think of others and of other things. They say their vows to the community as much as to one another, and the community gathers around them to hear and to wish them well, on their behalf and on

its own. It gathers around them because it understands how necessary, how joyful, and how fearful this joining is. These lovers, pledging themselves to one another 'until death,' are giving themselves away, and they are joined by this as no law or contract could ever join them. Lovers, then, "die" into their union with one another as a soul "dies" into its union with God. And so here, at the very heart of community life, we find not something to sell as in the public market but this momentuous giving. If the community cannot protect this giving, it can protect nothing. . . .

[T]he marriage of two lovers joins them to one another, to forebears, to descendants, to the community, to Heaven and earth. It is the fundamental connection without which nothing holds, and trust is its necessity.[51]

Marriage was historically understood in American law, even from a secular viewpoint, as a three-party arrangement, with the state as a conscious party reflecting society's enormous stake in the outcome and the offspring of each marriage. Indeed, it is precisely the *public* part of marriage—the high degree of social interests involved in the very concept and function of marriage—that distinguishes it from all other relationships and contracts. To marry is to make a public commitment that one accepts a fundamental responsibility to the community and its basic social values. For this reason, the society itself must retain the primary role in determining which relationships, which privileges, and which duties reflect the kind of marriage that satisfies the social interests.

Our present legal definition of marriage has not yet altered this time-honored understanding, but our recent public conversations have obscured it and the outcome of the debates on divorce and same-sex marriage could obliterate it. Before we do that, let us reconsider the social interests in marriage, not only when we discuss gay marriage and divorce reform, but in all legal and social policy discussions about children, marriage, and family life.

Notes

1. "All in the Family," *Time*, (June 16, 1980): 31.
2. UMDA, Section 201.
3. *Bowers v. Hardwick*, 478 U.S. 186 (1986).
4. Karst, "The Freedom of Intimate Association," *Yale Law Journal* 89 (1980): 624.
5. "[A]t law, children are but adjuncts to adult interests." Donald S. Moir, Putting Children First: *A Reconsideration of Family Law* (unpublished manuscript presented at The International Society of Family Law, Quebec City, June 14, 1996).
6. *The Abolition of Marriage* 4 (1996).
7. *Olmstead v. U.S.*, 277 U.S. 438, 478 (1928).
8. See Mary Ann Glendon, *Abortion and Divorce in Western Law* (Cambridge, Mass: Harvard University Press,1987) 78.
9. Id. at 63.
10. H. Maine, *Ancient Law* 163-65 (1st American ed. 1870)

11. National Public Radio, Morning Edition Series on Divorce in America, May 13, 1996, NPR Transcript #1866.

12. Janet Dolgin, "The Family in Transition: From Griswold to Eisenstadt and Beyond," *Georgetown Law Journal* 82 (1994): 1519, 1520.

13. Id. at 1570.

14. Id. at 1571.

15. "Developments in the Law—the Constitution and the Family," *Harvard Law Review* 93, (1980): 1156, 1248-49.

16. Robert Bellah, et al, *Habits of the Heart (Berkeley: University of California Press, 1985).*

17. "The collapse of marriage can be summed up in just two statistics. Almost one-third of all American children (and two-thirds of African American children) are now born out-of-wedlock. [And] demographers [now] estimate that up to 65 percent of all new marriages now fail." Maggie Gallagher, *The Abolition of Marriage* 4-5 (1996). Also see the data summarized in Barbara Dafoe Whilehead, "Dan Quayle Was Right," *Atlantic Monthly*, (April 1993): 47.

The effects of these trends on America's children are especially disturbing. For example, "Children in single-parent or stepparent families are more likely than children in intact families to be poor, to drop out of school, to have trouble with the law—to do worse, in short, by most definitions of well-being." They are also more likely to be abused, to have physical and emotional problems, and to abuse drugs. And, contrary to some popular assumptions, these children do not always "bounce back" after divorce or remarriage; instead many of their problems continue. Ibid. In significant part because of the higher proportion of children in single parent families, a national commission recently concluded, "never before has one generation of American teenagers been less healthy, less cared for, or less prepared for life than their parents were at the same age."

The disturbing number of children now living in poverty is also directly related to single-parent families. Senator Moynihan found that while poverty historically derived from unemployment and low wages, today it derives primarily from weak family structure. Elshtain and Popenoe, *Marriage in America* pamphlet.

See also David Popenoe, *Life Without Father: Compelling New Evidence that Fatherhood and Marriage are Indispensable for the Good of Children and Society* (New York: Martin Kessler Books,1996); Sara McLanahan and Gary Sandefur, *Growing Up With a Single Parent: What Helps, What Hurts* (Cambridge, Mass: Harvard University Press, 1994); Leslie Margolin and John L. Craft, "Child Sexual Abuse by Caretakers" 38 *Family Relations* 450 (1989); Martin Daly and Margo Wilson, "Child Abuse and the Risks of Not Living with Both Parents" 6 *Journal of Ethology and Sociobiology* 197 (1985); other sources quoted in Maggie Gallagher, *The Abolition of Marriage* (1996).

18. *Marriage in America* pamphlet.

19. Dolgin, supra, at 1570.

20. *Maynard v. Hill*, 125 U.S. 190 (1888).

21. G.K. Chesteron, "The Superstition of Divorce," 1920, in Marlin, G. (ed.), *Collected Works, G.* Marlin ed. (1987, Vol. 4), 239.

22. NPR Morning Edition, Series on Divorce in America, May 13, 1996 (transcript).

23. ABA Presidential Working Group, "American's Children at Risk: A National Agenda for Legal Action," 1993.

24. James P. Grant, Executive Director of UNICEF, "The State of the World's Children" (1994), 1,2.

25. Id. at Panel 14.

26. "Family Cannot Be Forced," Editorial, *Salt Lake Tribune*, 17 January 1996, A8.

27. H.R. 3396, 104th Congress, 2d Session.

28. *Bowers*, supra.

29. *Romer v. Evans*, 1996 U.S. Lexis 3245; 64 *U.S. Law Week* 4353, May 20, 1996.

30. Walter Berns, "Marriage Anyone?" *First Things*, (April, 1996): 7,8.

31. E.g., Nancy D. Polikoff, "We Will Get What We Ask For: Why Legalizing Gay and Lesbian Marriage Will not Dismantle the Legal Structure of Gender in Every Marriage," *Virginia Law Review* 79, (1993): 1549; Nan D. Hunter, "Marriage, Law and Gender: A Feminist Inquiry," *Law & Sexuality* (1991):118-119; Steven K. Homer, "Against Marriage," *Harvard Civil Rights-Civil Liberties Law Review* 29 (1994): 506.

32. Bruce Dunford, "Governor: Take state out of marriage role," *The Honolulu Star-Bulletin*, January 9, 1996, A-5.

33. Andrew H. Friedman, "Same-Sex Marriage and the Right to Privacy: Abandoning Scriptural, Canonical, and Natural Law Based Definitions of Marriage," *Howard Law Journal* 35 (1992): 173.

34. Mary Ann Glendon, *The Transformation of Family Law* (Chicago: University of Chicago Press, 1989) 26.

35. Id. at 34.

36. *Maynard v. Hill*, 125 U.S. 190, 205, 211 (1888).

37. *Boddie v. Connecticut*, 401 U.S. 371, 376 (1971).

38. *Boddie v. Connecticut*, 401 U.S. at 389 (Black, J., dissenting).

39. A recent *Newsweek* national poll found that 33% of those sampled believed that same-sex marriages should be sanctioned by law. *Newsweek*, June 3, 1996, p. 27. The same poll found that 84% believe gays should have equal access to job opportunities.

40. Richard Bernstein, "When One Person's Civil Rights Are Another's Moral Outrage," *New York Times*, October 16, 1994, (Section 4) 6; Dennis, "Shaky Ground: Gay Rights Confront Determined Resistance From Some Moderates," *Wall Street Journal*, 7 Oct. 1994, A1.

41. Arland Thornton, "Changing Attitudes Toward Family Issues in the United States," 51 *Journal of Marriage and the Family* (1989): 873, 891. Another study concluded that perceptions among white college students "considered the traditional nuclear unit as a family, and the majority perceived marital status and parental status to be important features when defining a family." The students tended to "exclude cohabiting couples without children [and] same-gender partners." Donna Y. Ford, "An Exploration of Perceptions of Alternative Family Structures Among University Students," *Family Relations* 43 (1994): 68.

42. Henry Foster, "Relational Interests of the Family," *University of Illinois Law Forum* (1962): 493, 493.

43. Roscoe Pound, "Individual Interests in Domestic Relations," *Michigan Law Review* 14 (1916): 177, 177 (emphasis added).

44. Id. at 182.

45. Roscoe Pound, "A Survey of Social Interests," *Harvard Law Review* 57 (1943):1, 2.

46. Carl Auerbach, "Comment," in *Is Law Dead?* 208 (E. Rostow ed. 1971)(replying to Ronald Dworkin, "Taking Rights Seriously," in *Is Law Dead?* 168 (E. Rostow ed. 1971)).

47. *Roth v. United States*, 354 U.S. 476, 484-85 (1957).

48. E.g., *Pierce v. Society of Sisters*, 268 U.S. 510, 535 (1925).

49. See *Bowers v. Hardwick*, 478 U.S. 186 (1986). The Court has included the right to abortion and the right to obtain and use contraceptives within the protected sphere for both married and single persons. See *Roe v. Wade*, 410 U.S. 113 (1973); *Eisenstadt v. Baird*, 405 U.S. 438 (1972). Although some commentators have inferred a right of sexual privacy from these decisions, my analysis reaches the conclusion stated in the text. See Hafen, "The Constitutional Status of Marriage, Kinship, and Sexual Privacy: Balancing the Individual and Social Interests," *Michigan Law Review* 81 (1983): 463.

50. *Bowers v. Hardwick*, 478 U.S. 186 (1986), 478 U.S. at 199, 204, 211 (Blackmun, J., dissenting).

51. Wendell Berry, *Sex, Economy, Freedom & Community* (1993): 125, 137-39.

11

How Current Constitutional Law Undermines the Family

Gerard V. Bradley

Christian Scientists practice the art of spiritual healing and reject medicine because they think matter is an illusion. Disease is unreal; it can be overcome by getting one's mind straight. While it may not make Christian Scientists subscribe to different articles of faith or force medical treatment upon them, their government funds cancer research, tells them all the time that cigarette smoking causes cancer, and taxes them for Medicare and Medicaid. Still, no one to my knowledge has ever suggested that Christian Scientists have an immunity against those and other practices that promote, foster, aid, and encourage the medical arts. That is because almost no one denies that the common good includes health and medicine.

Many Amish reject formal schooling, both because they believe that it is unnecessary to their lifestyles and as a sign of worldliness, of conformity with earthly powers. The Amish are famously exempt from compulsory attendance at high school, and have won some other privileges from legislatures, as well as courts, due to their religious beliefs. But the Supreme Court held in *U.S. v. Lee*[1] that they were not exempt from Social Security withholding. The Amish also pay the property taxes that are commonly the source of public school funds. "Stay in school," saith also the state, in public service sermons during televised sporting events. This conveys, to be sure, an endorsement of what the Amish conscientiously reject, and may make them feel like second-class citizens. But they have no legal cause of action, for the common good includes education.

No one suggests that a latter day Luddite, or someone with the views but not the hobbies and mailing habits of Theodore Kaczynski, has an immunity from government industrial policy, even though those policies signal to Luddites that they are, to put it mildly, "outsiders" in our political community. That is because there is a common good in economic development.

Christian Scientists, the Amish, and our Luddite have an absolute right to think what they please about God, the modern age, and our polity. They enjoy a substantial but limited immunity against forced participation in practices to which they object. But, frankly, it never occurs to us or to them (and maybe not even to the ACLU) that they have a First Amendment veto over public authority's pursuit of the common good in health and medicine, education, and material prosperity. The common good includes their right to dissent, but the common good is not trumped, held hostage, or even modified by their dissenting views.

Now let us consider a different type of dissent. A new resident in your town notices a lighted sign atop the municipal building that says, "Praise God." Then his child goes to school and encounters a century-old custom, hitherto welcomed by all parents and children, of opening the school day with a moment of silent prayer.

Dad and Junior sue. Neither alleges coercion. Neither says that these recognitions of a greater than human source of meaning and value are sect-partial. They agree, in other words, that these practices constitute a minimum philosophical understanding of religion. Neither Dad nor Junior alleges that they disagree with the affirmations themselves; there is, indeed, not a word in the record about what the plaintiffs believe. They allege only that they "object" to public, i.e., governmental, affirmation of them.

Dad and Junior prevail on summary judgment: God must go from public space. An incensed district court judge flails local public officials for ignoring the Supreme Court's rule that public authority may never promote, encourage, foster or aid religion, for relegating the plaintiffs to status of second-class citizens, for stigmatizing them as outsiders by these "endorsements of religion over nonreligion."[2]

This is the world of church-state constitutional doctrine. It is Anthony Lewis territory. Here, the lonely dissenter holds the trump card. These doctrines, of which the "no-endorsement" command is master principle, make no sense save on the presupposition that there is no common good in religion. The justices *say* that no governmental entity has care of the common good, if any there be, in religion. They *mean* that religion is a private matter.[3] This is an endorsement—of radical secularism—*and it is precisely this secularism that threatens the well-being of the family.* The constitutional doctrine of "privacy" that spawned rights to abortion, contraception, pornography, and other elements of the liberationist agenda (which often means liberation from the family or from family rights and duties) has its roots in, and is made possible by, the perversion of religious liberty by the courts.

An objector might say that, surely, religion has not entirely disappeared from the government radar screen. Don't some tax dollars go to Catholic colleges? Don't some nativity scenes survive the ACLU's annual purge? Did not believers win the two most recent Supreme Court cases, *Pinette*[4] and *Rosenberger*[5]? Yes, but in no case does evidence of religion or of its promotion get through constitutional scrutiny as a promotion of religion. Survivors instead emerge battle-scarred from constitutional litigation with strangers' dog tags, under some nonreligious description. Baby Jesus, amongst Rudolph and Nutcracker, is now a "neutral folk symbol," legislative prayer and the "In God We Trust" motto on the dollar bill are examples of a vestigial "ceremonial deism." The justices say flatly and constantly that aiming to help believers lacks a secular purpose. It is unconstitutional per se.

This means that aiming to help believers is not within the common good entrusted to the care of government.

The question in *Rosenberger* and *Pinette*, the cases decided in June 1995, was whether notwithstanding the general constitutional principle that forbids government discrimination among viewpoints, how much worse does the Establishment Clause allow—require—states to treat believers than nonbelievers? The question, put differently by Justice Scalia, is whether piety is on a par with pornography,[6] whether (in my words) the Madonna is on a par with Madonna. A minority of the Court—Scalia, Thomas, Kennedy, and Rehnquist—answered in the affirmative. A majority held that sometimes Madonna gets the edge.

So, let us say there is public school space let out to community groups for lectures on the subject of family life. Dr. Dobson surfaces in this realm of self-imposed value neutrality under the description as private speaker "A," and Madonna as private speaker "B," and Andrew Sullivan as private speaker "C"—if Dr. Dobson is permitted to speak at all.

A critic might now say that, surely still, the government promotes and encourages *religious* liberty. There is, for G-d's sake, a Free Exercise Clause and a Religious Freedom Restoration Act.[7] Religion must therefore be promotable, if only to accord it a proper liberty.

Yes, but consider the justices' consistent and regular admonition that the Constitution protects a "religious liberty" that treats religion and nonreligion equally.[8] Note well: Right from the beginning of the new judicial dispensation—*Everson,*[9] 1947—it has been equal religious liberty for atheists. The State, according to the *Everson* court, is commanded by Free Exercise to protect the religious freedom of Baptists, Mohammedans, Methodists, Catholics and Non-believers (with a capital "N").[10] The rationale for this "religious liberty" cannot be what it was for the Founders, that religion is good. That would endorse religion. What, then, is the doctrine—and the coherent rationale—for the Court's "religious liberty"?

Let's see.

In the 1994 *Kiryas Joel*[11] case the justices reviewed a classic example of special governmental care to assist believers to live out their commitments. The New York legislature carved out a village-sized school district to accommodate Hasidic Jewish children who could not conscientiously go to public schools, where they could get special education, which federal statutes guaranteed them.

The Supreme Court declared the revised accommodation an unconstitutional establishment. Why? The justices were not sure that the legislature would be equally solicitous of other "religious (and nonreligious) groups."[12] The governing principle of free exercise was stated by Justice O'Connor, in her concurring *Kiryas Joel* opinion: "Religious needs can [only!] be accommodated through laws that are neutral with regard to religion."[13]

Another earnest attempt to locate the rationale and scope of "religious liberty" is Justice Souter's opinion (for O'Connor and Stevens) in a 1992 public school graduation prayer case, *Lee v. Wiseman.*[14] Souter wanted to justify special "accommodation" of religious believers as such. He initially opined that "accommodation" of believers, without equal concern for the irreligious, *was* constitutionally acceptable. "Accommodation," he said, showed only "respect" for religion. He distinguished this permitted "respect" from a prohibited "endorsement" of religion.[15]

"Respect," Souter continued, allows us "to act without expressing a position on the theological merit of those values."[16] Fair enough." We do not necessarily affirm the truth of some Islamic tenet when we say that Muslims have a right to religious worship. But Souter then added, "or of religious belief in general." Souter is back where he began: On what basis do we act in some special way to "respect" or "accommodate" persons' religious practices without "endorsing" religion. How do we "respect" religion, completely apart from any judgment about the value of religion?

"What makes accommodation permissible, even praiseworthy," Justice O'Connor said in *Kiryas Joel*, "is not that government is making life easier for some religious group as such. Rather, it is that government is accommodating a deeply held belief."[17] Souter, more revealingly, in *Lee v. Weisman*: "In freeing the Native American Church from federal laws forbidding peyote use [to take a common example]. . . . the government conveys no endorsement of peyote rituals, the church, or religion as such; it simply respects the centrality of peyote to the lives of certain Americans."[18] But only "certain" Americans because, presumably, Native American sacramental use has a value or is good in a way that peyote use in a non-sacramental context is not. But saying that would endorse religion, which is forbidden.

The Supreme Court protects "religious liberty" precisely by the endorsement test: Public authority may not favor "one religion over others nor religious adherents collectively over nonadherents." The justices see themselves as promoting religious liberty just by making religion private, by excluding it from that part of the common good entrusted to the care of public authority. And so, "religious liberty" surfaces under another description, either "privacy," "autonomy," or just plain "liberty."

Question: How to promote "religious liberty" without endorsing "religion." Answer: It's the liberty, stupid—not the religion. Devotion to Madonna and the Madonna must be seen as exertions of the same right. If so, there is just one great big constitutional liberty these days, an autonomy right to give your own meaning to, among other things, family, marriage, life, death. "Religious liberty" is an aspect of the *Casey v. Planned Parenthood* megaright to create your own moral universe.[19] Harvard's Laurence Tribe put it aptly in the title of his treatise's chapter on the topic: "Rights of Religious Autonomy."[20] There is one great big right. See *Casey*. People exercise it in various ways, some ways religious, and some not.

Does this content-less account of rights seem too depraved, too perverse, even for the Supreme Court? Well, the *Casey* plurality opinion—by three Republican appointees—not only affirmed *Roe v. Wade* but argued for abortion liberty by saying that it participated in the same autonomy that justifies a woman's right to carry a baby to term.[21] Really. The *Casey* plurality said that it could not find a constitutional right against government-mandated killing (think of Chinese family policy) *without* finding an included private right (of women) to kill their unborn children.[22] The justices must believe that the common sense moral distinction which ordinary people have no trouble making—between bringing life into being and extinguishing it—is not a fit basis for constitutional line-drawing. And the justices think *that* probably because they must, in their view, remain entirely agnostic about values, like the values of life and religion.

My deeper point is this: The "no-endorsement" "religious liberty" regime was—is—the essential precondition of *Casey*. Put differently, getting rid of God—secularism—was and is the necessary condition for christening the *Casey* court's radical autonomy principle.

Did the Court simply stipulate this? Or is it fairly discoverable (as the justices often say it is) in the Founders' constitutional command? What was the general understanding of the principle of nonestablishment before the beginning of the modern jurisprudential era in *Everson*?

The *Everson* court said nonestablishment meant to the Framers and hence to the justices at least no support or promotion of religion, period.[23] But nonestablishment meant instead, for a very long time before *Everson*, no preference for one religion over another.[24] The Founders' insight, at the end of the eighteenth century, was this: The common good of their society did not depend upon the truth of the matters that distinguished the Protestant sects. What distinguished Methodists from Presbyterians—finer points of doctrine, modes of worship, church disciplinary practices, and governing structure—could be safely declared beyond the competence of public authority. The law knew no heresy, no dogma, and established no sect. And a glance at the historical record from the Founders up to *Everson* reveals public support, promotion, encouragement of religion.

In *Zorach v. Clauson*,[25] the Court said that "[w]e are a religious people whose institutions presuppose a Supreme Being." In 1961 the Court said that the "Founding Fathers believed devotedly that there was a God and the unalienable rights of man were rooted in Him is clearly evidenced in their writings, from the Mayflower Compact to the Constitution itself."[26] The implication is that the Founders believed secularism would undermine our rights. Is that true? All too briefly, the acceptance of divine revelation by Jews, Christians, and Muslims led them to treat as false (because unreal) the various sources of meaning and value other than God and human persons—the many gods, spirits, world souls. Apart from God the creator, there remained only the created world, and in that world, only God and created persons could give meaning and value. But, so long as God is in the picture, God-given meaning and value is logically prior to and regulative of *our* attempts to give meaning and value. For no rational person would deny that the Creator's plan is not normative for his creatures.

Secularism leaves nothing but human thoughts and desires to serve as sources for the meaning and value of everything, including human persons. So, only when God is dead, or at least presumed to be irrelevant, will sane people credit the extraordinary assertion of human creativity that is the *Casey* "mystery passage."[27] In a secularized regime we should expect that the question of who or what counts as a subject to whom moral duties, like the duty not to kill, are owed is resolved according to the interests of those who already count as persons. So it is in the *Casey* regime; the alleged instrumental necessity of abortion to women's lifestyles is, arguably, the major premise of the joint opinion. In a secularized society, a genuine common good, which transcends people's *de facto* interests and desires is strictly inconceivable. In place of a common good, including inalienable human rights, we should expect a discourse about ordering our life together that is, in reality if not confessedly, a more or less stable consensus of the articulate on an agenda. Does not *Casey*'s exaggerated emphasis upon precedent and doctrinal stability suggest just such a pattern? Does not the exclusion from respectable discourse (i.e., "public reason") of those defending the inalienable right to life of the *in*articulate further evidence it? Does not the judiciary's privatization of religion confirm it?

What this leads to in constitutional matters involving family law is this: Groups defending traditional (monogamous, heterosexual) marriage as, simply, the truth about marriage will be received by courts as just another interested group pushing its private agenda in the public square. Thus arrayed as merely a majoritarian "interest," there is little hope that these groups can prevail against other persons' "fundamental liberty" to create and, it seems, to inhabit their own universes—in which their own private notions of "family" and the rights and duties regarding marriage and family life will trump any mere majoritarian interest "masquerading" as the truth about marriage.

Notes

1. 455 U.S. 252 (1982).

2. See, e.g., *Rosenberger v. Rector & Visitors of U.Va.*, 115 S.Ct. 2510, 2525-2528 (1995) (O'Connor, J., concurring).

3. See, generally G. Bradley, "Dogmatomachy: A 'Privatization' Theory of the Religion Clause Cases," *St. Louis Law Journal 30* (1986): 275.

4. *Capitol Square Review Bd. v. Pinette*, 115 S.Ct. 2440 (1995).

5. See note 2, infra.

6. *Pinette*, 115 S.Ct. at 2449.

7. 42 U.S.C. 2000 bb (1993). Or at least there was—see *City of Boerne v. Flores* 138 L.Ed.2d 624 (1997).

8. See, e.g., *Rosenberger*, 115 S.Ct. at 2521-2523.

9. 330 U.S. 1 (1947).

10. 330 U.S. at 16.

11. *Board of Ed. of Kiryas Joel v. Grumet*, 114 S.Ct. 2481 (1994).

12. Id. at 2491.

13. Id. at 2496.

14. 112 S.Ct. 2649 (1992).

15. Id. at 2677.

16. Id.

17. 114 S.Ct. at 2497.

18. 112 S.Ct. at 2677.

19. See 112 S.Ct. 2791, 2807 (1992) (joint opinion of Kennedy, Souter, O'Connor, JJ.).

20. L. Tribe, *American Constitutional Law* 1154 (2nd ed. 1988).

21. 112 S.Ct. 2811.

22. Id.

23. See 330 U.S. at 15-16.

24. This is the thesis of G. Bradley, *Church-State Relationships in America* (New York: Greenwood Press, 1987).

25. 343 U.S. 306, 313 (1952).

26. 366 U.S. 420 (1961).

27. 120 L.Ed.2d 698 (1992).

12

The Moral Logic of No-Fault Divorce

Maggie Gallagher

Let me state the twin facts of the matter rather baldly: First, marriage, as a lifelong childrearing union, is on the brink of extinction. Second, marriage, as a formal, legal institution, has already been abolished.

The decline of marriage can be captured in a few swift statistics: At least half of marriages fail.[1] Meanwhile one-third of our children are now born outside of marriage. As recently as the 1940s just 14 percent of married white women (and 18 percent of married black woman) would divorce. One generation later, half of women who married in the late sixties and early seventies, have already divorced.[2]

As fewer adults marry, the divorce rate appears to have leveled off, albeit at an unprecedentedly high level. Meanwhile the illegitimacy rate continues to skyrocket. In the most recent National Center for Health Statistics data, the jump in out-of-wedlock births (from 31 percent to 32.6 percent) was the largest single-year increase ever in recorded American history.[3]

In just a few years, if current trends continue, half of all our kids will be born outside of marriage; half of the remainder will experience the breakup of their parents' marriage. In short, if current trends are allowed to continue, marriage will swiftly become a cult practice, the domain of a small, relatively affluent minority.

The collapse of marriage is undoubtedly the result of a number of complicated social forces, from the rise of the feminism to the decline of male wages, from the rights revolution unleashed by the Me generation to the explosion in out-of-wedlock sex.

But underlying social forces are not the whole story. Over the last twenty years culture and public policy have conspired to weaken marriage as an institution, to parcel out its rights to the unmarried, and to undermine the supports the married have generally relied on to help them fulfill their responsibilities to children and to each other. These changes in adoption and foster care, in tax law and zoning, in credit, child care, and housing policies might each individually seem small. But cumulatively they have sent out a consistent public message: Marriage is one of many equally valid lifestyle choices. Such an abrupt (if generally unremarked) shift in public policy must have played a role in weakening the special place of marriage as an institution.

But the law has gone even further still. Not content merely to weaken marriage, the law has, in substance if not in form, actually abolished it. If this sounds radical, consider the following. One of the unacknowledged side effects of the no-fault divorce revolution is this: The law will no longer allow you to make a permanent legal commitment to your spouse. With no-fault divorce, judges and state legislatures have gutted the marital contract. Under no-fault, the law no longer cares who wants to break up the marriage or why. Instead the law uniformly sides with the spouse who wants out, in the process transforming marriage into a legal relation best described as cohabitation, with insurance benefits.

What are we doing when we say "I do"? Under our current divorce laws the marriage commitment has been reduced to this: "I promise to live with you and care for you until I feel like doing something else, at which point I have an absolute right to get out for any reason, or no reason at all." What is the difference between this and living together?

Recently I wrote a column proposing reforming no-fault divorce law by adding a five-year waiting period for a contested no-fault divorce. This long waiting period (which would bring America's divorce laws in line with much of Europe) would do two things: (1) slow down the divorce process and save some marriages that could and should be saved, and (2) give some power, dignity, and leverage back into the hands of the abandoned spouse. If you want a quick, no-fault divorce, the law would say, you are going to have to negotiate with the man or woman you married in order to get it.

In my mind, this is the least a civilized society can do to enforce the marriage commitment and to demonstrate concern for the well-being of both spouses.

The idea provoked quite a bit of mail that fell rather neatly into two categories: applause from spouses who had been abandoned, and outrage from spouses who had ended their marriages.

This was not a gender divide. I received anguished letters from both men and women who felt their lives have been ripped apart by the cruelty of divorce. And I received at least as many letters from women as men who simply could not understand the reasoning behind such a proposal.

"What good excuse would keep a person in an unhappy, unrewarding relationship?" asked one respondent, a woman who left a twenty-five year marriage because she was "tired of trying to please, gain love, do the 'right thing'." "Would it be denial of a problem," she asked, "would it be financial gain, would it be 'for the children', would it be for all the wrong reasons? My question--why would an unwanted spouse wish to stay in a marriage? What is, therefore, wrong with no-fault divorce?"

This is, judging from conversations I've had with many Americans over the last few months in the course of publicizing my book, *The Abolition of Marriage,* a not uncommon sentiment among Americans, one way we resolve the moral conflict of interest between two spouses, one of whom wants a divorce and the other of whom does not: You want to hold onto someone who doesn't want you any more? What kind of loser are *you*?

On the other hand, another woman wrote to tell me of her husband's divorce decision, "At age 57, he announced he would seek a divorce. All my dreams, hopes, and looking forward to some well earned 'golden time' were dashed and smashed to smithereens. Our 37-year marriage was to be erased. My former standard of living was obliterated and can never be reached again. Our laws," she complained, "do not differentiate between 4 months or 40 years."

They do not differentiate as well between a woman who wants to leave an abusive husband or a man who wants to trade in an aging wife. Our laws make no distinctions at all because their aim is now to facilitate the party who wants out, no questions asked.

The right to leave is judged so compelling that it must override our right to make (and be held responsible for) our commitments. For twenty-five years we have talked and written and legislated about no-fault divorce as if it represented an increase in personal choice. As the letters I received from divorcees suggest, this is a simplification and a falsification of our experience with no-fault divorce. For in most cases, divorce is not a mutual act, but the choice of one partner alone. "[W]e might expect that both partners would be ready to end the relationship by the time one leaves," note family scholars Furstenberg and Cherlin, "But the data suggest otherwise. Four out of five marriages ended unilaterally."[4]

No-fault divorce does not expand everyone's personal choice. It empowers the spouse who wishes to leave, and leaves the spouse who is being left helpless, out of control, overwhelmed and weak.

The spouse who chooses divorce has a liberating sense of mastery, which psychologists have identified as one of the key components of personal happiness. He or she is breaking free, embracing change, which, with its psychic echoes of the exhilarating original adolescent break from the family, can dramatically boost self-esteem.

Being divorced (as the sudden popularity of the movie *The First Wives Club* attested) reinforces exactly the opposite sense of life. Being divorced does not feel like an act of personal courage, or transform you into the hero of your own life story, because being divorced is not an act at all. It is something that happens to you, over which, thanks to no-fault divorce legislation, you have no say at all.

The spouse who leaves learns that love dies. The spouse who is left learns that love *betrays* and that the courts and society side with the betrayers. In court, your marriage commitment means nothing. The only rule is: He who wants out, wins. Thus, no-fault divorce represents not an increase in personal choice, but a one-sided transfer in power in which the state seeks to facilitate as rapidly as possible the desires of one partner over the other. In the process, no-fault divorce denies to individuals both the ability and the right to make any kind of enforceable marital commitment.

Could there be any relationship between the legal and formal abolition of marriage and its subsequent collapse? For years the answer the academic researchers came up with was, No. "Nearly every study of divorce and the law has concluded that legal changes have little or no impact upon the rate of marital dissolutions," wrote Princeton social historian Elaine Tyler May, repeating the conventional scholarly wisdom.[5]

But evaluating the effect of law on divorce rates turned out to be tricky. Not only do state statutes vary, but different states changed different aspects of divorce law. Some states merely added no-fault to other grounds for divorce. Others abolished fault altogether. Still others cut waiting periods.

Many of these earlier studies assumed all the changes lumped under the no-fault rubric had the same effect on divorce rates. Moreover in many cases states officially passed no-fault laws only after judges had already effectively changed the law to ease divorce. In these cases, statutory changes merely codified what the common law practice already was.

To add to the confusion, many other states were suddenly labeled "no-fault" states not because the law had changed but because they were added to a catalog of no-fault jurisdictions assembled for a 1974 listing in the influential journal *Family Law Quarterly.*[6] Since early researchers sometimes relied on this listing as definitive evidence of when states adopted no-fault (when in fact the law had not changed or had changed much earlier), they concluded (naturally but wrongly) that the law had had no effect on the divorce rate.

Several recent studies however, using different methods of analysis, conclude that some of the changes in divorce law did increase the divorce rate in some jurisdictions.[7]

What legal changes appear to increase divorce the most? The research suggests the answer is changes in timing, such as reducing waiting periods. When lawmakers try to speed up the divorce process, as well as make it more nonjudgmental, more spouses and children will be exposed to the cruelties and losses divorce entails.

No-fault divorce is just one of a series of ways the law has weakened marriage. Federal statutes, originally intended to protect single and divorced women from discrimination, now make it illegal for private individuals as well as local governments to distinguish between married and unmarried couples for a variety of purposes including housing, credit, and zoning.

Prior to 1968, for example, most cities that offered low-income housing offered strong preferences to poor married couples. The federal government, in its wisdom, denied federal housing monies to municipalities that "discriminated" on the basis of marital status.

At about the same time, the federal government transformed unwed teenage pregnancy from a social wrong into a constitutional right: Henceforth, on pain of losing federal education funding, schools could no longer segregate pregnant girls (or unmarried fathers) in special schools, nor could they even restrict their extracurricular activities. (When one Texas community tried to bar pregnant cheerleaders, the school had to back down when the National Organization for Women threatened to sue.) In foster care and adoption, the one-time preference for married couples has been largely abandoned. Race-matching, for example, is pretty much everywhere considered a higher priority in adoption than obtaining for a child a married two-parent family.

Meanwhile, our welfare policy continues to define failure to work, rather than failure to marry, as the prime problem. For the purpose of ending a culture of dependency, a five-year time limit on welfare benefits may be worse than useless. For the average teenager (much less a poor, inner-city kid) five years seems like an eternity. Our current welfare law thus invites a vulnerable young girl to have a baby she cannot support and then cuts her off after she makes decisions (like quitting school or having another baby) that make it virtually impossible for her to become self-supporting. Similarly, while one can imagine asking her to give up for adoption a baby she cannot take care of, one cannot really ask the same woman, five years later, to ditch a kindergartener just because she is poor.

Perhaps the most important step the law could take in this regard is ending welfare for teenage mothers. In 1993 about 30 percent of all out-of wedlock births were to unmarried teenagers. If we aren't willing to tell these poor, undereducated, unmarried categorically that they should not be having children, we aren't serious about ending poverty or making a start on restoring marriage.

Instead of routinely giving custody of babies to girls too young to drive a car or sign a contract, the law should require that every baby born in America be under the guardianship of a competent adult. If the girl cannot find an adult willing to assume full legal responsibility, the baby should be placed for adoption.

These are just a few examples of the ways in which law and public policy, which previously privileged marriage, now actually intervenes to prevent private individuals, organizations, and local governments from supporting marriage as an institution, which the federal government has largely redefined as "discrimination on the basis of marital status." In short, the sudden collapse of marriage was far from inevitable. It is, at least in part, the product of bad public policy, which could and should be reformed. To a much greater extent than most of us have been willing to acknowledge, a 50 percent divorce rate and a 33 percent illegitimacy rate is not just something that happens. It is something we do to ourselves, to each other, and to our children.

Try this thought experiment: What would happen if courts treated property and business contracts as we now treat the marriage contract? What if American law refused to enforce business contracts and indeed systematically favored the party that wished to withdraw, on the grounds that fault was messy and exposed judges and attorneys to unpleasant acrimony? What if property were viewed, as marriage increasingly is, as a strictly private matter, so that when disputes arose, thieves and owners would be left to work things out privately because, after all, you can't legislate morality? If the corporation were required to operate on the same legal principles that govern our marriage laws, the economy would collapse. So it is not surprising that, under the same regiment, marriage is on the verge of doing just that.

This summer, just as the country seemed to forge a new consensus on the value of marriage, the cultural elite struck back. A slew of highly praised books such as Ruth Sidel's *Keeping Women and Children Last*, Michael Lind's *Up from*

Conservatism, Kristin Luker's *Dubious Conceptions*, and Judith Stacey's *In the Name of the Family* have been published, which argue that the family is not collapsing, that teen pregnancy, illegitimacy, and divorce are not on the rise or do not represent a social crisis but an evolution of family form.

But the most powerful argument these divorce advocates muster is this: "People who are unhappily married aren't going to stay together. Teenagers aren't going to have a mass conversion and choose abstinence until they marry—if they do marry. And members of the impoverished underclass . . . aren't ever going to be able to live like Ozzie and Harriet," as Carol Travis, a social psychologist put it in her review of Judith Stacey's book.[8] In other words, good or bad, the collapse of marriage and the rise of the unwed mother are inevitable. There's nothing we can do but accept these changes and try, through government subsidies, to ease the worst of the economic deprivation children and single mothers are now experiencing.

The argument from despair has played a powerful role in paralyzing the American public and American policymakers. But even a cursory survey of the international data suggest that marriage and modernity are not nearly as incompatible as these preachers against traditional family values would have us believe.

While it is true that rates of illegitimacy and divorce are on the rise throughout the Western world, the rate at which nations have been able to resist such trends varies wildly. Germany, for example, has an illegitimacy rate of 15 percent, half that of America. In Italy the rate is 7 percent. In today's Japan just 1 percent of babies are born outside of marriage,[9] the same proportion as in 1970, and the divorce rate is so low that almost all minor children live with both their married parents.[10]

While America may never return to the low divorce and illegitimacy rates of the last century, there is every reason to believe that these two simple goals can be accomplished: (1) to stabilize marriage, so that the majority of lovers who marry succeed in making a permanent union, and (2) reconnect marriage and childbearing, so that each year more and more (rather than fewer and fewer) American babies begin their lives under the protection of a couple publicly joined by marriage vows.

The law of marriage exists not to punish people but to help them achieve their goal—to take two biological strangers and create, out of them and their children, a new family.

A hundred years ago romantics, living in a time when marriage could be taken for granted, imagined that heroic acts of love must take place outside of its bonds. But they were wrong, these wistful romantics. Today we have learned through a painful process of experimentation that it is not free love but the vow that is daring. To dare to pledge our whole selves in love to a single person is the most remarkable thing most of us will ever do.

With the abolition of marriage, this last possibility for heroism has been taken from us.

Notes

1. See, for example, Teresa Castro Martin and Larry L. Bumpass, "Recent Trends in Marital Disruption," *Demography* 26 (1989): 37ff.

2. Dennis A. Ahlburg and Carol J. DeVita, "New Realities of the American Family," *Population Bulletin* 47, no. 2 (August 1992): 15.

3. Murray Op. Cit.

4. Frank F. Furstenberg, Jr and Andrew J. Cherlin, *Divided Families: What Happens to Children When Parents Part* (Cambridge, Mass: Harvard University Press, 1991), 21-22.

5. Elaine Tyler May, *Great Expectations: Marriage and Divorce in Post-Victorian America* (Chicago: University of Chicago Press, 1980), 5.

6. Herbert Jacobs, *Silent Revolution: The Transformation of Divorce Law in the United States* (Chicago: Univeristy of Chicago Press, 1988), 81-82.

7. See Thomas B. Marvell, "Divorce Rates and the Fault Requirement," *Law and Society Review* 23, (1989): 557ff Martin Zelder, "The Economic Analysis of the Effect of No-Fault Divorce Law on the Divorce Rate," *Harvard Journal of Law and Public Policy* 16, no. 1, 241ff; Paul Z. Nokonezny et. al., "The Effect of No-Fault Divorce Law on the Divorce Rate Across the 50 States and Its Relation to Income, Education, and Religiosity," *Journal of Marriage and the Family* 57, no. 2, (May 1995) 477ff.

8. Carol Travis, "Goodbye, Ozzie and Harriet," *New York Times Book Review* (September 22, 1996): 27.

9. Amara Bachu, "Fertility of American Women: June 1994" (Washington D.C.: Bureau of the Census, September 1995) page xix, Table K.

10. June Axinn, "Japan: A Special Case," in *The Feminization of Poverty: Only in America?* Gertrude Schaffner Goldberg and Eleanor Kremen eds. (New York: Greenwood Press, 1990): 101.

13

The Case against Divorce

Diane Medved

In discussing the alarming phenomenon of popularized divorce, most observers focus on its impact to the members of the torn nuclear family. They acknowledge the trauma of a spouse rejected by the other, of children thrust into single-parent families and denied a father's presence, of starting over amidst financial handicaps. The usual stance is to view each failed family as an isolated unit, which with divorce becomes various permutations of units, all of which earn the title "family." In a perverted expression of our national motto, E pluribus unum ("from many, one"), many social scientists consider a marital breakup as "from one, many," providing them more units to study and service, just as honorable and "whole" as the single unit the couple had formed before.

Three "Ruinous Ripples"

I tend to look a bit more broadly at the impact of divorce. Instead of viewing each marital dissolution separately, I see it as the stone tossed into the water, causing a series of "ruinous ripples" that greatly disturb the surrounding tranquility. Divorce is particularly damaging to three "ripples," three classes of individuals hurt by the termination of a single marriage.

At the center of the devastation are of course the two married partners. But even the partner who instigates the divorce, perhaps seeking freedom from a situation deemed intolerable, cannot emerge unscathed. Standards of living, particularly for women, plummet; men often must radically diminish their lifestyles to support two households.

The character of divorced people is inevitably altered. Experiencing failure of what was once a "permanent" commitment is at some level a disgrace, a public statement of either poor judgment or inability to cope. No one feels proud of a divorce. And after divorce, no individual looks at marriage the same way, with the same kind of trust, enthusiasm, hope, or goodwill.

The second "ruinous ripple" consists of those around the divorcing couple.

Primary among these are, of course, the children. My colleague David Blankenhorn, founder of the Institute for American Values and author of *Fatherless America*, has documented well the harm suffered by children in every sphere of life, in both the short and long term. Judith Wallerstein, known for her longitudinal studies of children of divorce, has found that the effects of the ordeal shadow children into their own marriages—frequently causing a fear of marriage altogether. Awkward feelings about relatives on both sides—often with strangers "blending" into family—dog children of divorce as long as they live.

But the "ripple" surrounding the divorcing couple includes many others. Writers and researchers seldom acknowledge the emotional pain of grandparents wrenched away from regular contact with their grandchildren. The divorce process often estranges these elders from their own children's lives, and they watch with heartbreak the reorganization of factors that affect them, including complicated custody arrangements, moves to lesser living quarters, and bitterness on both sides. I have talked to many grandparents who lament, "how can my children make a decision that impacts my life so much—it's not fair."

Divorce also hurts friends. Clients in my psychology practice often express their shock and dismay when they hear about the separation of friends they thought were models of a happy marriage. They think, "Is my marriage safe? Do we really have the love relationship I thought we had? If it can happen to Joe and Mary over there, it can happen to us." Divorce therefore calls into question everything they believe about their own marriages, and by extension, everything they believe about the validity of their neighborhoods and friendships and society.

Which brings me to the third "ruinous ripple" of divorce, its impact on society at large. The 50 percent divorce rate, while a popularized statistic, is not only misleading, as I'll discuss later, but appears everywhere—because in our divorce-rife society, any opportunity for validation is welcome. The old adage "misery loves company" might apply here, for there is comfort in feeling part of a large group. Statistics suggesting that half of all marriages fail lets a divorcing person dismiss his own failure as simply his bad luck in falling in the "wrong half," diminishing his motivation to work to save his union. When divorce becomes "no big deal," then the value of marriage erodes destructively.

Statistics about the failure of marriage also affect wider social problems such as out-of-wedlock births. We know that 30 percent of births overall and 70 percent of those in the black community are to unmarried women. Figures like the "50 percent divorce rate," confirming that marriage cannot be stable, fuel a refusal even to bother. Today's mores have changed so dramatically that now classic young women's magazines such as *Glamour* and *Mademoiselle* have changed their editorial "norm" to the following progression. A young woman meets a guy, dates him once or twice, at which time it becomes appropriate for her to go to bed with him. If she falls in love, she and her young man cohabit for a while, as she continues with her career. In perhaps two or three years, she might want children, and the couple marries. Or they split apart. This new norm is radically different from the one we older baby boomers absorbed from these same publications, which assumed we reserved sexuality for marriage, an event ideally occurring immediately after college. I think labeling divorce "just another choice" contributes greatly to the revision in young peoples' expectations and their permissive behavior.

Causes of Divorce

So divorce hurts the individual, those around that individual, and our society at large. But rather than elaborate on the impact of divorce, I'd like to shift to something new—its causes. I'd like to talk about this "bad news," not so much in terms of what it is, but about why it is happening. Three types of factors fuel the proliferation of divorce: economic, cultural, and personal.

Economic Factors

There is a dirty little secret that, instead of being a growth experience— which we all thought divorce was during the sixties and seventies and even up into the beginning of the eighties—divorce is not a growth experience. Instead, it has become a growth industry.

It's a fact that many professions benefit from divorce. Though workers in these fields might want to support family values in their own lives, professionally they foster divorce, spurred by economic incentives. I'm going to look at a few examples of this in unexpected places.

I'm the fifth generation from Southern California. My husband and I have lived in the same house in the Los Angeles area for twenty years, where reside all our family, long-term friendships, and deep roots in our Jewish Community. But recently Michael received a job offer he couldn't refuse—so we have been looking at advertisements for homes in Seattle. One striking feature of many of the ads is phrases like "sellers motivated, divorce"; "sellers motivated, buy now, divorced"; "divorcing couple." Now, realtors have two inches of space to write something to draw buyers—and they write that the couple is getting divorced! It's crazy but realtors are chomping at the bit for divorces, not because they like to see families die, but because they want commissions. The more households that split up, the more financial opportunity. As a realtor, wouldn't you rather sell one property and buy two, than have none? And when the transaction is complete, others gain finacially. Ask any moving company how much of their business arises from the dissolution of households due to divorce. Packers, movers, U-haul renters, apartment cleaners all have an investment in divorce.

Then there is a new kind of occupation that has emerged—arbitration. I don't remember as a child growing up hearing that as a career option. The idea of marital arbitration or mediation has proliferated in the last few years, since divorce has become so widely accepted and so prohibitively costly. Suddenly, custody battles are de rigueur, and after tying up courts for so many years we have now become wise enough to devise a separate occupation of specialists, also with a stake in the rising divorce rate. Very few arbitrators will say "hey, why are we sitting here—go home." They say "alright, how can we divide this," "how can we make this work"— and "how much time are we putting in here," because they probably charge by the hour.

Then there's the "family attorney," which is probably an oxymoron. "Family Attorneys"—what do they do? Do they typically say, "stay together?" No, they say, "let's see how we can get the wheels of the legal system to run more smoothly for you." They very rarely would say, "gee, you know I shouldn't be working with you." Instead, they focus on the task at hand: "Let's look at the technicalities here: if 'a,' then 'b'; this is how we can use the law to further your case."

And finally we turn to my own colleagues--some of whom will probably recoil from my remarks--because therapists are in most cases also motivated toward divorce rather than toward saving marriage. I get calls every day from different parts of the country saying, "I've read your book, *The Case Against Divorce*. Now, can you give me a referral to a therapist in my area who wants to save marriages, because I've been to a handful of them and they all say, 'why do you take this? You ought to get a divorce,' but I don't want to get a divorce." Few therapists are willing to express a bias in favor of marriage, to figuratively "shake the shoulders" of their clients and be "judgmental." It has been a sin amongst therapists to be judgmental, though reserving any opinion is also a judgment of another kind.

I was trained at UCLA at a time when Rogerian Therapy was popular. I remember being taught to empathetically nod our heads, like one of those dolls in the back of a car, no matter what the client said. We were to deliver unqualified acceptance and reinforcement until the proverbial lightbulb suddenly appeared over clients' heads, and they figured out on their own not only the source of their problem but also how to solve it. That very rarely works, of course. Therapists often can't bring themselves to say that one course of behavior is superior to another out of a fear of appearing judgmental. And so they "enable" divorce.

Oops—that's another buzz word that enjoyed a period of favor. I've heard clients justify ending marriages because spouses were "codependent" on each other, a misuse of a concept meant to apply to destructive behaviors such as drug or alcohol abuse. When couples come to me and say "we're codependent," my immediate thought is, "that's what marriage is all about, so, what's new? It's a problem that you see it as a problem. It isn't a problem that you are codependent," though I like to rephrase the term: Spouses in healthy marriages are really "interdependent."

I've encountered therapists who say "I want to help you achieve your goal." But they overlook the question, "what are your goals?" These therapists let the client sit there and complain for an hour, and they wouldn't dare say, "do you think that a major contributor to your problem could be that you are self-pitying?" I think it is important to let people see that there is a continuum of right and wrong, and that there is some behavior that is more correct or constructive than other behavior. Unfortunately, that is not commonly accepted today. The more therapists nod their heads and the less they say, "it's likely you're making a mistake," the more money they are going to earn.

Now this is not to say that therapists are inherently evil-minded or selfish—nothing of the sort. Every ethical therapist absolutely believes that she is doing the right thing for the client. But at the same time, a competing, underlying influence is the financial opportunity. Is it irrelevant that a therapist wants to earn money? Is it irrelevant that she can bill the insurance of those who come to her? I don't think so. So what we see here is an economic incentive, silently pushing even dedicated therapists toward prolonging the therapy, and, unfortunately, that in a sense can mean prolonging the pain. I think this contributes to the choice to divorce rather than to heal the marriage. One way to begin combating these subtle influences is to recognize that they are part of a self-perpetuating industry.

Cultural Factors

The second source of "bad news" about divorce is cultural factors. The strong and ubiquitous influence of the media drives people apart and encourages them toward divorce. I mentioned earlier the 50 percent divorce rate, bandied about undisputed. In fact, this came about as a predictive statistic based upon figures from 1983 showing half as many divorces as there were marriages. Frankly, there is controversy about this figure, and arriving at a prediction so dire depends on manipulation of the statistics. But more importantly, the fabled "50% divorce rate" is destructive for anyone contemplating marriage, and powerfully discourages marriages while causing those in marriages to take them less seriously than they deserve. More crucial are U.S. Census Bureau figures showing the likelihood of divorce for a given individual. And those statistics reveal that among those who have ever been married, only 20 to 25 percent ever get divorced. The "50 percent divorce rate" applies to marriages, not people. And it is inflated by the Elizabeth Taylors of the world whose multiple divorces count over and over though they apply to only a single individual. So your chances of divorce at the outset of your first marriage are just one in four or five; there's a great difference between that and one in two. Those kinds of misrepresentations in the media tend to have a life of their own, and work to drive couples apart.

Then you go to movies. Now, despite my husband being a movie critic who attends seven screenings of new films every week, I must confess that I see very few movies. But I do read his reviews in the *New York Post*, where he is chief film critic, so I can know a lot about them without actually subjecting myself to them. One of the movies that he reviewed a few years ago was called *The Last Married Couple in America*. Just the existence of that title tells you something about how movies portray marriage. In this film, the couple's marriage is slowly dying, withering away, and pretty soon there is going to be only one couple left. That's the way it feels for married people when they view movie stars in tabloids at the supermarket checkout, and see the products of their talents on the large screen.

Television provides a similar view of marriage. In the book I coauthored with Dan Quayle, *The American Family*, I preliminarily surveyed a thousand families, and then zeroed in on five from diverse parts of the country. I was surprised to hear members of healthy, happy, intact families, say, "Well, we are no *Ozzie and Harriet* family"; "We're no *Leave it to Beaver* family." Do you believe it: *Leave it to Beaver* and *Ozzie and Harriet* presented successful, functioning families and nobody wants to admit that they can have the same? The image of *Ozzie and Harriet* has become denigrated and ridiculed, and it has been replaced by images of families like *The Simpsons* and *Married with Children*.

As marriage is denigrated, the single's life is venerated. I call this bias media's "lie and lure of the single's life." For example, it's apparent in the shows *Friends*, *Seinfeld*, *ER* or *Baywatch*, which filmed on our synagogue doorstep in Santa Monica. What is the message of these TV shows? It's that everyone should aspire to the young, hip, exciting, sexually active singles life. Because you don't want to be like *The Simpsons* or *Married With Children*. You want to aspire to be like *Baywatch* babes. Those are the two contrasting options: a *Baywatch* singles life or *Married With Children*. Viewers receive a lot of messages that set up impossible standards for marriages to meet, and contribute greatly to divorce. If your partner isn't passionate, like the lovers that you see on screen in all their singles glory, you're going to compare yourself to that unfavorably and ask, "where has the spark gone?" concluding, "It has died for us." For my psychology clients, this often translates into "we've fallen out of love."

We've fallen out of love. What does that mean? Every time you see the other person your heart doesn't go pitter-patter? Is it supposed to? Is this what life is? Well those of us who are happily married for a long time know that perhaps that is not the idea. But if you watch TV, you think that is the idea and you think you're missing something.

No one is immune from the impact of media, even those of us with no TV, and those of us who don't go to movies. If you read *Hollywood vs America*, my husband's book, you probably read of an incident where he took me to a movie that its publicists promised would be a cute little fun "dark comedy." The word "dark" should have been the clue. It was *The Cook, the Thief, His Wife, and Her Lover*, and I spent almost the entire time under my coat, humming. This a depraved, gross, gory product of a twisted imagination. Forks flying into cheeks, rotting wild bird carcasses, cannibalism. And those disturbing images remain with me, stored involuntarily in my brain.

More ubiquitous are damaging messages about marriage bombarding us in the media. The accepted stance on television networks and among all but a very few filmmakers is that marriage is not sacred. In fact, it's optional, just another choice on the same level of worthiness as divorce, choosing to have a child out of wedlock, or living with a homosexual lover.

Even adjacent to our Jewish day school, there is a billboard for a tanning company, portraying two unclad men and a woman reclining on each other on a beach. It implies that if you bathe nude at the beach you are going to have a happy life, you are going to be like these smiling attractive people. This is not a pro-marriage message and you can't miss it—it is right outside my children's school. Avoiding such constant and multidirectional messages is like the saying, "if you don't like the smog, just stop breathing." You can't stop breathing the media's anti-marriage poison.

So we must expand our awareness beyond economic factors encouraging divorce to the powerful effects of cultural messages as well.

Personal Factors

Over the past thirty years, divorce has skyrocketed due to Americans' sliding standards regarding acceptable personal behavior. Though the divorce rate has leveled off, and even declined slightly, the reasons people offer for their divorces reflect increased focus on personal feelings of continuous happiness and less attention to "old-fashioned virtues" like duty, loyalty, service to others, integrity.

People come to me with selfish reasons for divorce like "I am having an affair and I can't give up the love of my life," or "this person is such an opportunity." Many excuse their infidelity with "I can't give him up because this person thrills me and arouses my passion." They say, "I have a lust for life now that I haven't had in ten years, how could I possibly give that up?"

Of course, they may have four children at home and a loving husband who does not know anything about it, and a great job and a beautiful house and friends who care about them and care about their marriage—but they have the gall to ask, "how could I give up my affair?"

The personal factor causing divorce is what I call "Heart over Head." We have changed our perspective from acting according to our heads—considering the long term, logical sense, what is good for those around us, morals, values and virtue— to valuing and behaving according to "what feels good for me now," the emotions of the heart. The liberationist selfishness of baby boomers in the sixties and seventies, rightfully dubbed "the Me-decade," with its slogans about feeling good and questioning authority, shifted values toward immediate rewards, inability to defer gratification, and glorification of the "here and now." This is the essence of "Heart over Head." The corollary is that nowadays, when head and heart battle—such as when deciding between an exciting affair and an existing long-term marriage—the heart wins. To the detriment of individuals' characters and long-term happiness.

The priority of the heart results in spouses requiring constant satisfaction. For example, I see wives who come in and say, "He's being so mean to me; we're fighting every day; I can't stand it and I have to get out," negating the eight years of fulfillment they enjoyed prior to this last six months of discord. We have to shake some shoulders and tell people to look beyond their toenails, to look further out into the future. To look beyond themselves and see their children and their parents and their community. Sliding standards have changed individuals' focus from the outside to the inside, from the head down to the heart as the source of all wisdom and knowledge.

Specifics of these sliding standards: We have gone from believing that "Marriage is for Keeps" to "Marriage is until Passion Fades." Maybe you have seen wedding ceremonies where the bride and groom say "I pledge my love to you, as long as love shall last." "As long as love shall last" means "maybe tomorrow, maybe the next day, I don't know, we'll see."

Another standard lost is the idea of divorce as a shameful failure. A child of a divorce was from a "broken home," and he was considered "disadvantaged." This is replaced with the notion I mentioned before that divorce is no big deal. "Since it affects 50 percent of the population, you can't expect that you are going to be in the 50 percent that is going to make it, right?" Nonjudgmentalism means that to be single is honorable, no judgment. To be married, that's honorable—no judgment. To be divorced, that's equally good. You can be gay and live with somebody else. In fact, you can do two of them together--be gay and be married, that's fine too—no judgment. This is a decline in our society, an example of sliding standards. We have to recognize when popular beliefs are counterproductive, stand up and say "that's not true, that's a mistake that we must correct before we spiral into social chaos."

Responding to the Factors Encouraging Divorce

So three types of factors fuel divorce: economic, cultural, and personal. Now let's take a look at how to counteract these anti-marriage influences.

On the economic front, I think we have to take some of the profit out of the divorce industry. I'm concerned about the effort to revise no-fault divorce laws to reflect one party's fault, and have even advised several states on this issue. I worry that even where a "fault divorce" is optional, children might be irrevocably harmed. For example, if, say, a wife has been wronged and seeks her financial due, in charging her husband with fault, accusations and negativity are bound to be overheard by children, causing them to suffer. Forever changed are kids' feelings about their father or their mother, their images of their home, their belief system about their parents, and, ultimately, their own marriages. I fear for the children and I am worried that while no-fault divorce law revision may help some children financially, it may at the same time harm them, by revealing lurid facts of marital life that perhaps should be saved until an age when their innocence will not be ruined.

My husband and I are co-authoring a book called *Saving Childhood: Protecting our Children from the National Assault on Innocence*. Divorce is a major destroyer of innocence, taking away that special, protected time. Divorce takes away a child's necessary feelings of stability, predictability, and security. If a child cannot count on his own family, his own home, his trust in the rest of the world is shattered. One of the major benefits of reversing attitudes about divorce is the restoration of childhood to children. The way to diminish economic incentives to encouraging divorce is not through laws but through public attention, discourse, and action. When choosing a therapist, couples should interview the therapist and ask "what are your feelings about divorce?" "To what lengths do you think couples should go to save their marriages?"

Now, I admit people often come to me when it's too late, and I can't save their marriages. Does that mean I am a bad therapist? I hope not. But I'm direct in expressing my bias in favor of marriage, even though some situations make divorce necessary. Physicians, friends, relatives, and legal advisors should urge hostile partners to seek out therapists expressing a priority for saving a marriage over divorce. An experienced therapist can offer a prognosis for couples when given a good description of the circumstances. For example, I've learned that if I see a couple where one of the partners wants to save the marriage and the other is involved in an affair, the likelihood is that the philanderer will choose heart over head. As ill-conceived as that may be, as wrong as that may be, it still turns out that in a majority of cases where there is an affair, male or female but particularly female, that the heart is going to win out over the head. However, this certainly does not preclude giving every possible effort to saving the marriage.

I think we need to educate mental health professionals, clergy, and parents on how they can promote marriage and talk about these issues in appropriate ways from the earliest ages. This begins a positive ripple effect, ultimately outweighing the economic benefits that accrue to the divorce industry.

On the cultural front, we have to set up a counterculture. We have to send out pro-marriage messages, as many people associated with the authors in this volume are doing effectively. Participants here will disseminate the messages they are hearing. We need to demand more media exposure for pro-marriage ideas. We need more talk at PTA meetings, not just about PTA business, but about achieving the grander agenda of saving families, of providing a haven in our schools and our classrooms for people who care about marriage and want to prevent divorce. Doing so will help our children enjoy the security that is the birthright of childhood.

Another cornerstone of the effort to curb divorce is promoting pro-family behaviors of individuals. Excellent headway has been made by groups promoting fatherhood. Marriage-enhancement courses and programs proliferate and can spread even further. But in particular I think that we have to offer more support to mothers. Since the seventies, the mother who chooses to stay home with her children has been stigmatized. She's been told "oh well, you're just a housewife" or "You're just languishing until you can do something intellectual"—they expect her to revert to the level of a three-year old, toddling along using three-letter words. I think we have to give some glory and dignity and honor to the idea that the best person to raise a child is that child's mother. Providing greater daycare options and doing all kinds of things to enable her to go into the workplace is perhaps counterproductive to a solid marriage and to raising children who view parenting as a joy, a pleasure, a privilege and not just as an obligation.

In my research for *The American Family*, the mothers I interviewed across this nation universally agreed that being a mother, being a wife, having a family life is the most exciting, thrilling, fun aspect of their lives. Yesterday, my husband chided me because I could not resist giving up the gym and three appointments to go with my children on their last-day-of-school picnic. I also happen to be a Brownie Girl

Scout leader, and such endeavors are not just fluff, not just playtime but very important foundations for lifelong attitudes about the family and motherhood. We must give them much more attention; more attention to mothers and to the benefits of raising children as a full-time occupation.

I'd like to discuss some surprising findings from my research for *The American Family* that can help retard divorce. Vice President Quayle and I zeroed in on five specific families: a farm family in Virginia, a Hispanic family in East LA, a single mother of five in Indianapolis, a black family in inner-city Chicago, and a mixed race adoptive family in Hawaii. And across all these families we found some commonalities, two of which were very striking.

The first was that each family had a well-ingrained sense of place. Moving is bad for children. Establishing roots into a community offers a grounding, a sense of place and security that goes beyond the family. Without this basis, families are all working in isolation. Children crave the feeling that "this is my home." My three young children feel comfortable on Ashland Avenue. It's too easy for parents to look at moving in terms of economic benefits only, or moving to a nicer house in a nicer neighborhood. Instead they need to look at the disorientation of uprooting and the lack of confidence that results for their children. Though it's somewhat ironic that I lecture on this while on the verge of a northward move, this change only underscores for me the precious nature of being surrounded by the familiar, of proximity to family, friends, church or synagogue, and the little conveniences and details that make a particular neighborhood "home."

A second personal value that parents can teach to combat a propensity toward divorce is, surprisingly, the value of a dollar. Each of the five spotlighted families valued money—but not in terms of what we see on TV, the media messages, what can you buy. TV commercials urge viewers to want—a new Lexus, a new cereal, anything new, new, new. Money is only good in terms of what it can buy. In contrast, the successful families I interviewed taught their children to view money in terms of what it took to make it, the work, the dedication, the sweat, the effort. I think we need to look in that direction.

Most importantly, the propensity toward divorce is counteracted by Judeo-Christian religious values. Being Jewish and observant plays a central role in the lives of the Medveds. Professor Hafen notes that marriage is seen now as a unity or a bond between three different parties—the husband, wife, and the state. Jewish tradition also envisions three entities forming a partnership in marriage. But under the Jewish "chupa," or wedding canopy, there is a husband, there is a wife, and there is God. When people get married in a situation where they believe that God is literally present to sanctify their marriage, there is a much stronger bond. The state I don't care about—I am moving to a different state!—but I do maintain the state of bliss because we really have a basis for that.

Also there's a sense of contacts in a religious community. My husband recently had an article in, *The American Enterprise* called "Banish the Honeymoon." In the Jewish religion, when a couple gets married, all the people invited to a wedding say "mazel tov," congratulations, or literally good luck—not to the bride and groom, but to each other. The guests say "mazel tov" to each other because a new family being formed enhances the community. It means as much for the individuals who are present at the ceremony as it does for the couple. Then after the wedding the couple doesn't dash off to a honeymoon in the Poconos with a heart-shaped bathtub, or take off on a plane for Tahiti. Jewish tradition holds that you stay in your community for seven days, and people in the community honor you at dinners every night of the week. Part of the tradition is to include someone new at each dinner, someone who did not attend the wedding, emphasizing the importance of a new family to the community. Now, the message is wonderful for the community—a sense of joy, a sense of growth—but it is more important for the couple, because they learn that their marriage is not just based on themselves, but rather on a context. They see that if they separate or divorce, the entire community mourns the loss. The events of every marriage send a message to every other couple, who see, feel and celebrate it. They renew their grounding in the community at every wedding celebration throughout their lives. That is why even with great secularization in America, Jewish couples continue to enjoy a significantly lower divorce rate than the population at large.

With that supportive context and the blessings of a third, divine partner in marriage, couples can gain strength to combat these enemies of marriage, the economic, the cultural, and the personal.

Part Four

The Market, the Media, and the Family

14

The Family in Capitalist America

Doug Bandow

Capitalism is perhaps the most powerful engine of social change in history. As such, its impact reaches all aspects of human existence, including the family. Of course, the effect on the latter is but one measure of a market system; that impact is increasingly important, however, at a time when the family as an institution seems to be weakening almost daily.

In general, markets are the most moral and efficient means to organize economic life. Built on the principle of free exchange, they maximize individual liberty.[1] Capitalism also generates wealth. Indeed, history's move from rampant poverty to increasing abundance is a tribute to the power of free markets.

Moreover, capitalism has proved its superiority over every competing system, including communism, socialism, and the welfare state. The twentieth century has provided perhaps the closest thing to a laboratory experiment in social organization, pitting free markets against a variety of forms of collectivism, and the former have uniformly triumphed, providing people with more liberty and prosperity. In practice, capitalism, a system built on consent rather than coercion, has also proved to offer a better environment for the development of other moral values, such as care for the poor and political freedom.[2] Better, but not ideal. Explains American Enterprise Institute scholar Michael Novak:

> Admittedly, the morality of democratic capitalist systems is low when compared with the supernatural standards of Christianity and other codes of spiritual perfection. But its daily practice in supplying opportunity to the poor is superior to the daily practice of any other historical system, traditional or socialist. It does not pretend to offer a moral paradise, only greater liberties and more flexible supports for moral living than any other system. It brings temptations, but also incredibly high moral possibilities. That is why people migrate in such numbers and with such passion toward it.[3]

However, though markets are better than any authoritarian economic system, they remain neutral to moral and social values. It is this very neutrality, "its indifference to the notion of moral choices," as historian Paul Johnson puts it, that poses problems.[4] While capitalism has no conscious design to undermine social institutions, like the family, the operation of the market system may nevertheless adversely affect them. Understanding those impacts will help us develop countermeasures to bolster institutions and values that may be harmed. As economist Peter J. Hill puts it, "although the private property order is, of itself, not a complete embodiment of all that is moral, it does offer the potential for moving closer to an ideal order when overlaid with Christian compassion and concern."[5] Some mechanisms for moving closer may come from government, principally by eliminating public policies that undercut civil society. Other remedial measures will be purely private efforts to strengthen the moral framework within which markets operate.

What Is the Market?

In order to assess the impact of capitalism on the family, it is important to define the term. In general, I equate free markets, free enterprise, and capitalism, by which I mean an economic system ordered by private participants rather than political authorities, in whatever form. To speak of a market does not, however, mean that every decision in society is determined by economic analysis, only that most economic decisions are made privately by people acting as they choose.

Moreover, while the market has tremendous social impact, it is not the only transformational force in society. As Dr. Hill points out, a committed Christian or Jew would point to "our alienation from God," rather than "the result of a particular institutional structure," as the root cause of materialism and family breakup.[6] Moreover, some of the dramatic changes over the last two or three centuries have resulted as much from modernity and industrialization as capitalism. Soviet communism no less than American capitalism uprooted traditional social institutions. My hope in this paper is to isolate, to the extent possible, the unique impacts of the market on the family.

The Characteristics of Capitalism and Their Impact

Private Economic Planning

Despite their appearance of chaos, markets are not chaotic. Planning occurs, but is highly decentralized. Individuals, families, businesses, and other social organizations (e.g., churches and fraternal groups) all work together to organize the market. This characteristic is almost certainly good for families, since it allows families to control their own destinies. In contrast, in authoritarian economic systems—communism and socialism most obviously—such decisions are made politically by governing elites, whether real majorities or varying coalitions of minorities.

Obviously, participating in the marketplace, individual heads of households and even families may undervalue the family as an institution and make mistakes. But, in general, there would seem to be little doubt that family members not only best know their own interest but also have the greatest appreciation of the interest of the family unit. Today, at least, it would seem to be the larger culture that most underestimates the importance of families.

Private Property Ownership and Control.

Capitalist systems require that individuals have the right to own and exercise control over property of all sorts.[7] This factor, too, gives the family a large degree of autonomy and legal protection. It also imposes responsibility on the family unit to manage its resources and determine its own fate. Obviously, the ability of families to make decisions for themselves may at times be a mixed blessing: Who has not seen a dysfunctional family and desired to make choices on its behalf? Moreover, the family autonomy engendered by the legal protections that accompany property ownership may weaken some broader communal ties—within extended families, for instance, churches, and other organizations. Still, the American experience with slavery dramatically illustrated how such autonomy is a necessary precondition for a strong family.

Competition

Perhaps the most heralded, and damned, characteristic of capitalism is competition. But it is competition of a special kind—competition to cooperate. Ultimately, people succeed in a capitalist system only by cooperating with one another.

Of course, the chief incentive to do so, money, may seem crass, but alternative inducements are either unrealistic (altruism) or brutal (state coercion). And organizations formally bound together by economic interest, that is, businesses, often develop an *esprit de corps* that reflects nonmaterial values. This contrasts sharply with other spheres of life. There is cooperation in politics, but the process is generally winner-take-all. (Come every political election, only one candidate wins a given position. Come the ongoing economic election every day, a host of competing products survive, even if they all cannot come in number one.) Although competition may be the hallmark of a market economy, it has no clear impact on the family.

Acting in One's Economic Self-Interest

Participants in markets are presumed to act based on their perceived self-interest. This much maligned characteristic of capitalism is much misunderstood. Self-interest is not the same as selfishness, though the two may be present in the same person. However undesirable the latter, there is nothing wrong with the former—to desire the best possible for oneself and one's family.[8]

Anyway, to act in one's economic self-interest is a natural characteristic of being human, not of living in a market system. The form of interest pursued may vary by system, but self-interest is a constant under collectivism as well as capitalism. Moreover, in no system do people act only for economic reasons. Even today many decisions are, or at least hopefully are, based on very different considerations: family, marriage, religion.

Of course, the role of economic self-interest is arguably magnified through business, in the sense that people not only act on their economic self-interest, but typically work for organizations that act on their economic self-interest. However, this is for good reason. Companies are far more effective at providing goods and services than in, for instance, promoting morality.[9] Thus, they should concentrate on doing the former rather than the latter, though such economic tasks don't necessarily exhaust their legitimate responsibilities.[10] Indeed, companies that take a more expansive view—including the need to treat employees well—tend to do better in the marketplace. As the late Warren Brookes has pointed out, companies that focus only on short-term profit-maximization tend to lose out over the long run.[11]

Still, the existence of an economic system driven by economic self-interest may ultimately influence the way participants look at the world, including decisions involving their families. At the margin, one may be somewhat more likely to choose economic over other values—to accept a promotion at the cost of time with one's family, and so on. This characteristic of capitalism, then, may pose a negative for the family.

Access to and Acquisition of Information.

Authoritarian economic systems predetermine individual choices. Capitalism, in contrast, presents scores of choices daily to every person and family. Which toothpaste to purchase alone can require a consumer to choose between a dozen or more brands. Defectors and former residents of collectivist systems have found this abundance, even tyranny, of choice to be one of the most difficult aspects of capitalism with which to cope.

There are obviously both costs and benefits of increased choice, but the latter predominate. On the one hand, it takes time to become informed and to intelligently make choices. And the images that spew forth in various media undoubtedly help to shape the attitudes of family members. Argues Harvard sociologist Theda Skocpol, "The major way children are learning morally questionable standards is through the mass media and advertising. What's missing in this conservative discourse is that they don't identify free market capitalism as a part of the threat and yet it surely is."[12]

On the other hand, being able to make choices that are good for one's family improves one's life. After all, since family members have the most understanding of the needs and desires of other family members, they are most likely to make good decisions for one another. In fact, the opportunity to choose is integrally related to the autonomy and responsibility that naturally accompanies the formation and growth of a family. And access to information is integral to making good choices. Advertising usually gives substance to already existing if latent desires rather than creates new ones *ex nihilo* (people don't want things because they are advertised; people's natural desire for things is channeled to specific items through advertising). Moreover, families can help control how much advertising comes into a home and how it is received.

Labor Specialization

Another important aspect of capitalism is labor specialization, symbolized by the industrial assembly line, on which workers perform a small but often routine task in the manufacture of a product. The benefits of this practice are almost incalculable—dramatically greater production and wealth creation.

But the downsides are real, too. For instance, piecework is often less satisfying for workers, and such frustrations may have a negative impact on other family members. Author Richard Cornuelle decries the "regimentation of work." He goes on to ask: "How can people see the value of independence and self-propulsion when they work in a system in which they are dependent and subordinate."[13] Moreover, labor specialization reduces the viability of small economic units, such as the family business and farm. While such activities are still not impossible, they become relatively less efficient and are therefore less likely to form and be maintained through succeeding generations.

Thus, on balance, labor specialization is probably a negative for the family, though the productivity gains nevertheless make the burden worth bearing. As Pope John Paul II observed, "many goods cannot be adequately produced through the work of an isolated individual; they require the cooperation of many people in working toward a common goal." This specialization is, he adds, "a source of wealth in today's society."[14] Not surprisingly, then, few people would likely want to be transported back to the year 1700. Moreover, labor specialization has more characterized industrialization than capitalism, with collectivist regimes also relying on larger units of production. To reverse the process would therefore require the abandonment not only of market economics but also industrial society, a very unlikely event.

Capital and Labor Mobility

The economies of the U.S. and most other nations have steadily moved from a multiplicity of local economies to a single global marketplace. Even nonmarket economies have been dragged into the international system, but capitalism has acted as the primary engine of transformation.

This economic change has dramatically expanded the opportunities for a family's breadwinner—if a person loses a job, he or she can likely find one elsewhere. But this phenomenon, in turn, tends to disperse families and dilute communities. Extended families are less likely to grow together in the same area. Moreover, the traditional safety net for members of a small community is less likely to exist in a larger area; that is, where populations are more mobile and personal associations less permanent, neighbors are less likely to aid one another. Without doubt, then, this aspect of capitalism is to some degree negative for families.

The Philosophical Underpinnings of Capitalism and Their Impact

Undergirding market economies are a number of assumptions around which people order their lives and which affect families.

Market Exchange Is Beneficial

At base, every market is the setting for bargaining between people. It operates voluntarily, not coercively. Mutual exchange per se has no obvious impact on families, since the decisions reached can be good or bad. However, the ability to act when one believes it to be in one's, and one's family's, interest is more likely to redound to the benefit of families than are decisions made by one or another political entities. Explains Dr. Hill: "Individuals' preferences, skills, and abilities are much more likely to be used in ways that the individual finds satisfying under" a market system.[15]

Decisions Are Economically Motivated

Although most economists understand that the economic man of abstract academic analysis is just an analytical tool, a system of free exchange will place some pressure on people to act for economic reasons. And if habits matter, the habit of thinking in economic terms may affect the way one weighs competing values, such as the prospect of a promotion and salary increase from a corporate move and the resulting impact on family stability.

However, the market doesn't require that people act only for economic reasons. To the contrary, average Americans obviously have various motivations for their actions, or else there would be no gift giving or charity. Even many relationships that start out as economic—consumer and small businessman, for instance—often turn into friendships. Here, again, while capitalism may magnify the impact of people acting selfishly and shortsightedly with regard to the family or anything else, market economies are not necessary for them to do so.

Financial Rewards Go with Economic Success

If nothing else, capitalism directs material benefits to those in certain high-demand occupations—inventors, entrepreneurs, artists, athletes—and much less to others, such as those involved in charity or other forms of public service. This, too, probably has an impact on the family, since it changes the relative reward system between being, for instance, a good doctor and a good father/mother. Indeed,

Charles Murray has noted how professionals have access to an additional reward system even if they fail in their roles as members of families and communities, something people with less remunerative and satisfying work are less likely to enjoy.[16]

Of course, society needs good doctors. The issue, then, is balance. Although market pressures emphasize financial benefits, authoritarian economic systems are no better. In the Soviet Union one was rewarded for being a good communist apparatchik rather than a good person. If one has to choose between economics and politics in creating some measure of objective reward, the former will come much closer than will the latter. In either system, then, one has to reach beyond the market (to civil society and religion, for instance) to ensure, as F. A. Hayek put it, that material rewards are not considered to reflect "the esteem in which [a person] is held as a whole person for his moral merit."[17]

The Purpose of Work Is to Fulfill the Material Wants of Others

Capitalism is consumption oriented. Success therefore means fulfilling the desires of others. This may or may not be good for families. After all, some of the products that abound in a market economy (a Porsche, say, or any number of other adult toys) may compete with one's family for attention, or otherwise hurt a family (e.g., pornography). Moreover, the fulfillment of some wants may hurt the producer's family in less direct ways—demand for less expensive goods, available only through labor specialization, makes family and neighborhood enterprise less likely, for instance.

At the same time, a consumer-oriented economy means that other people will produce what a family wants. And that means many things: A family can get better goods at less cost, acquire products that enhance its members' lives (new medicines and surgical techniques, for instance), and so on. Thus, on net, but not in all cases, the market benefits families by being oriented toward consumers.

Individual Responsibility

Most decisions in a market economy are made by individuals and family units; thus, family decisions will be made by households (in a process that may be dictatorial, cooperative, or somewhere in between) rather than larger collective social units. As noted earlier in the context of private planning and markets, some families will make mistakes. However, in general, families are better able to choose what is in their interest, which suggests that they are likely to be better off than in a system where an outside actor, whether local tribe or national bureaucracy, makes the decision.

The Outcomes of Capitalism and Their Impact

The social manifestations of market economies probably have the greatest impact on families.

Freedom

The most important practical aspect of capitalism is the maximization of individual (and family) liberty. A market economic system allows people to choose amongst a host of activities. Some of the resulting decisions will actually be harmful to families—such as gambling, prostitution, drug use. Some choices, such as bad investments, will simply be mistakes. But most, hopefully, will be good. Overall, a family with free choice in the economic world seems likely to do better than one with artificially constrained options.[18]

At the same time, economic freedom tends to encourage cultural and political freedom. This occurs in part because the acquisition of wealth allows one to concentrate on other values.[19] It also occurs because market forces are too powerful to remain isolated from other areas of life, like sexual mores.

In general, then, freedom is good for the family, since members are able to choose their own destiny. But there doubtless are bad aspects, since the freedom to choose means the freedom to choose bad options, some of which will be chosen.

Wealth

The second most practical, and perhaps most visible, manifestation of the market is affluence. Economic growth clearly improves people's lives. It yields improved health, through the ability to control and cure disease. It continues to generate labor-saving devices, leaving people more time for leisure and one another. It advances personal comfort and the opportunity for education and self-advancement. It yields more resources to help one's extended family and others in need.

As important as the benefits of wealth are, there remain some negative impacts on families. Increased earnings enable individuals and their families to rely less on other family members and those within their communities. It probably makes it more likely for distracting "thorns," to use a Biblical concept, to grow up within families and disrupt them.[20] With greater economic possibilities money is more likely to be become a family's goal, and to be seen as the solution to other problems (the purchase of a new gadget in response to a spouse's unhappiness).

Wealth also promotes autonomy within the family that may not be best for strong family relationships. For example, teens increasingly have their own cars and televisions. There is nothing wrong with automobiles and TVs, but the former make it easier for children to escape family oversight and the latter open up kids to greater influences beyond family control. As one parent worries, "having a car makes it easy for kids to cut loose and take part in activities far from home. Needing that ride from Mom and Dad helps to keep a family connection."[21] In short, these sort of products lessen the experiences that draw families together and ease members' participation in other, nonfamily communities.

The availability of goods also may focus greater attention within a family on material values—to keep up with the Jones's, so to speak. Of course, materialism is evident everywhere, including in the most impoverished collectivist economies. Nevertheless, the unique ability of capitalism to satisfy material wants may create its own problems.

Expanded Opportunities

Market economies, with an abundance of freedom and wealth, provide opportunity. Opportunity, like so many other things, is double-edged. People have a greater chance to find fulfillment, build happy lives, and support a family. Money also makes it easier to leave one's family—to get off of the farm, move across the country, and otherwise disperse the extended family.

A multiplicity of economic opportunities also increase the availability of certain forms of work and work habits—e.g., pornography and lengthy corporate/legal hours—that are anti-family. Expanded opportunities may make more families look at their members, particularly mothers but also high school students, as potential workers; such employment may end up being detrimental to the operation of the family as a family (whatever the obviously real financial benefits). Indeed, more expansive assumptions about the women's earning capacity may have encouraged the shift toward no-fault divorce laws, which has probably spurred family breakup.

Technological Change

Capitalism has helped generate a profusion of new gadgets in people's lives. Beepers, cars, cellular phones, computers, washers, and much more. The benefits of technology to the family are obvious: They make us more productive, leaving more time for our families, and increase our earnings, allowing us to better provide for loved ones.

But there can be negatives as well. New technologies can divert the attention of family members from one another. The internet, for instance, has proved addicting to some; it has even spawned a new term, cyber-adultery. A cellular phone for a workaholic may ruin his or her family's vacation. Moreover, technology may make family members and the family itself more autonomous than is healthy for the family unit and larger community. Increasingly, every child of driving age has a car, the ultimate source of personal mobility. The simple garage door opener reduces interaction with neighbors by eliminating the spontaneous contact that results from stopping in one's driveway.

Of course, in most of these cases technology only exacerbates preexisting tendencies. Technology per se doesn't make or break community. But still, it probably helps change human behavior, and accentuates actions that may be good or bad.

Creative Destruction

With increased wealth and technological development come instability. Markets reward and punish without regard to the consequences on social institutions such as the family. Companies fail, family members lose jobs, living standards decline, communities shrivel, and the sense of security is disrupted or destroyed. These sorts of changes can put enormous pressure on families and can disrupt the larger community networks within which families are nestled and nurtured.

Of course, there are countervailing advantages of the creative destruction of capitalism: increased prosperity, additional opportunities to advance one's career and enhance the living standards of one's family; the absence of class or caste, which preordains that some will fail; and creation of additional options for even the most disadvantaged and disfavored. The foregoing benefits are substantial, but can't disguise the fact that economic and social change, which naturally accompany free markets, can impose often substantial costs on individual families.

Rewards for Success of All Sorts

Those who are hardworking, talented, and/or lucky in any number of ways, tend to reap substantial material benefits in capitalist economies. In general, this is good and moral, since it usually rewards individual characteristics rather than collective ones, like gender or race.

But such economic rewards do not reflect a particular moral judgment about a person's character—that, for instance, a worker is a good person or good father/mother. Moreover, the perceived unfairness of financial inequality may be galling to those who earn less. Indeed, the market system often seems biased against those who put their families first (as noted earlier, capitalism's benefits are likely to push a worker toward working longer hours, relocating for a promotion, and so on).

Yet, for all the apparent arbitrariness of some of the activities and characteristics rewarded by market economies, this phenomenon is really not unique to capitalism. Collectivist economic systems, too, provide rewards that are, if anything, even more arbitrary and less favorable to families. In communism, for instance, ideological correctness, personal connections, and ruthlessness tended to be the features with greatest material value.

Moreover, in a larger sense, markets tend to reward broader virtues that also benefit families. As Francis Fukuyama points out: For capitalism to work, it "must be leavened with reciprocity, moral obligation, duty toward community, and trust, which are based in habit rather than rational calculation."[22] Although these characteristics are not always evident in market transactions, businessmen and firms who exhibit such characteristics tend to prosper.

Social Harmony

Many people view the market as the antithesis of polite society—the famous image is of "cutthroat" competition. But markets actually tend to encourage cooperation, since mutual exchange requires that both parties perceive the transaction to be beneficial. And absent perfect knowledge about other people, only the price mechanism in a free market allows people to efficiently coordinate their activities.

Free exchange also mutes otherwise contentious issues—we typically don't inquire about the moral values, religious positions, or political views of a gas station attendant. And we don't run political campaigns and have votes over which toothpaste to buy. Such decisions become neither public nor heated controversies.[23]

In fact, at base, capitalism is more democratic than democracy. In politics, there is but one president and elections are winner-take-all. But there are lots of colas—the market allows "losers," like Pepsi (which trails Coca-Cola in sales), to also win. Virtually everyone has access to products which they, but not a majority of their neighbors, favor. This kind of environment—which yields a more harmonious society—is probably better for families, though the impact is admittedly indirect.

On Balance?

What is capitalism's *net* impact upon the family? Probably positive, though attempting to balance many very different effects is not easy. The chief virtue of capitalism is not that it is pro-family, but that it promotes freedom and prosperity. And it is these results that have both good and bad effects on the family.

Can one imagine an economic system that is more pro-family? Yes. Would it be possible to construct it in practice? Probably not. And even if it were, would it yield the overall benefits of a free market? Almost certainly not.

Instead of attempting to replace capitalism, it would be better to examine the negative impacts of market economies and review ways to moderate those effects. The law may provide some answers. For instance, tax relief would help reduce the pressure on both spouses to work. Welfare reform might moderate or eliminate artificial incentives that inhibit family formation and promote family breakup. And lawmakers could choose to outlaw particular choices perceived to be particularly destructive to families—gambling, perhaps, or drug use.[24]

More appropriate and effective, however, are likely to be remedies advanced through civil rather than political society. People need to establish a larger moral framework within which to nestle a market economic system. There is, for instance, little that the law can do to make someone into a good father. People acting as individuals, families, churches, and communities need to supply the extra penalties and rewards to encourage him to be a "good family man." Similarly, people acting freely together need to accept as their duty helping to protect those who prove vulnerable to the creative destructiveness of capitalism. Private charity is far more likely than public welfare to provide the kind of personal attention necessary and to avoid the counterproductive effects of today's bureaucratic system.[25] And this task is likely to be easier in a society that remains free rather than one in which the political authorities attempt to take on such a role.

Conclusion

Is the market pro- or anti-family? Neither. Rather, it reflects the values brought to it by members of society. Capitalism neither advances existing human virtues nor corrects ingrained personal vices. Nevertheless, the market system does have a strong impact on the family—especially by generating instability as a result of constant economic change and capital and labor mobility. But authoritarian economic systems are worse. Limiting freedom and choice inevitably do more to harm than help families. As economist Wilhelm Ropke puts it: The concentration of political power "destroys the middle class properly so called, that is, an independent class possessed of small or moderate property and income, a sense of responsibility, and those civic virtues without which a free and well-ordered society cannot, in the long run, survive."[26] But, as the experience of communist states has dramatically shown, the consequences of trying to implement an alternative to capitalism would be truly catastrophic, including to the family. Writes Paul Heyne:

> Capitalism consequently cannot be rejected without simultaneously repudiating the basis of contemporary life. Christians who want to reject capitalism ought to know what else they are rejecting at the same time: the coordination of complex cooperative activities in the only way they can be coordinated. The cost would not be just the loss of some luxuries; it would be famine, disease, and a new dark age as the communities of science, literature, and art disintegrated right along with the institutions that provide our "necessaries and conveniences."[27]

Thus, the task of those of us who are concerned about strengthening the family is to use our freedom responsibly, especially to create countervailing social forces and ensure that markets do not operate in moral vacuum. Pope John Paul II has written of the importance of putting capitalism "within a strong juridical framework which places it at the service of human freedom in its totality and which sees it as a particular aspect of that freedom, the core of which is ethical and religious."[28] Thus, to flourish, families require economic liberty, but within a larger moral environment capable of supplying the social ballast necessary to help them adjust to the inherent instability of a free society.

Notes

1. All of the impressive trappings of advanced industrial capitalism, like the most primitive open-air market, grow out of the same basic freedom of consenting adults to contract with one another.

2. For a discussion of some of these issues, see Doug Bandow, *The Politics of Envy: Statism As Theology* (New Brunswick, N.J.: Transaction Publishers, 1994), 3-35; Doug Bandow, *Beyond Good Intentions: A Biblical View of Politics* (Westchester, Ill.: Crossway Books, 1988).

3. Michael Novak, "Democratic Capitalism: Moral, or Not at All," *Freedom Review* 22, no. 3 (May-June 1991): 13.

4. Paul Johnson, "The Capitalism & Morality Debate," *First Things*, (March 1990): 13.

5. Peter J. Hill, "Private Rights and Public Attitudes: A Christian Defense of Capitalism," paper presented to Liberty Fund conference, Tucson, Arizona, (February 20-22, 1985), 4.

6. Hill, p. 2.

7. Historically, land was typically the most important form of property; today intellectual capital has become increasingly important. The distinction between formal ownership and practical control is great: A government-recognized title to land means nothing if it conveys no right to actually use the property to, for instance, build a house, manage a farm, or otherwise generate an income.

8. This issue is discussed in greater detail in Brian Griffith's *The Creation of Wealth: A Christian's Case for Capitalism* (Downers Grove, Ill.: InterVarsity Press, 1984), 68-69, and Paul Heyne, "Christianity and 'the Economy'," *This World*, (Winter 1988): 31.

9. See, e.g., Doug Bandow, "Is the Good Corporation Dead? Should We Even Bother to Mourn?," *Business and Society Review*, (Fall 1993): 16-17.

10. See, e.g., Michael Novak, "Profits with Honor," *Policy Review*, (May-June 1996): 50-56.

11. Warren Brookes, "Goodness and the GNP," in *Is Capitalism Christian?*, Franky Schaeffer, ed. (Westchester, Ill.: Crossway Books, 1985): 40-43.

12. Quoted in Laura Sessions Stepp, "Who's in Charge?" *Washington Post*, 15 July 1996, D5. Similarly, Pope John Paul II has warned about the creation of "consumer attitudes and lifestyles . . . which are objectively improper and often damaging to his physical and spiritual health." John Paul II, "Centesimus Annus," *Origins* 21, no. 1 (May 16, 1991), 15.

13. Richard Cornuelle, "New Work for Invisible Hands: A Future for Libertarian Thought," *The Times Literary Supplement*, undated: 4.

14. John Paul II, *Centisimus Annus*,(May 1, 1991); 13.

15. Hill, p. 11.

16. Charles Murray, *In Pursuit of Happiness and Good Government* (New York: Simon & Schuster, 1988): 280-86.

17. F. A. Hayek, "The Moral Element in Free Enterprise," in *The Morality of Capitalism*, Mark Hendrickson, ed. (Irvington-on-Hudson, N.Y.: Foundation for Economic Education, 1992): 68.

18. A market system may still exist if government constrains some decisions—e.g., the consumption of drugs. A market fades as an ever larger number of decisions is dictated by politics.

19. This phenomenon has been demonstrated in practice in such countries as South Korea and Taiwan, where demands for democracy and environmental protection followed economic prosperity.

20. Matthew 13: 7.

21. Lyla Fox, "Hold Your Horsepower," *Newsweek*, 25 March 1996, 16.

22. Francis Fukuyama, "The Economics of Trust," *National Review,* (August 14, 1995): 43.

23. See, e.g., Hill, pp. 8-9.

24. Of course, policy should not be judged solely on the basis of its impact on families. Preventing the great mass of people who can gamble without harming their families is a high price to pay to attempt to restrict gambling by the vulnerable few. And drug prohibition creates a host of practical problems, such as increased crime and gang warfare, that adversely affect not only families, but the entire society. See, e.g., Bandow, *The Politics of Envy*, pp. 245-99.

25. See, e.g., Marvin Olasky, *The Tragedy of American Compassion* (Washington, D.C.: Regnery Gateway, 1992).

26. Wilhelm Ropke, *A Humane Economy: The Social Framework of the Free Market* (Indianapolis: Liberty Fund, 1971), 32. Similarly, Pope John Paul II simply observes that "The Marxist solution has failed," and goes on to explain why. John Paul II, p. 17.

27. Heyne, p. 38.

28. John Paul, II, p. 17. See also the discussion in Ropke, pp. 90-91; Johnson, p. 19; and Brookes, p. 20.

15

Television as a Medium Undermining the Family

Michael Medved

I would like to share something new and different with readers that may surprise them, because—in a volume where I suspect the authors tend to agree on most fundamental issues—this will be a point that even in this context may seem a bit radical. And I want to begin by asking a question related to many of the other chapters in this book. They tend to come to the same conclusions about what is happening to the family in the United States and they also reach the same conclusions—which are inescapable—about when that began to happen. Demographically, statistically, and in terms of real life the way people live in this country, things began to fall apart for the family sometime around 1960. The question I want to pose is, "what happened?"

You know, I remember at the time I was still a kid, that there were people that were worried about fluoridation of the water. Well, I don't think you can explain what happened to America by some alien plot to fluoridate water. There are suggestions in this volume, and of course everyone agrees on it, that the easy availability of mass reliable forms of birth control clearly had some impact. But I think we can agree that in and of itself that is not sufficient to explain the magnitude of the earthquake that began to shatter the very foundations of the traditional American family. So I want to suggest to you that the principal, though certainly not the exclusive, cause for all the lamentable changes that we began to see in this country back in 1960 was that most ambiguous and influential of all American institutions, television.

If you think about it, the timing is perfect. Nineteen sixty is precisely that point at which the first generation to grow up principally on TV was just entering those dangerous adolescent years. Nineteen sixty-five, which one could say marked a further and much more dramatic deterioration, represented a point by which virtually everyone coming of age had grown up on TV.

But at this point someone surely must be thinking: "Medved, what are you talking about? Because the TV that existed in the 1950s and the early 1960s wasn't slash and burn TV, it wasn't shock TV, it wasn't *Ricki Lake*, it wasn't *Married with Children*. It was *Ozzie and Harriet*, it was *Leave It To Beaver*, it was *Father Knows Best*—precisely the kind of wholesome traditional shows that conservatives and traditionalists are supposed to long for and support. So how can you say television was a major cause of the demise of the family when the television at the time was almost universally positive in its depiction of the family?" And the answer to that is the burden I want to place upon the reader at this point: It is the notion that the fundamental problem isn't the content of TV, but the medium itself.

A long time ago Marie Winn, who wrote an interesting book called *The Plug-In Drug*, got in a great deal of trouble—and I subsequently got into trouble by quoting her—by saying the only difference between good TV and bad TV is the difference between good heroin and bad heroin. The bad heroin will kill you faster, but the good heroin is also addictive and it is also dangerous. And what I want to submit to you today is that television in and of itself as a medium is destructive of the very foundations of the family, and it is destructive because of the nature of the medium. The nature of that medium tends to make people (1) impatient, (2) depressed, and (3) selfish—all of them attributes that are absolutely deadly to the survival of marriages and families. Let me take these one by one.

Impatience

First of all, the issues of impatience. Do people here know how frequently an image shifts on television today? (And, by the way, it has been changing and been getting shorter and shorter.) A typical image is held on TV just nine seconds before you get a new image on the screen. In motion pictures they hold images on screen for the lavish, luxurious, and leisurely total of eighteen seconds, but on TV it is every nine seconds. On MTV, it is every four seconds on average, and on *Sesame Street* the average is every five seconds. The very nature of television as a medium creates impatience and tends to undermine any attention span. There is a wealth of empirical data on this point, there is a wealth of survey studies and education reports. Or, you can simply talk to any preschool or elementary school teacher that you know, and they will tell you it is easy to tell the children in the classroom who are particularly addicted to television, because they tend to be afflicted by a condition best described with a Yiddish word—"spilus." Spilus is one of those words I don't think you need to translate. Now I say this at some risk with my three children waiting at the moment very patiently in front of me because I don't want anyone to say that any of them are displaying spilus, and I hope they don't, but the truth is that anyone who works in education can talk to you about the way that attention span is directly impacted by people who are accustomed for a great deal of their time to watch flickering images passing one after another and bang, bang, bang, bang, bang, bang. No teacher can equal that.

But it is not just the images—it is the whole structure of television as entertainment. The whole idea of a TV show is that everything begins and ends in neat one-half-hour or one-hour chunks. Every problem is posed and then solved very quickly. And even if it is a very lavish TV show, it is ninety minutes and then everything is tied up.

And the commercials on television are exercises in impatience. It is not just the quick cutting where the imagery in commercials goes across much more quickly than even the imagery in the programming. But it is that the whole idea of commercials is to make you impatient, to make you want things and to want them now, immediately. And commercials work. Anybody here who has children, who has ever seen children exposed during holiday season to TV ads, knows what I am talking about. It is a very common thing. Kids come back after seeing a toy advertised in December and all of a sudden they want that toy and they want it now and no substitute is accepted. There is a sense of encouraging desire, and even a desperate edge to that desire. All of this has to do with shortening the long-term view that is necessary for any family health or survival. .

Depression

But it is not just the impact of television in terms of creating impatience that is harmful to families. Television also promotes depression. And here let me pose a question that many of you, perhaps in your work, have confronted many times. There's an anomaly when you read all the survey data about how Americans feel about this country at the moment and the anomaly comes up again and again. If you ask people how they feel about their own family life, their own children, their own parents, about the state of their own family, people overwhelmingly—in percentages ranging from two-thirds up to three-fourths—are very satisfied. They tend to be very optimistic, they tend to be very grateful for their own families. But then when you ask them what's the state of family life in general, the percentages are reversed. It's three-quarters who are very dissatisfied and feel that things are terrible. It's the "I'm O.K.—everybody else is in terrible shape" syndrome.

What does this have to do with TV? It seems to me that it has a great deal to do with the fact that the focus of the media is relentlessly negative. And, you know what, this is one of those areas where it is almost built into the medium itself.

There are things that television does well. Television dramatizes violence very well; it shows disasters very well. We have all seen great footage of tornadoes, floods, and fires, and there is a natural tendency to focus on the negative. To use one example, if someone living in southeastern Washington goes to church, works at three jobs to support five children, is knocking himself out, comes home every night at 3 a.m. in the morning and kisses each one of those five children and asks God's blessing on those kids, it is not "news." If that same person goes out one night and shoots each of the five children, it is big news. You hear about it all over the country.

Tolstoy said a long time ago in the opening to *Anna Karenina* that all happy families are the same and all unhappy families are unhappy in their unique and fascinating manner. And that obviously gives a great push for the media to focus on dysfunctional, and that of course is what you find. The saying in local news is "if it bleeds it leads," which is why so many Americans seem to be utterly unaware that there has been some good news in this country in the last five years concerning the actual rate of criminal violence. It goes against what they continue to see on television.

And it is not just the news, it is not just the focus on dysfunction, it is also the visions of the future and here it's a very bizarre thing. Look at the way that the future is portrayed any time we portray the future in motion pictures today. David Gallanter wrote a very interesting book about the World's Fair of 1939. The point of that book is that, while the world was on the very cusp of the most disastrous event in human history, World War II and the Holocaust, what happened at the World's Fair in Flushing Meadow was hugely optimistic. The most popular ride was sponsored by General Motors and was called Futurama, and it saw the future as magnificent. The interesting point that Gallanter makes is that at that moment of history that was so dark, those future visions almost all were positive ones.

The problem we have today is exactly the opposite. We live in a moment of history which in objective terms is pretty good. It's not great if you are a Bosnian, certainly not great if you're a Rwandian, but in terms of the overall sweep of history, look at the moment we live in. And yet our visions of the future are incredibly bleak—fed profoundly by the media.

Regarding film visions of the future, they are doing a new movie called *Escape from LA*, which is sort of a companion piece of *Escape from New York*. It is another postapocalyptic vision of Los Angeles. In *Waterworld* last year, the most expensive movie ever made, the polar ice cap has melted and there is no dry land and you have to rely upon Kevin Costner, you will pardon me, drinking his own urine, which is the opening scene of the movie, to save humanity. Or look at the *Mad Max* series, the *Terminator series*, or *Blade Runner*. Whenever the future is portrayed it is shown as bleak, hopeless, and horrible. (The only exception to that is, by the way, the *Star Trek* series, which is rooted very firmly in a different consciousness from the 1960s.) But what is the impact of all of this? The impact is to convince America's children that their lives are going to be more bitter, more difficult, and more hopeless in the future than the lives they lead today or the lives their parents had the opportunity to lead.

One of the particularly fascinating aspects about these visions of future destruction is how neatly and effortlessly people in the media were able to shift their attention from a vision of nuclear apocalypse to visions of environmental apocalypse. The end of the cold war was a big disaster for Hollywood filmmakers, because you could no longer have visions of the world in ashes, blown up by thermonuclear destruction. So without missing a beat—and there were literally scripts that were changed—it became environmental disaster, with the same result: people running around in animal skins in a debased future. But the commitment to horror and negativity remained consistent.

And yet, someone might ask, what about all those other things on TV? Because it is not all dark, it is not all destructive, and it's not all homicide, life in the streets, and gritty realism. There is a lot of revolting fluff on television as well.

Anybody ever see *Baywatch*? No one could accuse *Baywatch* of being gritty and pessimistic and realistic and horrifying! But it is horrifying in another sense, and it contributes to the impact of television on making people depressed. And that is because it creates this whole vision of unattainable expectations, a vision that leads you to compare your own life to the impossible life that people lead on this show—a possibly superficial and idiotic life, but nonetheless one that is sold in the best tradition, with a great amount of glamour and a great amount of appeal. And the gap between that glamourous world and any reality recognizable on this planet is a gap, it seems to me, which contributes greatly to this depressed mood that afflicts the country.

Because I am convinced that the biggest epidemic in the United States today and the most deadly epidemic ultimately is not the epidemic of AIDS, as serious as that is, it is the national epidemic of whining. And it strikes every corner of society. And it has very little basis in reality.

Selfishness

Television is a medium that not only contributes intrinsically to making people impatient and making them depressed. I also would submit that it contributes to making people selfish—and this bears a bit more explanation. I will give you a statistic—to go with all the other horrifying statistics provided by David Popenoe and David Blankenhorn and other contributors to this volume—I'll give you a statistic that particularly horrifies me, that they may even be unaware of: 58 percent of American households with children—58 percent!—allow those children to have televisions in their bedrooms. That is HORRIFYING!

First of all, it is unbelievably stupid, because there is nothing that so immediately removes any parental role at all in determining what a child can watch. There is nothing that ensures even the old idea by which they use to try to sell TV in 1950s: That it is the new "family hearth" and everybody gathers together around the *Milton Berle* show and the family will be closer than ever because they watch "We Are the Men Who Wear the Star." (For those of you who are too young that was a featured commercial on the *Milton Berle* show, sponsored by Texaco.) In any event, far from that idea, you have people retreating to separate corners of the house and the atomization of society proceeding so far and so fast that it not only involves families that are isolated from one another but it involves family members that are isolated from one another because everybody wants to be watching something separately.

Moreover, it is not only television in children's bedrooms by the way—I think an almost equally idiotic idea is the idea of television in the bedroom the parents share. Now this is something that my wife talks about a lot. She's a clinical psychologist who specializes in trying to help people avoid divorce. One of the first questions she poses to couples who are having difficulties, because those difficulties most often are difficulties in communication, is "do you have a TV in the bedroom?" The easy advice is: If you want to try and make this marriage work, get rid of it. Ideally, throw it out the window, but at least put it in the closet, because—it is not just the interference with sexuality (although that's serious enough)—you have to ask yourself what is the message that this machine sends when at the end of a long and busy day, and God knows we all have long and busy days, when you lay your weary body down and finally sleep arrives to take your soul and you turn your weary eye and the last face on earth you see is David Letterman. This is not a healthy message for any marriage.

But it is not just the David Letterman image that interferes with marriages, that tends to make people selfish, that tends to break down the unselfishness that is required for any successful family unit. It is also the images of physical perfection that are so regularly promulgated on television. Now, here I don't blame the TV broadcasters. You know, if you owned a TV network, it is obvious that you are going to sell more of whatever it is you want to sell by having beautiful people on the air than having the Hunch Back of Notre Dame (which is, by the way, a film you should all miss—just saving you a good deal of money on that!) Of course you are going to have pretty people. But the impact of all of that—to be constantly surrounded by these visions of physical perfection—is devastating. We all know famously how devastating it is on adolescent girls, who can't possibly measure up to the visions of female perfection and female beauty—and by the way it's not just adolescent girls who can't measure up: You know the stars themselves can't measure up. Most major Hollywood stars use body doubles because they are not perfect enough and so you have body doubles who specialize in legs, in rear ends, in shoulders. If you take a look at these films, it's astonishing. I just saw this film with Demi Moore (*Striptease*—a nude film), who's famous for her body, but she clearly uses a body double in some scenes. And these images of physical perfection not only invade our adolescent girls, but also, in a very real and very destructive way, invade the imaginations and the expectations of American men. And this clearly contributes to a sense of dissatisfaction, of restlessness, of inevitably comparing a real human being to a perfect composite human being made up of various body doubles, makeup effects, cosmetic surgery, and brilliant camera angles. You know, I mean, wouldn't it be great if we all had body doubles in real life. There are occasions when you know everybody could use one!

But all of this creates one of our most destructive syndromes in this country, which is the syndrome of entitlement, and I am not now just talking about government programs that are going to bankrupt the society. I'm talking about the sense of sexual entitlement, the sense that every American is entitled to an absolutely perfect physical specimen, and if you don't have it, you had better go out and look for one—that everyone is entitled to ceaseless arrays of ecstatic pleasures just like the people on *Friends*. After all we know that that reflects reality, everybody looks like that— NOT! And yet the message comes across . . .

And there is even a most destructive form of entitlement that is encouraged by television and that is the sense that everybody is entitled to unending entertainment and fun. And if something isn't fun, isn't entertaining, and isn't exciting at one given moment then you have to go off after something exciting, change the channel, press the remote control, move along. Now what's wrong with fun? Let it not be said that conservatives are against fun. Fun is nice, fun is good, but there's a very big difference between fun and happiness, and that is something that has to be acknowledged and emphasized ceaselessly.

The main differences between fun and happiness are two. Fun is fleeting, and you can have lots and lots of fun—and afterwards how do you feel? There is usually a sense of emptiness or I need more fun right away. And the other difference between fun and happiness besides the fact that fun is fleeting and happiness can last is that happiness is something that has to be earned. Happiness is something that you have to work for, happiness is something you have to achieve and make sacrifices for, and that's the whole essence of the approach to family happiness.

Television and the Family

So, to summarize, why then does television have such a destructive impact? Why is television at the very heart of our undermining of the family as an institution as a unit in this country. Because television undermines precisely those attributes that are most necessary for successful families, most necessary for family survival. First, for family to thrive and exist to achieve happiness you need patience, not impatience. You need to emphasize deferred gratification, you need to emphasize a long-term view rather than a short-term view.

Second, regarding the point that television encourages people to be depressed and self-pitying and unhappy and restless: Optimism is a crucial element in any family's survival—and here I'll just speak very personally, from my father's experience—especially growing up in very difficult circumstances. My grandfather was a barrel maker, he never learned to speak English, he came to this country from Ukraine in 1914, and he grew up under tough circumstances. My dad used to tell stories about, literally every night, having to go to his father's bloody hands and pull the splinters out, and there was a knowledge that he could only work as a barrel maker for a certain limited amount of time until his hands could not function any more. And they lived in difficult circumstances. My grandparents didn't speak English and you know I talked to my dad, what was it in that experience, how were you able to overcome these obstacles with not a penny? He said, "because we knew it was going to get better." We had no question it was going to get better. We believed in America, and his father knew that, even though things may not be better for him, they would be better for his children. Optimism is essential. If you are convinced that the world is getting worse, that the future is going to be bleak, that you are going to have fewer opportunities than your parents, then your motivation to dedicate yourself to any kind of work, to any kind of long-term commitment, to any kind of long-term horizon is undermined. Optimism is essential and is much better achieved when the TV is off. And the best way to achieve that optimism is through gratitude, through a recognition of all the blessings we do enjoy.

And on the final point—the point that TV makes you selfish, makes you isolated, makes you want things for yourself immediately, things meant to emphasize "fun"—what's necessary for families to survive is an emphasis on unselfishness and happiness and the whole idea that happiness lasts because happiness requires work and sacrifice. Here I would like to allude to a couple of things in the Jewish tradition. You know Jewish people are not known normally, even secular Jewish people, as sort of easygoing, "party-animal" types. This is not the stereotype, but does that mean that Jewish people don't ever have fun, that Jewish people can't celebrate and kick back? No, they can and they do. There are two occasions for Jewish people that are celebrated above all, where you actually have explosions of pure joy. One of them is a wedding and the other one is the holiday of Purim, which celebrates the events in the Book of Esther. What's fascinating about these two occasions—on both of which by the way it's traditional for Jewish people to imbibe "adult beverages," to dance, to show great joy—what's fascinating is that both of these occasions celebrate survival. A wedding celebrates survival and continuity, the miracle, in the case of the Jewish people, in the survival of our people against all odds. And of course, Purim represents the same thing. Haman in the Book of Esther is trying to exterminate the Jews, but the Jews have survived and then you celebrate. But there is something else that these two occasions have in common and it's very profound. It is that both of them are preceded by a fast day. In Jewish tradition, a bride and a groom fast the day before the wedding and then under the wedding canopy they break the fast with a cup of wine they share, their first shared meal, in fact, as husband and wife. And Purim, the most joyous holiday of the Jewish Year, is preceded by the Fast of Esther, by a full fast day. The message is very clear: The difference between fleeting fun and lasting happiness is work, is sacrifice, is commitment, is recognizing that it's not an entitlement, it is something you have to strive to achieve.

Conclusion

So with all of this it is very obvious that when I talk about the destructive impact of TV, I am not talking merely about the wretched quality of network TV today. It is wretched, but even if we turned around and all of a sudden made Governor Casey or Lawrence Jarvik, who I know is an expert on television or take anyone else in the room, David Blankenhorn, and made him chairman of the FCC and all of a sudden empowered him somehow to totally clean up the world of television and get rid of all the foul behavior and vulgar attitudes and the disgusting exploitation and the violence and the sexuality and all of a sudden we were back to *Leave It To Beaver* except artistically more gratifying—imagine that and, you know what, even imagining that—if the American people still watched an average of twenty-six hours a week of television, it would still be a disaster and you all know that. If your children are spending twenty-six hours per week and all they are watching is A&E and PBS (fat chance!), and C-Span (that's really fat chance!), if that's all they are watching . . . yes it is better than them watching MTV for twenty-six hours per week. It is better but it is still a disaster, and the analogy here is tobacco. Because I believe at this point of our debate and our understanding of the impact of media on the family, we are at some level comparable to the situation we had with tobacco.

You may remember when the Surgeon General of the United States—back forty years ago when we had a Surgeon General in the United States, (you will notice the Republic is not teetering on its axes because we don't have a Surgeon General at the moment—no one is safe, right?!)—discovered that cigarette smoking was not beneficial, that it was indeed hazardous to your health, the first response from sane people, from thoughtful people, was: we'll put better filters on the cigarettes. We are going to reduce the tar and nicotine. Remember that? It was a very good thing. Why not reduce the tar and nicotine, why not do better filters? It helps—but it doesn't help much. Ultimately you have to recognize that you've got to get rid of the level of smoking itself. You've got to cut down on the actual total volume of consumption of tobacco, not just the kind of tobacco or the kind of cigarettes you consume.

We are at the same point with the media. It helps to clean up the media. I've devoted a great deal of my life to it. I think it is a great thing, it would be better if there were more wholesome programming, it would be better if there was less destructive programming. But ultimately that's not the answer; that's just getting rid of tar and nicotine. The real answer is cutting down the level of TV watching itself. That's why I believe that one of the priorities of that counterrevolution that Gertrude Himmelfarb has written about must be, not simply attacking the irresponsible excesses of the media, but attacking the irresponsible excesses of the American people who consume so much of it. A primary focus has to be getting TVs out of the bedrooms, first of all, and maybe even for families that are willing to take the dare, getting rid of TVs altogether. And I will tell you that we have three children, and you can inspect them at your leisure—they do not have hair on their palms, they do not have little horns—they have grown up in a TV-free household, and I believe with all my heart that they are better for it.

And again, another analogy, you know I think we all recognize there is something to be said, not much, but something to be said for programs of so-called "Safe Sex." Is it better if people are going to have sex outside of marriage to use protection. Of course it's better—you're less likely to have pregnancy, a little bit less likely to have sexually transmitted diseases. Is that an answer? NO! The answer is abstinence, and by the same token reducing the amount of junk on TV is the equivalent of Safe Sex. It may be worth doing, but the real answer is abstinence. And here all I can say is that this has to be an answer that must be brought home to American families today. You hear so many times that people are worried about children watching so much TV—I'm worried about adults watching so much TV, about what it does to relationships, about what it does to communities, about what it does to any efforts to mobilize people for anything because they are all too busy being entertained.

Do you know that, given the average American who watches twenty-six hours per week of TV, that means that when we all go on to the next world—the average life expectancy in this country is seventy-five years eight months—the average person will have devoted thirteen uninterrupted years to television. Think about it, that's thirteen years, twenty-four hour days, seven days per week, fifty-two week years, no time for sleeping or eating, just TV. Thirteen years of life—do you want it on your gravestone? "Here lies our beloved husband and father who selflessly devoted thirteen years of his life to his TV set." Your TV set doesn't need it—your family needs it, your wife or your husband needs it, your community needs it, your church or synagogue needs it, you need it because you can't get it back.

So beginning with cutting down, maybe trimming down one hour per day, think about what that can mean. For an American family or an American individual to cut TV watching one hour per day still means the average would be nineteen hours per week, which I think is plenty. But one hour a day gives you seven extra hours a week, twenty-eight extra hours per month to maybe read a book—remember them? To read a book, to cherish your loved ones, maybe to talk to your spouse, to have a conversation, which is always a useful thing in a marriage, to work for some larger cause, to worship your God, maybe to start that exercise program, that vigorous exercise program you have been meaning to start for the last twenty years, to enjoy great music, or maybe just go outside in the beginning of summer and to fully appreciate this magnificent world the Almighty has given to you.

16

Family Values and Media Reality

Robert Lerner and Althea K. Nagai

While it is often stated that marriage and the nuclear family are universal social institutions, this may not remain the case. That there is a crisis of the family in modern society is taken here as given. David Popenoe, David Blankenhorn, Lawrence Stone, Maggie Gallagher, and William Galston have all presented data and analyses which provide evidence of the astonishing decline of the family in post-1960s America.

These authors' descriptions of the current crisis of the family is acute, detailed, and devastating. The explanations provided as to how this unprecedented situation emerged, however, are thin. For example, sociologist David Popenoe claims that somehow the modern nuclear family as an ideal disappeared during the 1960s and 1970s,[1] possibly because of the spread of belief in what he calls "radical individualism."[2] Is it really true that belief in the modern nuclear family, an institution purportedly the most universal for all of civilization, suddenly vanished? What *is* this novel, in effect subversive, belief system of radical individualism? How did it become widely accepted, if this is in fact the case?

Although this essay cannot provide definitive answers to these vast questions, we explore several subsidiary questions of great relevance to understanding how the values of "radical individualism," which we prefer to call expressive individualism, have been disseminated throughout the culture. What is expressive individualism, who believes it and who doesn't, and how did it come to be the dominant elite ideology of our times? Second, how is the ideology of expressive individualism transmitted to the culture at large? Third, and most difficult, what kind of impact does the media have on the society that receives it?

These questions are considered in four sections. Part one of this paper examines in detail the enormous gap in attitudes between elites in news, television entertainment, and current motion pictures, as compared to those of other American elites and the general public.

Part two examines the increasing infusion of expressive individualism into media institutions and productions. We use prime time television entertainment as our case study; the content of prime-time television has evolved (or devolved) from

173

Father Knows Best to *Roseanne.*

Part three compares depictions of sex and family in the media to social reality. We contrast media views with data concerning the actual distribution of current opinions and behaviors concerning issues of expressive individualism.

In part four, we raise questions as to the impact of television entertainment on the public's beliefs and practices, and speculate as to its indirect effects on the family as an institution.

Liberalism and Expressive Individualism Among News, Television, and Movie Elites

Familism and family values— *pace* Vice President Quayle—have not always been celebrated in the West. On the contrary, leading thinkers such as Plato, Engels, John Stuart Mill (*On the Subjugation of Women*), and Herbert Marcuse, as well as legions of feminists beginning with Simone de Beauvoir and Betty Friedan, have been sharply critical of the nuclear family for being a repressive, even reactionary institution, standing in the way of human liberation for both women and men, sexual fulfillment, and the creation of a just society.

Current articulations of expressive individualism are a direct ideological adaptation of these relatively "advanced" views of family relations to contemporary political and social practice. In *American Elites* (coauthored with Stanley Rothman),[3] we show that what we call "expressive individualism" has come to be the dominant view of sex, marriage, and family relations among American elites, especially those in the mass media, who take the intellectual trends of the day as their primary frame of reference. Expressive individualism is the adaption of contemporary liberalism to questions of sex, marriage, and family relations. Elites in news, prime-time television, and movies are liberal, compared to the general American public.

In the past fifteen years, social scientists have begun to survey these elites of popular culture. As part of a larger study of American elites, Stanley Rothman, S. Robert Lichter, and Linda S. Lichter surveyed 238 members of the news media elite, 149 directors, writers and producers of popular motion pictures, and 104 writers, producers, and executives of prime-time television. In 1990, David Prindle and James Enderby also surveyed Hollywood elites, comparing the views of 35 opinion leaders in the entertainment industry with those of the general public.

The results of both surveys provide unequivocal support for what many conservative commentators have claimed. For example, when asked to describe their own ideological leanings, 55 percent of the media elite consider themselves liberal, while 17 percent call themselves conservative; the rest labeled themselves middle-of-the road. Similarly, 67 percent of the movie elite and 75 percent of the television elite think themselves liberal. Only 19 percent of the makers of film and 14 percent of the creators of prime-time television call themselves conservative.[4] In 1993, a survey of the American public conducted by the National Opinion Research Center (GSS93), 26 percent of the respondents described themselves as liberal, 36 percent described themselves as middle-of-the-road, and 36 percent described themselves as conservative.

Prindle and Enderby found similar results in a 1990 survey directly comparing Hollywood elites with the general public. Sixty percent of Hollywood opinion leaders described themselves as liberal, compared to 30 percent of the general public. Fourteen percent of his Hollywood leaders see themselves as conservative, compared to 43 percent of the general public.

The liberalism of news, television, and movie elites, however, is most prominent when considering issues of expressive individualism.

In our book, *American Elites*, we statistically analyzed opinion data of 12 American elite groups.[5] These include American business elites, American labor leaders, partners in America's most prestigious corporate law firms, high-ranking members of the federal civil service, the American military elite, Congressional aides, federal judges, leaders of public interest groups, the media elite, the creators of our most popular movies, the makers of prime-time television, and American religious leaders.

We used the statistical technique of factor analysis which allows us to extract the underlying dimensions that constitute core values from correlations among responses to individual questions. The dimensions are ideal-type abstractions meant to represent and partially explicate the underlying link between otherwise disparate issue positions. Five underlying dimensions of ideology emerge: laissez-faire individualism versus collectivist liberalism; moral puritanism versus expressive individualism; system support versus system alienation; regime threat versus liberal cosmopolitanism; and lastly, support for versus opposition to affirmative action. For the sake of convenience, we refer to a dimension by the label assigned to its liberal pole (e.g., collectivist liberalism, system alienation, expressive individualism).

This essay focuses on attitudes held by the media, television, and movie elite on issues of expressive individualism, as opposed to what we call traditional values, and compares these views to those held by other elites and the general public.

In our factor analysis of elite opinion, four questions statistically fit together on the expressive individualism dimension:

- whether a woman has the right to decide regarding abortion;
- whether gays should be allowed to teach in public schools;
- whether extramarital sex is wrong;
- whether homosexual relations are wrong.

To compare elites' responses, we computed mean factor scores on the expressive individualism dimension for members of each elite group. Higher scores represent more liberal responses to these four questions than do lower scores (see Table 1).

The news, television, and movie elites are more liberal on these issues than are other elites. Conservatives accuse these cultural elites of being to the far left of most Americans; *they are also far to the left of most other elites*. Except for public interest leaders, they are more liberal than elites in the military, religion, business, labor, the federal civil service, the Congressional staff, corporate law firms, and federal judges. The ideological split between the extreme liberalism of news, television, and movie elites versus every other elite group (except for public interest leaders) is statistically significant.[6]

Table 1. Expressive Individualism Among American Elites (Mean Factor Scores)

Elite Group	Factor Score
Religious	90.89
Military	92.30
Labor	96.06
Judges	97.43
Business	99.92
Congressional Aides	99.63
Bureaucrats	99.92
Corporate Lawyers	103.36
News Media	105.43
Moviemakers	106.05
Public Interest Leaders	106.17
Television Makers	106.48

These elites are also significantly more liberal than the general public. Table 2 contrasts media, television, and movie elites' positions with those of the public.[7]

Table 2. A Comparison of Attitudes among Media, Television, and Movie Elites Versus the General Public.

	Media	Movies	TV	Public
Woman has right to decide on abortion	90% Agree	98% Agree	97% Agree	52% Agree
Gays shouldn't teach in public schools	15% Agree	13% Agree	14% Agree	38% Agree
Extramarital sex is wrong	46% Agree	42% Agree	49% Agree	77% Agree
Homosexual relations are wrong	24% Agree	28% Agree	23% Agree	65% Agree

In every instance, members of news, television, and movie elites are significantly more liberal than the general public.

- Almost all members of the media, television, and movie elite support abortion rights; roughly half the public believe a woman has a "right to choose."
- More than three of four Americans also think adultery is wrong; a majority of the media, television, and movie elite think extramarital sex is permissible.
- Similarly, roughly two out of three Americans think homosexual relations are wrong, while roughly three of four news, television, and movie elites think there is nothing inherently wrong with homosexual relations.
- Lastly, 38 percent of the public think gays should not teach in public schools, while only a small percentage of news, television, and movie elite think the same.

Prindle and Enderby[8] also found television and movie elites to be more liberal than the general public. Nearly every member of Prindle and Enderby's elite sample (91 percent) opposed changing laws on abortion to make abortions more difficult to obtain, while 41 percent of the public favored changing abortion laws in this way. While only 16 percent of Hollywood leaders favored prayer in public school, roughly three in four Americans surveyed felt the same. Only 6 percent of Hollywood leaders thought AIDS might be God's punishment for immoral sexual behavior, compared to 42 percent of the public.

Clearly, elites in the media, television, and movies hold significantly more liberal opinions on social issues than does the general public. What differences does it make? To what extent do these elites create a product reflecting their own values? To what extent do they produce something demanded by the public (i.e., driven by the free market)?

The next section reviews the findings of Rothman and his colleagues' content analysis of prime-time television, the news, and movies.

The Dominance of Expressive Individualism in Media Content

While traditionally separate from news coverage, the boundaries between entertainment and real life have blurred as never before. Moreover, television entertainment, rather than news, comprises the vast bulk of all television programming, and is watched by more people than television news.

It is easy to intuit a massive transformation of television content toward supporting positions of expressive individualism.[9] Yet large-scale quantitative summary statistics describing how much has changed with any degree of reliability or validity are nearly nonexistent. To our knowledge, only one study quantitatively analyzes changes in television content over the past four decades. S. Robert Lichter, Linda S. Lichter, and Stanley Rothman have produced detailed quantitative analyses of the content of prime time-television. Lichter et al. conducted one study based on a random sample of 620 prime-time television shows drawn from the Library of Congress video archives, spanning the period from 1955 to 1986. The same authors updated and slightly modified their study to study prime-time television of the 1990s, using prime-time television shows on the four major broadcast networks: ABC, CBS, NBC, and Fox.[10] Critical findings from these studies will serve as the basis of our analysis of the evolution of media content.[11]

Sex on Television

Lichter et al. find that while at one time television and the movies were relatively prudish in their approach to sex on television, today it is abstinence that is deviant. Lichter et al. tallied actual sexual activity.

- In the 1992-1993 season, of the 220 scenes that dealt with sex between unmarried partners, only 9 percent concluded that it was wrong. Sixty-nine percent treated sex as desirable, and the remainder rendered no judgment either way.[12]
- Teenage sex, rarely found before the 1990s but now commonplace, was criticized in 25 percent of cases, endorsed 42 percent of the time, and portrayed without judgment in one-third of the cases.[13]
- Prime time television in the 1990s presented masturbation, fetishes and fantasies, group sex, bondage and discipline, and sadomasochism among other lifestyle choices.[14]
- The word "condom" was first uttered on television in 1986.[15] Today, the word is commonplace.
- Homosexuality in contemporary prime-time television is treated matter-of-factly, even though the didactic approach has not died off.[16]
- Before 1965, half the scenes where extramarital sex occurred treated it as wrong in all cases. Between 1965 and 1975, this dropped to 6 percent, it continued at 7 percent in the decade of the 1980s. Seventy-eight percent of cases by the mid-1980s passed no judgment, or portrayed adultery as an acceptable lifestyle choice if recreational. Roughly 15 percent portrayed adultery as acceptable when the persons were in love.[17]

Above all, the bias toward expressive individualism in prime-time television is reflected in its portrayal of those who oppose such behavior as puritans and prudes. The "correct stance" is nonjudgmental. It is akin to anti-anticommunism.

The Family on Television

Atypical families have always been a part of prime-time television. However, the nature of the atypical family has changed. The family comedies of the late 1950s included widows and widowers as single parents; these same types of programs in the 1970s included divorced parents heading households.[18] The 1980s introduced a new type of family structure—the accidental family, formed from characters who are not blood relatives—single-parent families, single parents plus an outsider, guardianships, blended families, etc.

- From the 1950s until the 1990s, there has been a 50 percent increase in the number of single-parent families as a percent of all families on prime-time television.[19]
- By the mid-1980s, 42 percent of all families were some form of accidental family.[20]

These transformations from the 1950s to the 1990s add up to little short of a cultural revolution.

Sex and the Family in Society

Almost no work has been done systematically comparing media portrayals with social facts. In this section, we compare Lichter et al.'s findings with the results of a landmark survey of Americans' sex lives, the National Health and Social Life Survey (NHSLS), conducted by social scientists Edward O. Laumann, John H. Gagnon, Robert T. Michael, and Stuart Michaels, in conjunction with the National Opinion Research Center at the University of Chicago.[21] How do the findings of Laumann et al. compare with what the public sees on prime time television?

Marriage and Divorce

In the Laumann study, 54 percent of respondents were currently married, 28 percent were never married, 2 percent were widowed, and 16 percent were divorced or separated. About 90 percent of all adults marry by the time they are thirty; a large majority spend most of their adult lives as part of a married couple.

However, the divorce rate has increased. Those born between 1933 and 1942 had a one in five chance of divorce by the tenth year of marriage. For those born between 1943 and 1952, the chance was one in three; for those born between 1953 and 1962, it was roughly 38 percent.[22]

In real life, the rising rate of divorce has meant an increasing percentage of children not living with their biological fathers—from 17 percent in 1960 to 36 percent in 1990. In addition, an increasing percentage of children are born out of wedlock. In 1970, they accounted for 11 percent of all births, in 1980, 18 percent; and in 1990, 30 percent.[23]

On the issue of family composition, Lichter et al.'s findings on prime time television roughly matches Laumann's survey results and the census data. Fifty-eight percent of television families from the mid-1970s to the mid-1980s were the traditional nuclear families. Forty-two percent of all television families are some kind of "accidental family." Eighteen percent of prime-time television families were comprised of one parent with children.[24] Other types included blended families, single parents plus an outsider, and various forms of guardianships.

Lichter et al. fail to report instances of illegitimate births on television, despite the notoriety of *Murphy Brown*. This is presumably the result of too-few cases on prime-time television, in contrast to the social reality of a rising rate of illegitimacy. To the extent that members of the television elite seek to defy current television conventions (and in the absence of audience reaction), there is every reason to assume that a future study would be able to tabulate these occurrences.

Sex before and between Marriages

Teenage sexual behavior in reality is far more complex than that approvingly shown on prime-time television today. Despite prime-time television's nonjudgmental portrayal of a teenage sexual revolution, Laumann et al. found only a gradual decline in the mean age of first intercourse. The mean age of first intercourse has dropped; those born in the decade 1933-1942 first had intercourse at a mean age of 18; those born between 1963 and 1967 first had sex at roughly 17.5 years of age. It is a statistically significant, but not a staggeringly large drop. For those coming of age in the 1950s and 1960s, 35 percent of men and 19 percent of women reported first intercourse at age 16 (includes within as well as before marriage). For those coming of age in the 1970s and the 1980s, 48 percent of men and 37 percent of women had intercourse by the age of 16.[25]

The change in American sexual behavior is partly the results of the rising age of first marriage. In 1955, the median age of marriage for women was 20.2 and for men 22.6. By 1987, it had increased for both women and men, the former was now 23.6 and the latter was 25.5[26] Therefore, an increasing percentage of men and women have sex before marriage.

Laumann et al. found public opinion to be fairly tolerant of premarital sex. Only one in five survey respondents thought premarital sex was always wrong. Public sentiment, while tolerant of premarital sex and sex between marriages, is not supportive of premarital sex among teenagers. Sixty-one percent thought premarital sex among teenagers was always wrong.

Prime-time television is far more liberal regarding premarital sex than is either public opinion or public practice. Ninety-four percent of all scenes dealing with the issue either conveyed no point of view (19 percent), or concluded that sex before marriage was acceptable (76 percent). Television is also significantly more permissive regarding teenage premarital sex. Before 1990, Lichter et al. report that almost no teen sex occurred in prime-time television. Today, roughly three out of four relevant shows portrayed teenage sex in either a nonjudgmental or positive light in the 1990s.[27]

Adultery

Laumann et al. found that almost all Americans have relatively few partners over the projected course of a lifetime—a statistic that varies little by education, race, or religion. Current marital status was *the* determining factor. A currently married person is almost always monogamous.

As more adults are divorced, however, there are increasing numbers who have sexual intercourse between marriages. In other words, adultery in marriage is generally a myth. For example:

- A vast majority of the American public are monogamous while in marriage.
- Ninety-four percent of those currently married had one partner in the last twelve months.
- Seventy-seven percent of respondents believe that adultery is always wrong.

This is in sharp contrast to prime-time television depictions, which hardly ever portray adultery as immoral. Seventy-eight percent of prime-time television shows portraying adultery by the mid-1980s passed no judgment, or portrayed adultery as all right if the relationship was purely recreational.[28]

Homosexuality

The activist groups often quote the figure of 10 percent as the percentage of homosexuals in the general population.[29] The facts of the matter are different. Only 5.5 percent of women thought having sex with another woman very appealing or appealing. Four percent were attracted to other women; less than two percent said they had had sex with another woman in the past year; about four percent said they had had sex with another woman after age 18; and roughly the same percentage said they have had sex with a woman at some time in their life. Finally, 1.4 percent of women called themselves homosexual or bisexual.

Six percent of men said they thought having sex with another man very appealing or appealing; two percent had sex with a man in the past year, roughly five percent had sex with another man since they turned 18; and nine percent had sex with another man at some time in their lifetime. Finally, 2.9 percent of men in the survey called themselves homosexual or bisexual.

In contrast, roughly ninety percent surveyed found same-gender sex "not at all appealing,"[30] and 95 percent of the sample engaged in heterosexual intercourse the last time they had sex and found it "very appealing." Roughly 65 percent thought same-gender sex was always wrong.

Laumann et al. also compared sexual practices and partners between homosexual and heterosexual respondents. There are no differences in the frequency of sex, but homosexuals report more partners on average in a twelve-month period, in the past five years, and since age 18 than do heterosexuals. Self-defined homosexual men report three partners in the past year, compared to two for heterosexual men. They report an average of nineteen partners over a five-year period, compared to a mean of five partners in a five year period for heterosexual men. Lastly, while heterosexual men report a mean of sixteen partners since age 18, homosexual men report forty-three partners.

Despite the fact that two-thirds of the American public think homosexual relations are always wrong, such a view is strongly condemned on prime time television. Homosexuality, according to Lichter et al., is a common, generally positive theme in the 1990s. Before the 1970s there was no mention of homosexuality on television. The one or two mentions that occurred were negative. The 1970s and 1980s were periods in which treatment of homosexuality was rapidly and radically transformed. Shows became didactic about homosexuality and tolerance. Extensive lobbying by gay activists produced dramatic changes in coverage.[31]

In the 1990s, Lichter et al. found recent shows where characters discuss a tension between general tolerance for homosexuals and their personal ambivalence. Anti-homosexuality opinions, however, continue to be portrayed as simple bigotry, with homosexuals as the frequent victim of such prejudice.[32] While the first openly homosexual character was presented in 1981, such shows as *Roseanne* routinely include openly gay characters. At all times, however, little mention is made of typical homosexual practices. The promiscuity of homosexuals, especially men, is never mentioned.[33]

AIDS

Data from the Center for Disease Control as well as Laumann et al. show that the spread of AIDS to the general heterosexual population is highly unlikely. Homosexually active men have a greater tendency toward multiple partners and, hence, suffer a greater risk of contracting AIDS compared to heterosexuals in general. Laumann et al. conclude that AIDS will never become an epidemic disease among the heterosexual population. Lichter et al., however, find that prime time television portrays AIDS in the context of heterosexual promiscuity. Discussions of the subject tend to occur among heterosexuals regarding condom use.[34]

The sexual revolution on prime-time television clearly is not the one experienced by most Americans at any given time. Married life is generally monogamous and sexual practices and attitudes in the 1990s are significantly more conservative than values portrayed on and endorsed by television and its creators.

This is no accident. These impressions are reinforced by findings from the Rothman-Lichter studies cited above. Seventy-seven percent of the television makers and 73 percent of the moviemakers believe that their medium should be realistic, not the mere exercise of fantasy. Sixty-six percent of members of the television elite believe that television should be a force for social reform, and 69 percent of the movie elite feel similarly about their medium. Only 19 percent of the television elite feel that television is too critical of traditional values, a sentiment which 11 percent of the movie elite share. Finally, while majorities of both television and moviemakers agree that there is too much violence in television and movies respectively, only 30 percent of the television elite and 23 percent of the movie elite agree that there is too much sex on television.[35] We take these data to indicate definitively that the content of prime-time television and movies regarding expressive individualism self-consciously reflects the views of its creators, not the market or any other outside influence.

Media Impact: Defining Deviancy Down

The question of ascertaining the impact of the media generally, and of its success in diffusing the values of expressive individualism in particular, is surprisingly difficult to answer with certainty. Those in the business of creating and acting in media content adopt contradictory views, depending upon the nature of the interest at stake. What is the evidence *for* media impact?

First, as a matter of self-justification, television's creative elite argue that they attempt to be socially responsible in their programming and help to effect social change in the desired direction. Second, the argument remains the same when sponsors seek advertising. Gerald Jones, a television writer of long-standing, described how the control of the content of television was wrested away from sponsors because of the very reach of television programming.[36] At the very least, advertisers are likely to be afraid of not advertising for fear their rivals will best them in the continuing contest for customers, sales, and revenue. A third bit of evidence comes from our coauthored book with Rothman. We found that other elites routinely view the media as one of the most powerful institutions in society, greater than the federal government and, except for the most liberal elites, business.[37]

Arguments *against* powerful media effects are made when the issue of government content regulation is raised, or when critics of popular culture call for self-restraint on the part of the media. They also come from the dominant scholarly literature, for, with some significant exceptions, there is little evidence for immediate, overwhelmingly powerful audience effects from the media,[38] although there is considerable evidence for smaller, more focused effects. The bulk of the evidence for media effects is indirect[39].

What, then, of the notion of pervasive media effects? We believe media effects do operate, but they do not operate in a vacuum.

The power of the media rests in its ability to shape and transmit information. Modern society is characterized by an increasing specialization of work and greater separation of social networks. Professional and work-related networks, school ties, religious affiliations, neighborhoods, and voluntary associations are less overlapping than ever before. Even among American elites, there are few crosscutting occupational and social ties. Cultural, economic, and government elites share little in common in terms of values, politics, religion, ethnicity, school ties, and geographical locale.[40]

The complexity of modern life also means that information is compartmentalized. With sufficient time, interest, and energy, one could gather sufficient information to draw one's own conclusions regarding the major social, economic, cultural, and political issues of the day. Since no one can be the master of all, there is increasing reliance on knowledge substitutes—i.e., rhetoric. Rhetoric describes that presentation of all knowledge encountered by one who is outside the scope of specific academic or scientific specializations. Knowledge, such as an article in the premier journal of physics, mathematics, or economics, when appearing in unmediated form to the nonspecialized audience, is beyond simple comprehension.

The mass media is *the* primary national institution which performs the rhetorical function of transforming unintelligible information into common knowledge. This assumes that the media truthfully transform information into common knowledge. Our review of what viewers see on entertainment television versus social reality suggests a large gap between the two. Other studies done by Rothman and colleagues show a large gap between scientific consensus and news media coverage on such issues as nuclear energy safety, the reliability of IQ tests, and environmental versus other causes of cancer.[41]

The media's power to shape reality is even more importantly reflected in non-expert beliefs, especially those relating to moral questions. The capacity of any social system to endure rests in part on its characteristic ability to label and stigmatize actions deemed outside the pale. Social systems have only a limited capacity to tolerate large quantities of deviant behavior. When these are exceeded, several reactions are possible, but commonly deviancy is either defined down, to use Senator Moynihan's fine phrase, or redefined entirely "to exempt conduct previously stigmatized" from opprobrium and sanction.[42]

Tocqueville observed that majority opinion in democratic societies is the most irresistible power, including its threat to independence of thought leading to the tyranny of the majority. Tocqueville stressed the sheer power of the majority to impose its will on all. This power is nicely captured in one of the ambiguous meanings of the word "normal," which means both commonplace and morally decent. There are tendencies in both directions: What is commonplace becomes morally acceptable and what is morally acceptable become commonplace. The latter is true for all societies, but in democratic societies the former is of equal if not greater in importance.

An important locus of power and influence in a democratic society like ours, then, is defining what is commonplace. The characteristic form of media impact is the redefinition of what is commonplace. The very nature of a modern society accentuates this power because the extensive division of labor means that individuals have no idea as to what everyone else is doing, except through the media. The media therefore define what the majority opinion is.

When the media follows actual commonplace definitions of morality, it acts as an instrument of moral order. When it portrays the majority to be acting deviantly by promoting a conflicting ideal, one of two reactions follow. Either the media is censored or deviancy is defined down. To put it in colloquial language, "if everyone's doing it, then it must be acceptable." The effect of media content saturated with expressive individualism, then, is in the normalization of heretofore deviant behavior. By redefining majority opinions, the media shapes the culture's perception of itself and contributes to defining deviancy down on matters of expressive individualism. While it would be far too much to say that the media alone caused the explosion of expressive individualism, it likely made a major contribution.

There are two definite bodies of evidence here. The first consists of studies of the effects of agenda-setting. While the media cannot coerce people into holding the opinions its leaders deem desirable, it can prompt them to think about certain subjects to the nearly inevitable exclusion of others, time and attention being limited resources. The studies of Iyengar and associates, as well as the entire literature of McQuail,[43] demonstrate rather convincingly that the media tells the public what to think about with considerable success.

The second important consequence is the social psychological phenomenon known as "pluralistic ignorance." Pluralistic ignorance exists where a significant gap exists between what people perceive to be majority opinion or majority behavior, and what majority opinion or majority behavior actually is.[44]

What is the impact of prime-time television on public perception, public opinion, and public behavior? Ultimately, the media plays its most consequential role in the delegitimation of American institutions. In comparing responses of an experimental versus control group to a CBS documentary highly critical of the military, Robinson[45] found the experimental group significantly less trusting and more cynical, while also feeling less politically efficacious. Miller[46] found increasing reading of newspapers critical of government correlated with declining trust in government and declining feelings of political efficacy. They also found media impact to be inversely related to education; the less educated a respondent, the greater the impact of the media would be. Lipset and Schneider examined the decline in trust and confidence in American institutions over time. They believe that the significant decline in public confidence is partly a function of the mass media[47]. Moreover, Lipset and Schneider found that confidence in the press was inversely related to confidence in the presidency; that is, the more trust one had in the media, the less trust one had in the presidency. Conversely, the more one trusted the president, the less one trusted the mass media. Democrats and liberals have more trust in the media than Republicans and conservatives respectively.[48]

The messages found in the mass media make it harder to raise children well in modern American society. For example, teenage sex is commonplace on television entertainment today, and nonmarital sex is almost prosaic. Negative judgments on homosexuality and messages of abstinence are portrayed as prudish, puritanical, and intolerant. In reality, the overwhelming majority of respondents disapprove of teenage sex, and a slight majority of respondents who came of age in the 1980s (including 63 percent of girls) did not have sexual intercourse as teenagers.

If the media have an impact, we would probably find that most people think majority opinion is either indifferent or approving of teenage sex; that the perceived age of first intercourse is significantly lower than the real mean age of first intercourse; and that the perceived proportion of teenagers having sex is much higher than the real percentage. We also expect that increased watching of prime-time television and greater reliance on prime-time television for information would lead to perceptions of reality that better matched television life compared to social reality.

Another contrast is the instances of adultery on television versus the instances of adultery among survey respondents and strong public disapproval of adultery. Less than one-tenth of relevant cases on prime-time television portrayed adultery as always wrong, almost all respondents think adultery is always wrong, and most married respondents are monogamous. If we are right about the media's role in shaping public perceptions of reality, we would expect respondents to think a greater proportion of married persons engage in adultery than those who actually do; and that a greater percentage of the public are more accepting of adultery compared to the small percentage who actually are.

These ideas, however, are speculative. Quantitative studies examining the relationship between changing media content and pluralistic ignorance have yet to be done. Nevertheless it is clear that what the public sees on prime-time television is more in line with the values of the television elite, rather than reflecting the public's own values and personal behavior. The gap between television and reality ultimately serves to lower the threshold of acceptable behavior. In other words, prime-time television defines deviancy *down.* In doing so, it both contributes to the crisis of the family and even more to the sense of family crisis described at the beginning of this essay. To answer the question posed there, then, the acceptability of the nuclear family and its accompanying moral codes among the cultural elite vanished during the 1960s and 1970s. This elite did its best to transmit these values to the general public, resulting in some change and much confusion.

Notes

1. David Popenoe, "A World without Fathers," *Wilson Quarterly* (Spring, 1996): 17.

2. David Popenoe, "A World without Fathers," *27.*

3. Robert Lerner, Althea Nagai, and Stanley Rothman, *American Elites.* (New Haven: Yale University Press, 1996).

4. See Lerner et al., *American Elites.*

5. The samples and methods are described in Lerner et al., *American Elites.* All survey respondents were asked a common set of 17 attitudinal questions. All responses took the form of a four-point Likert scale, "strongly agree," "somewhat agree," "somewhat disagree," and "strongly disagree."

6. Lerner et al., *American Elites.*

7. The questions were asked in a survey of the general public's sexual attitudes and behaviors reported in Edward O. Laumann, John H. Gagnon, Robert T. Michael, and Stuart Michaels, *The Social Organization of Sexuality: Sexual Practices in the United States. The Complete Findings from America's Most Comprehensive Survey of Sexual Behavior* (Chicago: University of Chicago Press, 1994). The comparable questions are: "A woman should be able to obtain a legal abortion if she wants it for any reason; Extramarital sex is always wrong; same-gender sex is always wrong." The question asked of the general public regarding gays teaching in public schools is from the Times Mirror Poll (1994, p. 36). The actual question wording is: "School boards ought to have the right to fire teachers who are

known homosexuals." Public opinion on this question has shifted to the left, quite possibly in response to media portrayals of homosexuals. In 1987, 51 percent agreed with this statement, while in 1994 only 38 percent agreed with it.

8. David Prindle and James Enderby, "Hollywood Liberalism," *Social Science Quarterly* 74, 1 (March 1996).

9. The same is true for motion pictures. Michael Medved points out that in 1965, the movie *The Sound of Music* won The Motion Pictures' Oscar for the best picture of the year. In 1969, it was *Midnight Cowboy* (Medved, 1992, p. 278). Medved comments that this transformation was not motivated by the box office, since *Midnight Cowboy* drew an audience one-third the size of that for *The Sound of Music*.

10. The content analyses used both character and thematic coding systems. Details of their construction and use are reported in the appendix to Robert S. Lichter, Linda S. Lichter, and Stanley Rothman, *Prime Time: How TV Portrays American Culture* (Washington, DC.: Regnery Press, 1994).

11. Stanley Rothman (with David J. Rothman and Stephen Powers) produced a similar content analysis of Hollywood's most popular motion pictures.

12. Lichter et al., 39.

13. Lichter et al., 40.

14. Lichter et al., 41.

15. Lichter et al., 43.

16. Lichter et al., 44.

17. Lichter et al. do not present additional analysis of adultery for their 1992-1993 sample, but there is no reason to assume that television has become more critical of adultery.

18. Lichter et al., 159.

19. Stanley Rothman, S. Robert Lichter, and Linda S. Lichter, "Television's America," in *The Mass Media*, Stanley Rothman, ed. (New York.: Paragon House, 1992), 234.

20. Rothman et al., "Television's America," 234.

21. The NHSLS relies on well-established survey research methods, including questionnaire construction and probability sampling. Laumann et al. found that reliable statistics on Americans' sexual behavior to be lacking, so much so that experts still relied upon data gathered by Alfred Kinsey and his colleagues. The Kinsey data was gathered during the 1940s and 1950s and, more importantly, failed to meet even the most minimal standards of obtaining a representative sample of larger populations. The Kinsey and his colleagues ignored standard survey practices well-known even in the 1940s, and obviously lacked today's more sophisticated technical methods and survey research tools. Even worse, Laumann et al. found subsequent studies even less reliable. Despite the availability of social science methods, subsequent studies such as the Redbook Survey and the Hite Report ignored them, and produced scientifically worthless results. Other surveys by social scientists, while of considerably greater value, studied only limited segments of the general public such as college students or younger women or were not based on probability samples and thus can not be reliably used to infer characteristics of the larger American public (e.g., Blumstein and Schwartz, 1983).

Laumann and his colleagues conducted the first general survey of sexual behavior, preferences, and general attitudes, based on a probability sample of the general public. Roughly 3,400 persons were interviewed; the survey had a remarkably low nonresponse rate of 17 percent.

22. The commonly cited divorce rate of 50 percent reflects the ratio of the number of divorces to the number of marriages in a given year.

23. The statistics are from David Popenoe (1996).

24. Some of these 18 percent overlap with the accidental family type.

25. Laumann et al., 324-26.

26. U.S. Bureau of Census. *Statistical Abstract of the United States,* 1982-83, 82.; U.S. Bureau of Census. *Statistical Abstract of the United States,* 1991, 87.

27. Lichter et al., 40.

28. Lichter et al., 90-93.

29. Laumann et al. provide an interesting account of exactly how the 10 percent figure so often used came into widespread prominence (1995, p. 287-89).

30. Laumann et al., 145-46.

31. Lichter et al., 93-96.

32. Lichter et al., 43-44; 93-96.

33. Lichter et al., 43.

34. Lichter et al., 107.

35. Linda S. Lichter, S. Robert Lichter, and Stanley Rothman, "Hollywood and America: The Odd Couple," *Public Opinion* (December/January 1983); Rothman, Stanley and S. Robert Lichter, "What Are Moviemakers Made Of?," *Public Opinion* (December/January 1984).

36. Gerald Jones, *Honey, I'm Home! Sitcoms: Selling the American Dream* (New York: Grove Weidenfeld, 1992), 73-75.

37. Lerner et al., *American Elites.*

38. McGuire, William J., "Possible Excuses for Claiming Massive Media Effects Despite the Weak Evidence," in *The Mass Media in Liberal Democratic Societies* ed. S. Rothman (New York: Paragon House, 1992).

39. Robert Lerner and Stanley Rothman, "Rhetorical Conflict and the Adversarial Media, Part II," *International Journal of Group Tensions* 20, no. 4 (1990): 303-22.

40. Lerner et al., *American Elites.*

41. For a discussion of science in this context see, Robert Lerner and Stanley Rothman, "Rhetorical Conflict and the Adversarial Media, Part II," *International Journal of Group Tensions* 20, no. 4 (1990): 303-322; Rothman, Stanley, "The Media, the Experts, and Public Opinion," in *The Mass Media,* Stanley Rothman, ed. (New York: Paragon House, 1992), 177-200.

42. Daniel Patrick Moynihan, "Defining Deviancy Down," *The American Scholar* 62 (Winter 1993): 19.

43. Shanto Iyengar, *News That Matters* (Chicago: University of Chicago Press, 1987); Denis McQuail, "The Influence of Effects of the Mass Media," in *Mass Communications and Society,* J. Curran, M. Gurevitch, J. Wollacott, J. Marrionett, and C. Roberts, eds. (London: Edward Arnold, 1977), 70-94.

44. J. M. Fields and Howard Schuman, "Public Beliefs about the Beliefs of the Public," *Public Opinion Quarterly* 40 (1976): 427-28.

45. Michael J. Robinson, "American Political Legitimacy in an Era of Electronic Journalism," in *TV as a Social Force: New Approaches to TV Criticism*, D. Cater and R. Adler, eds. (New York: Praeger, 1975), 97-139.

46. A. H. Miller, Edie N. Goldenberg, and Lutz Erbring, "Typeset Politics: Impact of Newspapers on Public Confidence," *American Political Science Review* 73 (1978): 67-84.

47. S. M. Lipset and William J. Schneider, *The Confidence Gap* (New York: Free Press, 1983).

48. Lipset and Schneider, 122-25.

Part Five

What Public Policy Can Do
for the Family

17

Government Tax Policy and the Family

William R. Mattox, Jr.

My task is a difficult one. I have been asked to write in a fresh and interesting way about a tired, old subject that was never really that jazzy in the first place. The subject is taxes, and specifically the tax treatment of families. Tax treatment of families is a "tired, old subject" because every major commission or working group or comprehensive report or contract with voters for the last ten or twelve years has placed pro-family tax relief at the top of its policy agenda.

- In 1986, President Reagan's White House Working Group on the Family chaired by Gary Bauer issued a report which identified doubling the tax exemption for children as its number one priority.

- In 1990, a much-publicized report by William Galston and Elaine Kamarck of the Progressive Policy Institute offered doubling the tax exemption for children as the top pro-family recommendation of "New Democrats."

- In 1991, the bipartisan National Commission on Children (which included then-Governor Bill Clinton of Arkansas and Children's Defense Fund president Marian Wright Edelman) issued a policy agenda for children, which had, as its centerpiece, a $1,000 tax credit for children.

- In 1994, the House Republican Contract for America included a $500 tax credit for children, which GOP leader Newt Gingrich called the "crown jewel" of the contract.

Despite the fact that pro-family tax relief has been embraced by everyone from Gary Bauer and Newt Gingrich to Bill Clinton and Marian Wright Edelman, the average middle-income family of four is only this year seeing any reduction in its annual income tax bill. As of the 1998 tax year, parents of children under the age of seventeen will receive a tax credit of up to $500. As I will discuss below, this is no more than a good starting point for pro-family tax reform.

While there has been a lot of talk from public officials about the need to ease the economic burdens of the "hard-working people who play by the rules and raise the children," there needs to be much more action. And for the lack of action, leaders in both parties share at least some of the blame. Indeed, few issues better symbolize why Americans are increasingly cynical about politics than this one.

Now, without defending those responsible for inaction on this issue, because I do not believe their inaction is defensible, I want to explain why this powerful idea, which seemingly enjoys broad support, has failed to have more influence in our law. One of the major reasons is that many of those who shape economic policy in our country do not appreciate the economic rationale for pro-family tax relief in the same way that they appreciate the economic rationale for, say, lowering the capital gains tax.

Over the course of the last ten years, the case for pro-family tax relief has most often been made on sentimental, political, and historical grounds. The sentimental argument is clearly the least compelling of the three. It uses the size of family tax benefits as a measurement of one's sentiment about families. The more you like families, the higher you think the benefits should be. Or so some people seem to think. The problem with this argument is that while families are a good thing, yes even a very good thing, they are not the only good thing. And since public policy sometimes requires choices to be made between competing virtues, the case for pro-family tax relief cannot and should not be tied ultimately to the size of our sentiment about families. While pro-family sentiment is to be applauded—especially in a day when family ties are so fragile—a less arbitrary standard is needed for guiding the tax treatment of families. Otherwise, efforts to adjust tax benefits up or down will be characterized, accurately, as attempts to socially engineer people in one direction or another.

The political argument, which is similar in many ways to the sentimental argument, is probably the best understood and least acknowledged argument for pro-family tax relief. Recognizing the powerful public sentiment that exists for families, the political argument views pro-family tax relief as a way of attracting votes. It uses pro-family tax relief as a way to identify with common taxpayers, to balance other tax provisions directed to taxpayers perceived to be less deserving of relief, or to offset potentially unpopular spending cuts. While there is no question that pro-family tax relief can pack a political wallop, it would be foolhardy to make changes solely on this basis—especially since the revenue loss associated with any significant increase in pro-family benefits is substantial.

The historical argument is the most compelling argument pro-family tax relief advocates have commonly used over the years. This argument takes a historical benchmark—usually the tax treatment of families in 1948—and shows how the erosion in value of the personal and dependent exemption over time has left the average family of four today with a far larger tax burden than existed a half century ago. This argument has some real muscle. Indeed, the first calls for pro-family tax relief in the mid-1980s were sparked by a comprehensive analysis of tax trends by economist Eugene Steuerle, which showed that the decline in the value of family tax benefits represented the most consequential change of any kind in tax law during the post-World War II era. In fact, if the current personal and dependent exemption had been adjusted to keep pace with wage and price inflation over this time period, the exemption would now be more than $10,000 in size rather than under $3,000.

But, while the historical argument is quite compelling, it does have one serious weakness—it presumes that the tax benefits for families set in 1948 were the right standards, that they were neither too high nor too low. But is this, in fact, the case? Why 1948 instead of 1938 or 1958 or 1968? Why should 1948 be the benchmark? Some have justified the use of the 1948 standard by pointing out that a major tax law was enacted that year and that this law's favorable tax treatment of families helped usher in the domestic tranquility of the 1950s. These justifications should not be dismissed out of hand. But neither should they totally satisfy us. While the economic well-being of families certainly contributed to the social stability of the 1950s, it is not obvious that pro-family tax benefits were the chief cause or even a leading cause of this economic well-being. In other words, simply passing a robust tax cut for families today will not guarantee a dramatic reversal in Bill Bennett's index of leading cultural indicators. That's not to say the effect would be insignificant; it's just an acknowledgment that there are serious limits about how much good public policy can do.

Thus, even though historical benchmarks can be a useful guide, they cannot be our only guide—or even our best guide—in setting the appropriate levels of pro-family tax benefits. Which brings us to the economic case for pro-family tax benefits.

The Economic Case for Pro-family Tax Benefits

Over the years, some advocates have sought to make an economic case for pro-family tax benefits by linking such benefits to basic living expenses. They have argued that the size of the dependent exemption should be tied to the latest projections about what it costs to raise a child in America today. But this idea is fraught with both practical and philosophical problems. To begin with, projections about the cost of raising a child vary widely, in part because many Americans disagree about what expenses should be considered "necessities."

But an even bigger problem with this formulation is that it emphasizes the economic costs of childrearing with no consideration for the economic benefits. As such, it perpetuates the myth that children should be viewed as economic liabilities (consumption items for which one pays) rather than as economic assets (investments which, when managed properly, can pay long-term dividends). So long as children are viewed as consumption items, it is hard to understand why the tax code should be adjusted to give those who spend on children a special tax break not available to, say, those who spend on poodles.

It is true that parents today do not think of children as economic assets in the way that parents in an agrarian era did. But the demise of family farming is not the only reason for this shift. Indeed, part of the reason parents today are apt to view children as economic liabilities is because our nation's Social Security system robs parents of the social insurance value of their children. Consider: If there were no old-age social insurance scheme, adults in our society would have an economic incentive to invest a portion of their time and money in the rearing of children in order to protect themselves against the prospect of being destitute in old age.

Childrearing is not the only means of protecting oneself against poverty in old age, of course. Certainly, one can and should save for such purposes. Nor am I suggesting that this economic incentive is, or ever should be, the primary motivation for raising children. Certainly, moral imperatives are, or should be, far more significant factors. But I do believe moral principles and economic forces should work in harmony. Yet, in our current system, moral and economic forces are in conflict. In our current system, it is economically foolish to invest in childrearing, for under Social Security productive adults can live it up today on the resources that might otherwise be diverted to childrearing and live it up tomorrow on the resources Social Security takes from other people's adult children and gives to them. In other words, you may devote your resources to raising children, and I may devote mine to raising poodles, but in the end, we will both be dependent on your children—not my poodles—for our old-age benefits.

Thus, the economic case for pro-family tax relief should be directly tied to this anti-child feature of the Social Security system. So long as the federal government's old-age entitlement programs continue to be biased against families investing in childrearing, it will be necessary for the government to offset these anti-family effects through some other means—the most logical being per-child tax credits.

How much in per-child savings would be necessary to neutralize the Social Security system's anti-child bias? If you take the annual combined payroll tax of a median-income family of four, reduce it by 17 percent (the proportion of all Social Security payments that are being theoretically set aside for payments to future retirees), and divide by 2.1 (the number of births per woman necessary to replace the population), you get roughly $2,100. Thus, it would take a tax credit of roughly $2,100 per child to offset the Social Security system's bias against investing in children.

It has not been possible to induce the federal government to adopt a $2,100 per-child tax credit—or one even half this size; a benefit of $500 was the best compromise attainable in the 1998 budget deal. That is a step in the right direction. Perhaps it would be possible to expand it by linking per-child tax relief and old-age entitlement policy. More revenue for higher per-child tax benefits could be obtained by raising the age at which one becomes eligible for old-age benefits. This would acknowledge the fact that Americans today are living longer and are able to lead productive lives well into their late sixties and seventies.

In addition, it would be well for policymakers to consider a plan to phase down (and perhaps eventually phase out) the Social Security system by combining a reduction in the payroll tax on workers today with a reduction in the size of Social

Security benefits for these same workers when they reach retirement age. This would reduce future dependency on the Social Security system and reduce the anti-child bias in the current system.

Not only is it important to integrate Social Security into the debate about pro-family tax relief, but it is also important to integrate Social Security into the debate about other tax proposals, such as the flat tax. It should be noted that, for all practical purposes, we already have a flat tax. When one combines current income tax rates with current Social Security tax rates, nearly all taxpayers have a marginal federal tax rate of roughly 30 percent. Generally, for those making below $60,000, this rate is divided almost equally between a 15 percent income tax rate and a 15 percent payroll tax. For most of those making more than $60,000, this 30 percent is derived from a 28 percent income tax rate and a 2 percent Medicare tax. While this is a reality that most of the leading "flat tax" plans currently ignore, it is a reality that need not threaten many of the appealing features of such plans—features like eliminating tax withholding, simplifying tax forms, and getting rid of many tax write-offs and deductions.

One tax deduction that ought not to be scrapped, however, is the charitable deduction. From the standpoint of economic theory, I do not know how compelling arguments for preserving the charitable deduction truly are. But it really doesn't matter, because the short-run political argument for preserving the charitable tax deduction is so powerful that no other argument is perhaps necessary. If one of our major goals is, as it should be, dismantling government welfare programs that have failed to help the poor, then I think we should recognize that few Americans are likely to view as credible any agenda that simultaneously seeks to gut public housing and to eliminate tax incentives for giving to Habitat for Humanity. Unless we are more troubled by charitable tax deductions than AFDC and public housing, we should steer clear of any tax simplification plan that eliminates charitable contributions. Indeed, if we truly want to shift more and more responsibility onto the charitable sector and away from the state, I think we ought to be looking at ways to transform the current tax deduction for charitable giving into a tax credit that is available to itemizers and nonitemizers alike.

Tax credits should not, however, be narrowly confined to remedial programs that focus primarily on the poor, but should instead be available for contributions to other civil society organizations that serve social needs. Indeed, arguably, the best anti-poverty prevention program is the local church—not just when it offers remedial services to those that are hurting, but also when it offers preventive messages about successful living. Indeed, a Sunday morning sermon on self-control may help to prevent alcohol abuse every bit as much as an AA program helps to treat recovering alcoholics. For this reason, charitable tax credits ought to cover both remedial and preventive endeavors.

A few final points. First, a word about the relationship between tax policy and economic growth. Frequently, when policymakers think about tax cuts, they think in terms of short-term economic growth; that is, policies that stimulate economic growth (as measured by the GDP) are considered more appealing than those—like pro-family tax benefits—that do not produce significant economic growth in the short run.

There are several problems with this framework. First, growth is not the only objective of tax policy—equity is, or at least should be, another. Second, the GDP is an imperfect measurement of economic health. It fails to distinguish between horizontal growth (which comes from population growth or the movement of economic activity from the home economy to the market economy) and vertical growth (actual increases in productivity that lead to real increases in per capita wealth). Thus, the GDP should not be used as a crude way of measuring the quality of life in America (even though some like to use it in this way). Third, some tax changes that yield short-term growth often come at the expense of long-term gain. They are the tax equivalent of strip mining—penny-wise, pound-foolish. Indeed, to the extent that years and years of unfavorable tax treatment of families has contributed to our current cultural crisis, we are seeing this principle at work.

One last cautionary note. While it is important for us to recognize the virtues of pro-family policy reforms, it is also important for us to recognize the limitations of all policy instruments. Pro-family tax relief, for example, will not make husbands love their wives or children respect their parents. It will not clean up filthy TV or remove child predators for our streets. Pro-family tax relief will not, by itself, magically solve the various problems facing America's families, neighborhoods, and communities.

But pro-family tax relief will make it easier for families to thrive by reducing economic stress. It will make it easier for parents to monitor their children's TV viewing habits by freeing them to spend more time with their children. It will empower parents to address many family needs that only they can meet. This is why pro-family tax relief is so critical—and why it is time for politicians (who should be weary of talking about this tired old subject) to get around to taking more substantial action.

18

How Taxes Affect the Family

John Mueller

How do taxes affect the family, and how we might change things for the better? I assume we would all like to strengthen the economic basis of the family. The first question to ask, then, is "what *is* the economic basis of the family?"

Aristotle, in his *Politics*, explains that the household is the basic unit of society—the household, not the individual—because it is the smallest self-sustaining unit. He divides the economic resources that sustain the household into two broad categories: people and things. Or rather, they consist of the "useful" part of the people and things at the disposal of the household.

It is almost a definition of modernity that we have reversed the priority of the "useless" and the "useful." The "useless" parts of people are, of course, more important than the useful ones. Babies, for example, are entirely useless; they are "use-less" precisely because they are ends in themselves, and not to be used for some other purpose. Somewhere along the line we got things reversed. This volume is about the family and "civil society." But I think it might be useful here to introduce a distinction between "civilization" and "culture." Civilization has to do with those aspects of society—not just the economy—which are useful. But culture concerns the use-less, that is, the good. As the German philosopher Josef Peiper reminds us, the root of culture is the cult—that is, worship.

Economists often call the useful part of people "human capital," and the useful part of things, "nonhuman capital." A parent's ability to provide for the family is a kind of "human capital." The family car's ability to provide transportation services is " nonhuman capital." A share in a company, which provides income to purchase such services, is also "nonhuman capital."

For most families, human capital is by far the most important kind of wealth; the most important form of saving is the investment of time and money in childrearing and education; and wages are the most important kind of income.

There is a very good reason for this. For most people, the return on childrearing and education—in terms of increased future earnings—is far greater than the return from investing in the stock market. The return on the first year of caring for a child is astronomical. The return on the first year of formal education is almost as astronomical. With each additional year, the extra return gets a little smaller. Eventually, the cost of, say, one more year of college is less than the return you could get by putting the same money in the stock market. At that point—but not before—it pays to put savings into the stock market.

This is why lower- and middle-income families save mostly in the form of human capital and receive most of their income in wages. It's also why ownership of businesses and other kinds of property makes up a much larger share of the wealth and income of upper-income families.

This may seem basic, but it helps explain the economic pressures on the family.

When we take all American families together, we find that just under two-thirds of gross national income is earned by workers (as a return on their investment in "human capital"); and just over a third is received by property owners (as a return on their investment in "nonhuman capital"). These pretax income shares have remained remarkably constant for many decades—because workers consistently contribute about two-thirds, and property owners about one-third, to increases in total output.

The constant shares mean that gross labor compensation has almost exactly kept pace with the rest of gross national income. Libertarians on the right (for example, the Cato Institute) stop here and say that there is no wage problem; while libertarians on the left (for example, President Clinton's Council of Economic Advisers) say there is no wage problem for workers as a group, only income disparities among workers, which require more redistribution of income.

What both ignore is that part of the income is taxed and distributed as "transfer payments"—that is, government benefits to persons who do not contribute to current output. If we estimate the distribution of net national income after all taxes and transfer payments, a very different picture emerges. Since World War II, the "wedge" of national income devoted to transfer payments has risen by about 16 percentage points. This has reduced net property income by about 6 percentage points, and take-home pay by about 10 percentage points.

This squeezes working families from two directions. Some of the benefits (like welfare and Medicaid) raise the cost of hiring; while others (like Medicare and Social Security) reduce workers' take-home pay. Any benefits to nonworkers must do one or the other. This is the only possible explanation for the fact that the minimum unemployment rate has *risen* (from 1 percent in the 1940s to 3 percent in the 1960s to 5 percent in the 1980s), while the take-home pay of workers *declined* as a share of national income. None of the "usual suspects" in the discussion over lagging wages—trade, demographics, deunionization, corporate restructuring—can explain how the minimum unemployment rate could rise while workers' share of income declined.

This process not only lowers national income and reduces workers' share of it. Income disparities are also increased by the way in which the rising burden of benefits is financed. Unlike owners of business property, workers do not receive special tax deductions for depreciation and maintenance of their income-producing investments. The payroll tax, for example, starts at 15 percent on the first dollar of gross income. This is why the higher tax burden has fallen primarily on "investment human capital." Workers earn two-thirds of national income—but now pay four-fifths of all Federal taxes. As Theodore W. Schultz said in 1960, "Our tax laws everywhere discriminate against human capital" and "in favor of nonhuman capital." Because for most people the return on investment in human capital is higher than on nonhuman capital, the tax disadvantage makes total national income lower than if all income were treated the same.

Looking at the political landscape, it is difficult to say who does more harm: The libertarians, who deny that there is any real problem facing America's working families; or the liberals, who agree there is a problem but do everything in their power to make it worse.

For example, the libertarians propose shifting from an income tax to a so-called "consumption" tax; but they define all investments in childrearing as "consumption" instead of saving. As a result, they would increase rather than lower the tax burden on working families. I have shown that the revenue-neutral flat tax rate would have to be about 27 percent when such a plan is fully phased in, levied almost entirely on workers' incomes. Workers' share of the federal tax burden would rise from almost four-fifths to nearly 100 percent.

Fortunately, in political terms, this approach is a nonstarter, because it would mean a tax increase on the majority of middle class households. A flat tax rate combined with a "consumption" tax base that exempts property income (and most government benefits) is a "lumpy" tax, not a flat tax: It would shift virtually the entire tax burden onto workers in each income class, and onto the middle class as a group. I have shown that all this is true, even when the extra growth that could be expected from flatter marginal tax rates is taken into account.

Another libertarian proposal is to privatize Social Security. I am aware that some pro-family advocates favor this on the theory that rising payroll taxes make it harder to raise families. They forget that the net effect of Social Security on families depends on both taxes and benefits.

Social Security is a "pay-as-you-go" system: That is, each generation of workers pays for the benefits of the preceding generation. The first generation of workers covered by Social Security therefore received more benefits than it paid in taxes. But this was precisely the generation that raised the Baby Boom: Rather than spending the windfall on riotous living on the Riviera, it made the most massive investment in human capital in world history. By the same token, if we privatize Social Security, the last generation of workers would have to pay twice for retirement: They would continue paying taxes to support their parents, while also being forced to save for their own.

Also, Social Security is the last institution in American life that treats the family, not the individual, as the basic unit. Unlike welfare benefits, one has to work to receive benefits, even though the benefits are progressively skewed. Every worker pays the same tax rate, but a married couple receives an extra 50 percent of the basic benefit, which is greater than the benefits a homemaker would receive based on her history of market earnings. Social Security therefore reinforces a father's responsibilities and a mother's sacrifices. It also provides survivors' benefits. Privatization would remove all this.

For both reasons, privatizing Social Security would worsen the squeeze on working families. Plans to force saving in the stock market during the transition would lower, not raise, family and national wealth, because (as we have seen) the return on stocks is lower than the return on childrearing and education.

Meanwhile, the liberals are actively working to prevent the only possible relief for working families. President Clinton's refusal to reform Medicare and Medicaid is sheer poison for workers and their families. Without such reform the problem will get worse.

Instead, we need to relieve the burden on working families in two ways.

First, we must reform government benefits like Medicare and Medicaid to keep them in reasonable proportion to the wages out of which they are paid. This could be done by providing a flat cash payment instead of a guaranteed bundle of medical services.

Moreover, we should keep Social Security solvent on a pay-as-you-go basis. For example, we could cut payroll taxes, say, 20 percent today while there is a surplus, but reduce growth of future benefits up to 20 percent for those who receive the tax rates that are at first lower, and never higher, than they are today.

Second, the tax system must be reformed in two ways.

First, we should roll the standard deductions, personal exemptions, and earned income tax credit into a single Earned Personal Tax Credit. The credit would refund all federal income and payroll taxes on wages below the poverty line. The credit would equal the combined income and payroll on wages of about $5,000 per family member, which is roughly the poverty level. That would be a bit more than $1,500 per person with the current tax rates. This credit would match existing deductions for maintenance of business property. And it would remove a huge and unfair burden from lower and middle-income families.

Second, to complete the equalization of tax treatment, we should remove special income tax deductions for new investment in buildings and machinery. This is already done for investment in human capital. Such a tax base would be both fair and efficient. And it would so broaden the tax base that we could have a revenue-neutral flat tax rate of 18 percent, even after paying for the Earned Personal Tax Credit and Social Security reform.

America's working families face a very real economic problem, and both political parties seem bent on making it worse. The good news is that the problem can be cured by making the appropriate changes.

19

Privatizing Welfare to Help the Family: The Biblical Center

Marvin Olasky

I'm glad to be included in this distinguished gathering, and somewhat overawed to be here. My third oldest son, who is eleven, was in a Junior Toastmaster class this past year with a group of other kids his age. They all took turns giving speeches and had a great time. One seven-year old who wanted to join the class was also allowed in. When it was time to speak about a controversial subject, he planned to give a speech showing that dogs were better than cats. Stage fright, though, took over, so he simply said, "A cat and a dog. That's all." Then he sat down.

The good news these days, when we read regularly about children either killing or impregnating other children, is that these eleven-year olds were extraordinarily polite. They all critique each others' speeches, but the emphasis is on saying something that's helpful, so the judge of the cat-and-dog speech contented himself with saying, "That was a very strong argument, but the supporting evidence was a little weak."

It would be hard to say that any of the supporting evidence we hear concerning the family debate these days is weak. Everyone has plenty of footnotes, and now that computers regularly have terrific footnoting programs, supporting evidence is a dime per dozen footnotes. What computers cannot supply, however, and what is desperately needed in much scholarly work, is an internal gyroscope, an objective sense of right and wrong.

I'm amazed sometimes at the enormous gyrations my fellow academics go through. I've done such gyrations myself, even preparing abstract papers for conventions. But think of the scene in *Raiders of the Lost Ark* where Indiana Jones is confronted by a sword-wielding Egyptian of frightening prowess. It's clear that the swordsman can slice and dice Jones; he is confident of doing so. But all the gyrations do not work. Jones uses the modern Occam's razor for that situation—a revolver—and in one shot cuts to the heart of the problem. (The dead swordsman could be a poster boy for gun control.)

Now, I am Professor Indiana Jones only in my dreams, but I do see lots of gyrations in analyses of the welfare state, and it is time to go directly to the heart of the matter—the need for a true gyroscope. There are lots of analyses of what AFDC has done to poor families, and lots of recommendations about what to do now, but the single best analysis of the problem that I have seen comes in the context of a New Testament discussion about how to help widows and orphans. The passage is from chapter five of the apostle Paul's first letter to Timothy, and I can paraphrase it like this: The church should give financial support to older women who are widows indeed and widows in need. A widow indeed is one who has displayed good character by raising her children conscientiously and helping others; a widow who just lives for her own pleasure is dead while she lives. A widow in need is one who lacks family members capable of helping her. Do not put young widows on your list of those to be supported, because if you do they will stop being busy and will instead become busybodies; they will not work and remarry, but will waste their time.

Let me emphasize several aspects of this remarkable passage, and then apply it to our current crisis of welfare and family. First, throughout the Bible there is an emphasis on helping widows and orphans, both of whom are in a difficult position through the mysterious workings of God's providence; this is the class of suffering people who are nearest and dearest to God. Nothing in this passage or my comments on it should be taken to mean that those in material or spiritual need should be abandoned. But look at the precautions Paul takes when recommending even aid to widows within the church: first, family responsibility; second, an emphasis on marriage for young women as a road to fulfillment and a road out of poverty; third, help to those who have demonstrated good character and are too old to help themselves.

From all this we learn much about the particular problem of helping widows in the church, but we can also draw logical conclusions regarding welfare generally: Be careful before putting people on the list. Emphasize family responsibility and remarriage. Again, should any misunderstand, let me stress both the centrality of biblical compassion and Paul's strong injunctions against idleness among men in chapter three of Second Thessalonians. My point is that we must be very careful in making up a list of those to be aided by government.

The cornerstone welfare program to aid semi-families, Aid to Dependent Children, now AFDC, began during the Depression. It was designed to help widows and orphans, but the program did not emphasize the biblical principles from I Timothy just noted. That was one strike against its effectiveness. A clause of the program that went largely unnoticed at the time allowed for distribution of aid to mothers who had not been married. That was a second strike, although it could be argued that women who have been abandoned are akin to widows. The third strike, however, came in the 1960s, when questions of character were thrown out the window, and welfare became an entitlement regardless of behavior.

Be careful about giving aid, Paul warned; and we all know that government has not been careful. The strongest criticisms of governmental welfare that I have heard this past year have come not from conservatives but from conscientious inner-city moms themselves, those who are struggling to live by biblical precepts. They are irate that all around them government programs are leading their neighbors into temptation. All around them governmental programs are enabling the woman next door to forget about marriage. All around them the programs are encouraging men not to stand by their women but to show up once a month and become what they call in south central Los Angeles "county check pillow pimps."

What has been the mainstream Republican answer to this sad situation? I've described in my book, *Renewing American Compassion*, some strengths and weaknesses of the vaunted Wisconsin program, but let me note here one component of it: The triumph of feminism. An anti-marriage emphasis underlies the Wisconsin jobs program, from signs on the walls of training sites—"Don't wait for Prince Charming. His horse broke down"—to more elaborate whines about the declining importance of family. But what's missing is serious examination of the beliefs and values that underlie development of strong families and good work habits.

Wisconsin welfare reform, an improvement on past programs, has many impressive gyrations, but is that all we should push for? Does the proposed solution go to the heart of the problem? No, I would suggest. Other articles in this volume point out what went wrong in the sixties, and what we've heard is true. Yes, contraception is a culprit in the breakdown of family emphasis. So is television. But the key change in the 1960s was the answer that many of the nation's elites gave to the question *Time* magazine posed on its cover: Is God dead?

The answer was "yes," at least in everyday practice, and once you answer that question that way it's logical to go on as Dostoevsky's character Ivan Karamazov did: "Destroy a man's belief in immortality and . . . nothing would be immoral then, everything would be permitted . . . egotism, even carried to the extent of crime, must not only be tolerated but even recognized as the wisest and perhaps the noblest course."

Let me now go directly to the heart of the problem: Governmental welfare does not harm the family primarily through its bureaucracy, or its entitlement provisions, or its many other flaws, many of which might be fixable. No, the main problem is that governmental programs are not Bible based—and, given legitimate First Amendment considerations, I doubt that they can be within our polity. The main problem is that they put man at the center, not God—and any society, or any family, that is not centered on God is a good candidate to enter a black hole.

Many conventional academics can demonstrate skilled public policy swordplay, but they miss the core of the problem: That all of us—not only the poor, but those rich in money or academic degrees as well—have holes in our souls, holes that only God can fill. The central message of the Bible is that God saves sinners. We can't understand how both poor and rich can experience real change in their lives unless we understand that only God—not government nor any other institution—can save us. Furthermore, our anthropology along with our theology is mistaken unless we realize that we are sinners. We are not essentially good, and brought down by a flawed social environment. We are sinners.

This is realistic but it's also hopeful, for God who is in charge of everything is both completely just in condemning us and completely merciful in providing a way for our sins to be covered. Some people, of course, say that any talk of sin is judgmental, but it's possible to avoid both judgmentalism and a skirting from judgment by emphasizing a simple truth that we could even sing: *I'm a sinner, you're a sinner.* Or, to coin a potential best-selling book title, I'm not OK and you're not okay—but there is a way out. Theologians such as J. I. Packer and Francis Schaefer have developed these concepts very readably, and I recommend their works to you. What we need to realize is that government training programs that avoid the heart of the matter—that our gyroscope is twisted and needs to be replaced by a new one—just don't work.

This is very impolite talk. I heard a minister saying earlier this month, "God puts the cookies on a low shelf, so everyone can just reach out and take one." That sounds sweet, but let's face it: Have you ever seen a corpse reaching out? We are dead in our sins. Each of us is—and if we don't believe in God, such a statement is an affront to our dignity. We need a second birth. Government cannot mandate that second birth—but God can. His power is stronger and more mysterious than even Donna Shalala's. He changes lives in ways that no program emanating from even a vastly improved Department of Health and Human Services could.

We see this most spectacularly in alcohol and drug abuse programs, and I've seen a lot of them this past year. I've written a lot about the successes, but I've been working over the past two years with someone who at this point is a painful failure, and I've seen close up the limitations of programs in the absence of personal change. For some folks you can have the best work programs in the world. You can have housing. You can hand out thousands of dollars. And all the gyrations won't work, unless the person who is being helped develops, through God's grace, an internal gyroscope.

All this talk sounds very foreign at universities and in conventional Washington. We do not often hear talk of how God saves sinners. But those involved in effective, private groups that help people stay off or get off welfare almost always talk that way. The volunteers who help unmarried, pregnant women at 3,000 crisis pregnancy centers around the country talk that way. The people who provide job opportunities at Community Enterprises of Greater Milwaukee and other effective inner-city programs across the country talk that way. The people who provide basic health care at the Voice of Calvary Health Clinic in Jackson, Mississippi, and at many other inner-city clinics around the country, talk that way. People who help kids stay out of trouble and learn after school right here in the District of Columbia—people at Children of Mine in Anacostia, or the Darryl Green Learning Center in northeast Washington—talk that way.

The people at Hope House in Idaho who care for badly abused kids also talk that way. My good friend Hadley Arkes in a luncheon talk on the family spoke of growing up among many adults who doted on him. Hadley did not grow up without self-esteem, and he's terrific. But what do you do for a girl whose father, to punish her for a minor infraction, sliced off her dog's head right before her eyes? Kids who have been abused in that way, if they are ever to be rebuilt in spirit so they can one day build better families, need to be told not fables but the truth. That girl needs to know that the reason to have a positive self-image is not that people are naturally good—think of her beloved pet's severed head—but that we are made in the image of a wonderful God, so that there is something still wonderful in us, no matter how much we deface that image.

Many people in this country understand very well what I have just said. Others scoff at the notion that theology can help where psychology fails. There is now a tremendous divide in this country between grassroots programs where you'll hear the name Jesus Christ sworn by, and government offices where that name will only be used to swear.

The divide, by the way, is largely between biblically Christian groups and government officials, but orthodox Jewish and Islamic groups also can run afoul of government mandates, and they also need to be encouraged. (I am committed to the centrality of Christ, but I am perfectly happy to see a wide variety of religious and nonreligious groups compete to show their effectiveness, and we will see over time which understanding works best.) I find it interesting that Alcoholics Anonymous for years has used the vague term "higher power" and has done impressive work--but the founders of AA focused on Christ and for years most of their chapters did also. Recent reports suggest a lessening of AA effectiveness, with some of its veterans concerned that "higher power" is now being interpreted to mean a cohort, a girlfriend, or other human figures without soteriological authority.

We could spend time examining individual trees, but I do not want you to miss the forest—or, to be precise, the growth of two distinct forests. Overall, the gap between Bible-based programs and their secular, government-financed counterparts is enormous. In Washington, D.C. and at many leading academic institutions and in the media, the word *compassion* is still equated with passage of particular pieces of legislation. But "outside over there," in the world beyond the Beltway and those whose greatest ambition is to be recognized within the Beltway, it is understood increasingly often that Jesus Christ did not pass a piece of legislation, or send a check, and call that compassion. He took up the cross. He suffered with us. (That's the literal meaning of compassion, from the Latin *com*, with, and *pati*, to suffer: *Compassion* means "with suffering" . . . personal involvement.) Christ persevered in his assignment until the appointed time for his death on the cross. And he always stretched our thinking of how people could be helped.

The gap is enormous. I have been examining the Gospel of John and have seen in chapters five and six two good examples of how Christ teaches us to be agents of change. First, in John 5: Does anyone here remember how Jesus at the pool of Bethesda talks to the man who has been an invalid for thirty-eight years? When Jesus asks him, "Do you want to get well?" the man responds, "I have no one to help me into the pool when the water is stirred." Ted Kennedy would immediately propose supplying the invalid with a full-time helper, and Bob Dole would introduce a counterproposal to provide only a part-time helper, but Jesus does neither. He knows that the invalid is coloring within the lines, his expectations covered by thirty-eight years on relief. Jesus gives the man not what he asks for but what will radically change his life. Jesus says to him, "Get up! Pick up your mat and walk"—and the man does.

Now, none of us has miraculous power, but all of us should be working toward real change, rather than passing out spare change. All of us can be agents of change rather than enablers of continued poverty.

Then we come to chapter six, where Jesus turns five small loaves and two small fish into enough food to feed five thousand men, plus women and children. As we see by reading the parallel accounts in Matthew, Mark, and Luke, Christ was not providing an entitlement; the feeding came only after many hours of teaching by Jesus, and after the people who wanted to learn had come to a place far from food supplies. Across this country, in hundreds of gospel missions, this emphasis on providing spiritual as well as material food seems obvious, but I've gotten into extended discussions with people in Washington who think it unfair to give a gospel message along with dinner. (Those who run Bible-optional shelters should also feel at home on swimsuit-optional beaches.) The divide is enormous. It's almost as if we have two Bibles out there, the real one and the liberal Washington/media/academia version. The Bible known in many government offices has passages with titles like, "Jesus Food Stamps the 5,000," but it also has the Parable of the Prodigal Panhandler and descriptions of how outstanding pieces of legislation, including the Good Samaritan Act, were passed.

The prodigal panhandler parable is found in chapter 15 of the Gospel according to the Government Printing Office, and it goes like this:

There was a man who had two sons. The younger one set off for a distant country and there squandered his wealth in wild living. After he had spent everything, he was in need and took a job feeding pigs. The job was miserable, and the younger son visualized an alternative: 'I will go back to my father and say to him: Father, I have sinned against heaven and against you.' He got up and started back toward his father.

But while the prodigal son was still a long way off, an official from Beds for the Homeless saw him and convinced him to spend the night. The government-funded shelter offered free food, housing, clothing, and medicine, and did not require any work in return. One day turned into a week, and a week into a month, as the prodigal son became used to panhandling in the morning, drinking fortified wine and smoking some joints in the afternoon, and watching movies at the shelter in the evening.

Meanwhile, the father sat on his porch in the late afternoon, hoping to see the prodigal son trudging home. Day after day the father visualized the opportunity to hug him and prepare a feast, but the son never came.

The GPO Gospel also includes a description of how the Good Samaritan Act was passed:

A man was going down from Jerusalem to Jericho, when he fell into the hands of robbers. They stripped him of his clothes, beat him and went away, leaving him half dead. A priest happened to be going down the same road, and when he saw the man, he passed by on the other side. Then a Samaritan, as he traveled, came to where the man was; and when he saw him, he was outraged that some people were so poor that they were forced to steal clothes.

He returned to Jerusalem and, using rhetorical brilliance to overcome prejudice against his ethnic group, convinced the Sanhedrin to pass the Good Samaritan Act. The Act used temple funds to establish Midnight Shepherding leagues for disadvantaged youth who might otherwise turn to crime along the Jerusalem-Jericho highway. The Act also erected a monument at the spot where the robbery victim had died.

As you can all tell, there is a chasm between the biblical parables that emphasize individual action and responsibility, and the modern versions I have just given you. The breadth of this enormous divide suggests that some desperate government attempts to bridge the gap are likely to fail. A recent essay by Henry Cisneros, Secretary of Housing and Urban Development, illuminates the problem. In nineteen pages of a HUD-printed publication entitled *Higher Ground: Faith Communities and Community Building* ("church" is insufficiently pluralistic, "religious institution" sounds too stodgy, so "faith community" is the new hot term), Mr. Cisneros argues that "Faith Communities Have Unique Resources" and "Faith Communities Touch the Soul."

Faith communities, it appears, have a heritage and a reservoir of respect that other institutions lack, according to Mr. Cisneros. He writes that they are capable of instilling values and moral structure, along with providing "a friend to talk to, or shake hands with, or hug." That's all true, and good, as far as it goes: A hug can make a person feel better, for a while.

What's sad, however, is that Mr. Cisneros leaves out the single essential element in promoting true, permanent change. He leaves out God. That word does not make an appearance in his essay. Mr. Cisneros does quote the Bible once, selectively: Mr. Cisneros quotes Isaiah 61:4 about how Israel "shall repair the waste cities." (He passes by the statement two verses above about "the day of vengeance of our God," and also leaves out the somewhat important statement that the repair work will take place when the Messiah comes.)

References to God or biblical quotations by themselves would not prove anything—Mr. Cisneros's boss, President Clinton, certainly knows how to quote Scripture for his own uses—but the absence of even an effort signifies that this is not even a serious attempt to understand the unique role of religious institutions.

The danger is that the Clintonistas, and many Republicans as well, see churches as potential appendages of the state, useful not for their ability to challenge ungodly beliefs but for their ability to funnel funds through programs that look like government-issue ones but have greater credibility. Some churches still care enough about God's commands so that they will steer clear of such temptations, but others have already entered into a halfway covenant with corruption, and may be ready to go all the way. Like bankrobber Willie Sutton, who purportedly said he robbed banks because "that's where the money is," some charities have little sales resistance when a government official offers to break the bank for them. Only when it's too late do the religious organizations find that they are the ones who have been robbed of their spirit.

Any type of *direct* government funding of religious groups, I believe, is fraught with danger to many parts of society, including the religious groups themselves. Do any of us really want Henry Cisneros deciding which church organizations should receive funding and which should not, even if the decision is supposedly made on an objective basis, using all the statistics and footnotes that money can buy?

Would the Republican Party, even if Bob Dole had been elected president, have the strength to deal with such questions productively? I doubt it, because an emphasis on the God of the Bible is shunned among many elite groups within the Party. (It was said of early Christians, "they shared their wallets with everyone and their beds with no one"—in other words, they practiced charity but did not practice adultery. But some Republican officials, like some of their Democratic counterparts, see political advantage to be gained from becoming fiscal conservatives but social liberals—in other words, people who share their wallets with no one but their beds with everyone.)

So if neither Democrats nor Republicans can do the job through government, where does that leave us? With privatization of welfare, I'd suggest—but privatization with a twist. There is a legitimate concern about the size of the role that private charity could play; if it is not sufficient, then government will need to stay involved. I do not expect to see civil society, battered for seventy years, bounce back in full strength immediately, with most individuals resuming the role of citizen rather than passive taxpayer. Even if we are seeing a new great awakening in this country, and there are mixed signals on that, the process of renewal will still be long and painful. So, while Washington has done an adequate job in providing for the common defense but has failed abjectly in providing welfare, the central government could be helpful if it returns to its constitutional role of promoting the general welfare.

I won't go into the details here, but the public policy proposal that makes the most sense to me is the poverty-fighting tax credit bill that is being pushed by Dan Coats and others in the Senate, and John Kasich and others in the House. Here is a way to transfer resources from the control of Donna Shalala to the control of individual citizens, while moving toward replacement of the welfare state and not mere continuation or shattering elimination.

Let me stress that this is a beginning, and only that. In the July 1996 issue of *Commentary*, Les Lenkowsky concludes a thoughtful critique of my new book by saying, "what Olasky is calling for would require a moral, cultural, and spiritual revolution." That's unrealistic, Les says. Maybe so, but we need to go as far as we realistically can. Right now, most of the kids growing up in the feminist welfare-based culture are being shut out of a better, family-based culture. What if 50 percent of those children could be saved? Would we keep on doing the same old same old and forget about that 50 percent? What if 40 percent could be saved? Should we continue to fund the path of destruction and forget about that 40 percent? What if 30 percent . . . or 20 percent . . . or 10 percent? What if actions we take could help to transform the lives of even 5 percent? Should we say, "let

Sodom be Sodom," and then build our own walls higher to keep out the sight? What if you yourself can help to save one person—by tutoring or coaching or perhaps even adopting a child?

One final question: If the welfare state is replaced by a privatized system, will life for poor families in this country automatically improve? No, but we will have hope for improvement, and more lives will be saved. Since defenders of the status quo like to throw dirt at those who propose change, let me tell you a story Daniel Webster used to tell about the very dirty hands he had as a child one day at school. Daniel's disgusted teacher said, "Daniel, hold out your hand," so he spat on his palm, rubbed it on the seat of his pants, and held it out, with one cleaner spot and the rest still a mess. The teacher said she had warned him before and would punish him unless: "Daniel, if you can find me another hand in this school that is dirtier than that, I will let you off." Daniel Webster promptly held out the other hand, and walked away a free man.

Look, poor families have it so bad now that nothing that comes out of Washington will turn around the situation very rapidly—but if an alternative can be developed, even if it is small at first, those families and our country will be better off, even if only a bit of the dirt is lessened by the application of spit. Welfare replacement is fraught with difficulty, but let us not despise direct person-to-person help and then get excited about the prospect for big-time government/church partnerships.

If you want more supporting evidence about the welfare system's problems and the ways to begin replacing it through personal effort and measures like tax credits, read books like *The Tragedy of American Compassion* and *Renewing American Compassion*. But the major supporting evidence for what I've said is found all around us. The heavens do declare the glory of God, and the streets display the sinfulness of man. I've done some evidentiary gyrations in my time, but the gyroscope is what really counts. So my basic answer to problems of welfare, and much else, is that we need to privatize in order to give real running room to those who understand the one thing that is infinitely complicated, but at the same time simple enough so that even a child can state the basics: "God and man. God saves sinners. . . . That's all."

20

Reforming Welfare—the Right Way

John J. DiIulio, Jr.

We are who we are because of Him to whom we belong. There are today in America poor children who are growing up fatherless, Godless, jobless, abused, neglected, and forgotten. In too many cases, they are surrounded by deviant, delinquent, and criminal adults. As all the research shows, being born healthy to loving, responsible parents or guardians of whatever race, creed, color, socio-economic status, or demographic description is about the luckiest fate that can befall a human being. But not all children are born so lucky, and in this Nation's inner cities today there are children who have no one—absolutely no one—to protect and guide them, to educate and nurture them, to teach them right from wrong, to show them His love. These children are more likely to suffer violent criminal victimization or to become criminals than they are to graduate from college. These children are more likely to stay home from school in fear than they are to attend school and excel. These children are our children, are God's children. Yet with every justification, they can lift their eyes to heaven and cry, "My God, why have you forsaken me?" We are failing them, we are failing Him.

The right way to reform welfare is to acknowledge the plight of these precious children. The wrong way to reform welfare is to make these children pawns in somebody's electoral strategy, theoretical speculations, or ideological gamesmanship. The right way to reform welfare is to look at all of the relevant facts, figures, and findings, not just those that fit our preconceptions. The wrong way to reform welfare is to overgeneralize about "ending welfare as we know it," or about "civil society," or about the elasticity of civil, private, and philanthropic efforts in relation to government retrenchment or withdrawal.

The right way to reform welfare is with a counsel of realism. The wrong way to reform welfare is with a counsel of despair that accepts the status quo, or a counsel of optimism that assumes all will be well when government "gets out of the way."

The harm done by the facile liberal social engineers of the sixties cannot be undone by the equally facile conservative social engineers of the nineties. It took liberals about thirty years to appreciate that Senator Daniel Patrick Moynihan was not all wrong about welfare, the family, and children in the sixties. Sometimes I fear that it will take conservatives as long to recognize that he was not all wrong about welfare, the family, and children in the nineties.

Welfare Reform

As I have argued elsewhere, big government is like a big bull in civil society's china shop. It breaks things on the way in and while inside, and we know from experience that it will break things on the way out. Together with Marvin Olasky and others, I believe that civil institutions both can and should do more, government less. But the problems of making this historic transition are many and severe—one point with which I am finally in agreement with welfare state apologists and the heads of government-supported megacharities.

Conservatives, especially religious conservatives, need to manifest a better appreciation for the actual administrative complexities and potential short and long run human costs of welfare reform measures, including measures that "merely" decrease the rate of spending as the affected populations, young and old, are growing (and as they will continue to grow more rapidly after the year 2002).

When it comes to welfare policies, God is truly in the statutory and administrative details. Just as it was obvious to everyone in the 1960s that lots of folks were poor, it is now obvious to almost everyone that welfare has done at least as much harm as good, proven more expensive than anticipated, and had many perverse and unintended consequences (illegitimacy, dependency, voluntary joblessness, family destruction, crime). But what was not obvious to serious-minded people in the sixties, and what is not obvious to serious-minded people in the nineties, is precisely how best to fashion and administer policy responses that make things better.

To cite just a few of these realities, the 1992 welfare population consisted of 9.2 million children (half under age six, a quarter under age three), and 4.4 million adults, almost all of the adults mothers, under 8 percent of the mothers teenagers. The average AFDC family size has decreased from 4 to 2.9 persons since 1969. The monthly support levels available from AFDC and food stamps have fallen steadily since the late 1960s. In 1993, the average monthly welfare check per family was $373.

Most welfare recipients really do try at one point or another to get off the dole. Only about 15 percent of welfare recipients stay on welfare continuously for five years or longer. Based on numerous studies, it is clear that most people who leave welfare for jobs and then return to the welfare rolls do so for legitimate reasons: layoffs, involuntary terminations, loss of child care, individual or family medical problems, loss of housing, domestic violence, and so on.

In short, it is no more true that most welfare recipients are totally lazy, undeserving people than it is true that most prisoners are mere first-time nonviolent criminals.

Likewise, 34 million Americans are covered by Medicaid, over half of them children. Research shows that since 1990, were it not for Medicaid, the number of uninsured Americans would have risen from 41 million to 50 million. After 1965, AFDC and Medicaid together gradually replaced a hit-or-miss system of poverty and health programs sponsored by state and local governments, charities, community hospitals, and public emergency-care facilities for indigent Americans.

As Marvin Olasky has argued so persuasively, the old welfare system had its huge pluses, including getting help to many of those who needed it in a way that was personal, spiritual, and challenging, that bred mutual responsibility, and that averted dependence on impersonal, centralized, government bureaucracies. Still, writ large, the old system could be pretty lousy; in fact, for many Depression-era Americans, their children, and their children's children, it was literally a killer.

But whereas the old welfare system failed to make America's poor part of "one nation under God," the new system did more to make America's poor "one nation under HUD." The government-anchored system that replaced the old poverty patchwork has turned out to be just as lousy, just as much a killer—a killer of families, neighborhoods, and individual initiative. Yet, warts and all, the federal "welfare state" has dependably delivered food, funds, and medicine to scores of millions of impoverished children, pregnant women, and elderly Americans.

Strictly speaking, the new system did not replace the old, but became a hybrid version of it. Thus, there remains tremendous state-by-state variance not only in how much money welfare and Medicaid recipients actually get but how (and how well) the programs are staffed and administered. Indeed, "welfare" can vary greatly from one state to the next. And the degree to which the "welfare state" is actually a loose confederation of government-assisted private, for-profit, and nonprofit organizations (many quite small) has gone largely unnoticed by those who insist that we need to "devolve" programs that are already quite devolved, and have always been so. The perverse federal regulations about which conservatives like to groan are quite real, but they have grown up as weeds in a highly devolved, state-centric, government-by-proxy system of program administration.

To date, most efforts to move people from welfare to work have yielded only marginal benefits. Even where Washington has granted *carte blanche* waivers and gotten out of the way, those welfare-to-work programs that have worked best have normally involved more, not less, per recipient government spending and more, not fewer, administrators and case workers. Anyone who thinks block grants are the answer ought to know that we have had twenty-three of those, fifteen still in effect. Categorical spending has always risen faster than general spending, and Washington strings on social programs will be no less constraining when they are "conservative strings." Senator Moynihan knows all this, and more.

We may never know one way or the other whether given welfare policy changes increased or decreased the incidence of abortion. Based on my own best understanding of extant theoretical arguments, statistical evidence, and ethnographic observations, I believe, as many Catholic bishops apparently do, that the cuts will probably increase the number of abortions.

Private Charity

But let me step beyond welfare reform as such to address an even broader concern about the elasticity of civil institutions and individual efforts in relation to government withdrawal. My Princeton colleague Julian Wolpert has studied the state of America's charitable organizations. Let me summarize for you just some of what Professor Wolpert, a member of the National Academy of Sciences, has found.

There are about 125,000 organizations in America that operate as charities and qualify for favored tax treatment under section 501(c)3 of the IRS code, and report receipts of at least $25,000 a year. Their combined revenues and expenditures are about $350 billion a year—about a seventh of combined federal, state, and local government spending. About 63 percent of their revenues come from nongovernment sources (dues, fees, donations, etc.). The single largest category of government support for charitable nonprofits is health services.

Between 1982 and 1992, charitable revenues from government for such things as maternal and child health care dropped by $47 billion. Government support as a share of nonprofit revenues declined by 20 percent in the same period. But private contributions to nonprofits increased by only 7 percent, and the loss of government support was not made up by reinvigorated individual giving—not even close.

As Professor Wolpert shows, had the spending cuts proposed in the Contract for America been adopted, they would have meant a $254 billion loss in nonprofit revenues during fiscal years 1996-2002. For example, had these cuts been realized, charitable agencies serving children would have needed a 58 percent increase in private contributions to make up for the loss of government support. At the micro-level, some nonprofits would have survived, but others would have been buried. For example, Lutheran Social Services of Detroit, which runs nursing homes, adoption programs, and more, would have needed a 2,486 percent increase in private donations to stay afloat.

Of course, one could argue—as many conservatives now do--that there are many government programs and government-supported charities and agencies that ought to go under. That's fine, but let's be specific, and let's not be so Pollyannish about either Americans' marginal propensity to contribute to charities, or the capacity of civil, community-based institutions to pick up the slack for whatever activities and services we *do* want to see continue.

In 1993, 75 percent of American households gave to charity, but donations averaged about 2.1 percent of household income. Both individual and corporate giving nose-dive during recessions. All annual corporate giving amounts to roughly $7 billion, or less than 1 percent of the corporate sector's pretax profit.

Even if all of America's 34,000 foundations gave away all of their assets (not just income but assets), they could cover only one year's worth of current government social welfare expenditures.

Again, I am not disagreeing with the conservative, civil society, community-centered, family-anchored, faith-based destination. I am trying to be honest and prudent about the journey. Right now, I do not see any chance that—even with huge increases in giving, voluntary efforts, and efficiency gains (i.e., no more government "leaky bucket" effects)—we could replace the present system in a way that sustains the nation's truly disadvantaged, even at minimal safety-net levels. If we are to take this journey, then we had better pack for a generation's worth of effort, including enough food, money, and medicine for the weakest and most vulnerable among us. But neither the rhetoric nor the fine print of welfare reform proposals make such provisions.

Volunteers?

Of course, some say that we should simply brave the journey, and trust that there are tens of millions of Americans who will, when government "gets out of the way," volunteer their time, their dollars, their effort, including where our communal problems are greatest. I've heard a figure—90 million volunteers! 90 million! But I know of no evidence to support that number. I suppose the 90 million volunteers, the 90 percent of all prisoners who are mere petty criminals, and the 6 million homeless will have a convention next year in the land of "doesn't exist."

Indeed, for the last year I have been working closely with a coalition of inner-city black ministers. One of them, Pastor Ben Smith, leads a congregation that bought an old Philadelphia baseball stadium, tore it down, and built a huge church complex on the site. Located in the heart of the city's worst neighborhood, Pastor Smith runs some 80 programs out of the church, everything from drug treatment to crime watch, prison fellowship to literacy, and much, much more. For over 50 years, the 81-year-old Pastor Smith has been out there doing God's work. Not a penny does he ask of government. He has inspired younger black clergy in Boston to do the same; and he has surely inspired me.

But Pastor Smith, a model of the "civil society" approach, a man who has done it, not just talked it, lacks volunteers! He and others like him function as civil society's paramedics, ministering to the unmet needs—spiritual and material—of our most disadvantaged fellow citizens, especially our children. Or, to change the metaphor, they function as civil society's ants, each of them carrying ten times his weight in communal needs and human problems.

So where are the volunteers? Will reforming welfare liberate them to do what, in fact, they could be doing now? How much has "big government" become the conservative all-purpose excuse? Perhaps the paleoconservative critique of Social Security was truer than even its advocates knew. Perhaps the neoconservative critique of how the welfare state has destroyed the family and enervated civil society in the ghetto and beyond is all too true. Perhaps the people to whom Pastor Smith ministers have been so profoundly debilitated that no mere reversal of marginal monetary incentives will cure the spiritual and cultural conditions that afflict them—and us.

If welfare killed the two-parent black inner-city family, I fail to see how pulling the knife out of the dead, cold body thirty years after the fact will restore family life or resurrect civil society. If welfare has driven illegitimacy and crime, I fail to see how "ending it" will save abused and neglected kids or set budding juvenile super-predators on the right path.

In conclusion, I return to the children. We've had welfare caps in New Jersey. People—policy elites—love to debate the numbers. Fine. But I'm telling you that, whatever the good news, the condition of the children in Newark and Trenton's worst neighborhoods has not changed. I'm telling you that the mean streets are just as mean. I'm telling you that we're saving a little money ($64 a month per newborn) but not saving lives or souls. There's a profound disconnect between "welfare reform" and the problems it purports to address.

So, let's make the journey, but let's, as they say on the street, "Get real."

Ninety million volunteers? Pastor Smith would love nine.

21

How Government Schools [May] Displace the Family

Charles L. Glenn

"Must Public Schools *Re*place the Family?" would be a more typical title than the one I have been assigned for a public policy conference in Washington. All the talk about families, in recent years, seems to have been to the effect that they are fatally weakened by developments in the culture since the sixties and, when not actively dysfunctional, are at least incapable of raising children without professional—and thus government—interventions.

How Much Trouble Is The Family In?

Among the loudest voices proclaiming the collapse of the family are those of educators and human service professionals who see this as an occasion for further expanding their own role and that of their institutions, rather than for asking to what extent these institutions—public schooling, public housing, the welfare system, the "victim" mentality fostered by some psychological and social work interventions—have contributed to a loss of functions, depriving family life of much of its traditional significance for family members. We are told, in the words of a probably spurious African proverb, that "it takes a whole village to raise a child," but the ongoing effort to professionalize the human care of human beings suggests that it is not grandmothers and friendly neighbors who are considered capable of the job.

There is no denying that many children today cannot count upon the stability and effective functioning of their families, though it is easy to forget that this has always been true; think of the street urchins of Victorian England, or the many orphans (like "Anne of Green Gables") left dependent upon the kindness of strangers. We should be careful not to stress "the breakdown of the family" so strongly, however, that we lose sight of its primacy in the care and nurture of children *under normal circumstances*. "Normal" in the sense that most of us continue to do it reasonably well, and "normal" also in the sense that the family is the best arrangement we know of to ensure that a child is cared for, day and night, year after year, by someone who is "crazy about him" or her. We have found no means as effective as the family to teach the habits of thinking and acting, the virtuous dispositions, that are—or should be—prior to all that schools can teach.

And it does not help to speak of "the total collapse of the family in America's ghettoes," as both conservatives and liberals are too prone to do. I've been an active member and sometime minister of inner-city churches for forty years, and have learned to admire the often heroic efforts of parents and extended families to do right by their children. It is not true that only middle-class families, or indeed only two-parent families (desirable as they are), can provide the stimulation and support that children need. Reginald Clark's close study of poor black families in Chicago whose children were doing well in high school found that

> the family's main contribution to a child's success in school is made through parents' dispositions and interpersonal relationships with the child in the household . . . a family's ability to equip its young members with survival and "success" knowledge is determined by the parents' (and other older family members') own upbringing, the parents' past relationships and experiences in community institutions, the parents' current support networks, social relationships and other circumstances outside the home, and, most centrally, the parents' current social relationships in the home, and their satisfaction with themselves and with home conditions.[1]

Clark noted a clear relationship between student success and "sacred and secular moral orientations," as well as a disinclination on the part of these parents to allow their children to see themselves as passive victims of a racist and exploitative system.

> These parents do not believe the school should provide all or even most of the academic training and support for the child . . . They are likely to say that "The world don't owe you anything; you owe something to yourself."[2]

Families make a critical difference, Clark found, by what they do day by day, and how they do it, and how they understand the significance of what they are doing.

That essential reservation noted, it is undeniable that something fundamental has changed in the *authority* possessed by the family, and its capacity to create the little world of moral coherence described by Tocqueville in the 1830s. "Certainly of all countries in the world," he wrote, "America is the one in which the marriage tie is most respected and where the highest and truest conception of conjugal happiness has been conceived . . . When the American returns . . . to the bosom of the family, he immediately finds a perfect picture of order and peace."[3]

How times have changed! If there is now one point of agreement between political conservatives and progressives in the United States, it is that the family is in trouble. Democrats and Republicans compete to convince the voters that they have the more credible plans to address this crisis, which seems to threaten the very foundations of our society. Inevitably, American schools are being called upon to do their share of providing a solution. Educational leaders are quick to assure the public that they can add this mission to many others that schools have assumed (generally ineffectively) in recent decades.

Why is the mess that some people make of their family lives a fit concern for social policy? There are three reasons why society as a whole has a legitimate interest in the health of families.

The first is simply that our sense of the fitness of things is offended by a massive breakdown of families. After all, for most Americans a happy family life remains a central goal. Surveys consistently find that "the overwhelming majority of young people today still put forth as their major life goal a lasting, monogamous, heterosexual relationship which includes the procreation of children."[4] A 1993 survey of workers nationwide found that "effect on family life" was a very important consideration in choosing a job for 60 percent, while salary or wages had similar priority for only 35 percent.[5] A survey published in 1988 asked women to describe the best thing about being a woman: "Sixty percent said it is 'motherhood.' Being a wife was in second place, and the great achievement of feminism, 'Taking advantage of women's increased opportunities,' came in a distant fourth."[6] Employers find men increasingly unwilling to put their careers ahead of their families by working overtime or by accepting frequent moves around the country.

Families contribute to private happiness, and they also serve as essential building blocks of the civil society, the "space of uncoerced human association and also the set of relational networks—formed for the sake of family, faith, interest, and ideology—that fill this space."[7] Families are important not just for the sake of the sociability and support they provide, but because they are one of the buffers between individuals and the state. Robert Nisbet points out that families inherently limit state power over their members.[8]

The second reason for policy concern about families is that children are better off in families that are functioning well, with two biological parents who are making a reasonable success of marriage. In this instance as in many others, research has recently been confirming what everyone except researchers already knew. "The vast majority of children who are raised entirely in a two-parent home will never be poor during childhood. By contrast, the vast majority of children who spend time in a single-parent home will experience poverty."[9]

Put even more bluntly, "family structure is by far the best predictor of child poverty."[10] Important as the level of schooling attained is for the escape from poverty or economic marginality, marital status turns out to be even more significant.

The conclusion that the best antipoverty program for children is a stable, intact family holds even for families with modest levels of educational attainment. For married high school graduates with children, the 1991 poverty rate was 7 percent, versus more than 41 percent for families headed by female high school graduates. For married high school dropouts with children, the poverty rate was 25 percent, versus more than 62 percent for families headed by female high school dropouts.[11]

A nationwide survey published in 1991 found that both children and parents from two-parent families were more positive on a whole range of factors than were those from single-parent families.[12]

The third reason for a policy concern with families is less global but no less important: The success of children in school (and thus, in a credential-driven economy, in much of life) is directly though not inevitably related to the nature of their family life. The late James Coleman put the research results in characteristically direct terms: "Schools are successful primarily for children from strong family backgrounds. Schools are singularly unsuccessful for children from weak or disorganized families."[13] After all,

the family is the institution in which children have their earliest education, their earliest experiences in the learning of languages, the nurturance of cognitive, emotional, and motor competencies, the maintenance of interpersonal relationships, the internalization of values, and the assignment of meaning to the world.[14]

In view of the significance of education within the family, it is not surprising that studies by researchers at Princeton and Johns Hopkins concluded that growing up in a single-parent family tended to depress a pupil's academic achievement and attendance. One interesting finding was that, as a family broke up, parents became less involved in the education of their children; another was that what parents *do* cannot explain the entire difference in academic achievement, since "the *strength of the attachment* between parents and child" had a direct impact upon school success.[15] If there is any measure within the reach of public policy that can help parents to function more effectively, it would be at least as important as any of the school reforms to which we devote so much effort. By the same token, we should be extremely dubious about school "reforms" and agendas imposed upon the schools that weaken the role and the authority of families.

For several decades elite opinion was dominated by the contention that there is no ideal model of family life; there are only "families" in endlessly different, equally valid forms. It has been argued that there is a consistent pattern of hostility toward the traditional model of family life on the part of the "new class," which dominates the formation of public opinion in America.[16] The assumption that marriage is the normative basis for family life and for raising children has increasingly retreated, at least in the media and associated elite circles of American society, in response to claims that in fact the "traditional" family is a vanishing species in American life. This contention has been repeated so frequently and in such an apparently authoritative display of census data that it has been widely accepted, though a visit to any suburban mall on a Saturday—or to most churches on a Sunday—would call it seriously into question.

Critics of such statements have pointed out that they rest upon extensive manipulation of the data. For example, it is claimed that "fewer than 10 percent of families today fit the old model of homemaker Mother and breadwinner Father," but this result is arrived at by counting as "families" every household in the nation, including old people and students living alone, and then denying the "traditional" label to any family in which the mother works for any amount of time at any point in the year, or in which there are less than or more than two children! Actually, according to government statistics in 1987, only 28.8 percent of families with preschool children had both parents working full-time; in 33.3 percent of these families, the mother did not have any paid employment, and in 15.8 percent the mother had part-time employment. Employed single mothers headed 10.1 percent of all families with preschool children.[17]

Arguments over statistics conceal a disagreement over how to define the situation of the family in America. If most families are broadly "traditional" in the sense that they are headed by two married adults who share in some combination of earning income and caring for children, public policies might support this pattern by child allowances and other encouragements for mothers to remain in the home during the earliest years of their children's lives. If, on the other hand, marriage and shared childrearing were no longer the norm, it would be time, as some feminists argue, to discard such terms as "single-parent family" as implying that this is an abnormal condition.[18]

Modern society has a tendency to move away from ascriptive identities, of which membership in traditional families is the prototype, toward identities and associations which are freely chosen. The decline of the family-as-fate (typified by arranged marriages) is probably irreversible, nor is there reason to regret an arrangement which was often experienced as oppressive. The family-as-choice can be oppressive in its own way, however, particularly when it must function within a cultural context in which the gratification of individual needs is the primary measure of value. Ethicist Stanley Hauerwas stresses the importance, for children, of being made to feel part of an ongoing story, initially that of their family and then widening outward, a story that teaches what "we do" and thus places the habits that sustain virtue within a context of meaning. This has grown more difficult in contemporary American society, according to legal scholar Mary Ann Glendon:

> Neglect of the social dimension of personhood has made it extremely difficult for us to develop an adequate conceptual apparatus for taking into account the sorts of groups within which human character, competence, and capacity for citizenship are formed. In a society where the seedbeds of civic virtue—families, neighborhoods, religious associations, and other communities—can no longer be taken for granted, this is no trifling matter.[19]

Surely this is the justification for treating the health of families as a concern of public policy, despite our appropriate concern about government interference in what is the private business of citizens. After all, "the public has a much greater interest in the conditions under which children are being raised than in the ways that adults generally choose to arrange their lives. European laws and policies . . . routinely distinguish for many purposes . . . between households that are engaged in child rearing and other types of living arrangements,"[20] since "the institutions of civil society help to sustain a democratic order, by relativizing the power of both the market and the state, and by helping to counter both consumerist and totalitarian tendencies."[21]

Among those who have worked most creatively to link families and schools as partners is Yale psychiatrist James Comer, who argues that

> the crisis that we're concerned about—that American kids don't achieve as well as European kids and some Asian kids—won't kill us because [the American students are] scoring high enough to compete. The one that will kill us is the large number of bright kids who fall out of the mainstream because their families are not functioning.[22]

Schools Undermining Families

It is one thing to agree that public policy should seek to support families, and quite another to urge that schools take on the support of families as a major aspect of their mission. There are two primary dangers inherent in such an assignment of responsibility. The first is that it could further weaken the capacity of schools to carry out their primary function of providing instruction in those academic skills that are essential to a modern economy and society; school staff are already too distracted by the conflicting demands placed upon them. The second is that there is an inherent danger in encouraging government to use schools as an instrument of social policy, particularly when that entails seeking to influence the attitudes and beliefs of pupils.[23] This concern was given definitive form by John Stuart Mill in his celebrated remark that

> a general State education is a mere contrivance for moulding people to be exactly like one another; and as the mould in which it casts them is that which pleases the predominant power in the government . . . in proportion as it is efficient and successful, it established a despotism over the mind, leading by natural tendency to one over the body.[24]

When families are defined as part of the problem that schools should address, it is very likely that they will be seen as rival sources of meaning and authority, and we might expect to find this reflected in the curriculum and practices of schools. Philosopher George Santayana wrote in 1934 that

> while the sentiments of most Americans in politics and morals . . . are very conservative, their democratic instincts and the force of circumstances have produced a system of education which anticipates all that the most extreme revolution would bring about. And while no one dreams of forcibly suppressing private property, religion, or the family, American education ignores these things, and proceeds as much as possible as if they did not exist.[25]

Perhaps he had in mind John Dewey, then at the height of his direct influence upon thinking about education. It is notable that parents and families are almost completely absent from Dewey's voluminous writings, except in passing observations like this one from 1922:

> Parents, priests, chiefs, social censors have supplied aims, aims which were foreign to those upon whom they were imposed, to the young, laymen, ordinary folk . . . men in authority have turned moral rules into an agency of class supremacy [but] any theory which attributes the origin of rule[s] to deliberate design is false.[26]

The view that families are somehow to be left behind when entering the world of the school—the *real* world—has penetrated even into elementary school textbooks, as psychologist Paul Vitz found in his study conducted in the mid-1980s:

> [In forty social studies texts for grades 1 - 4] there is not one text reference to marriage as the foundation of the family. Indeed, not even the word marriage or wedding occurs once in the forty books [in an American context]! . . . neither the word husband nor wife occurs once in any of these books . . . Public school officials may constantly bemoan teenage pregnancy and the frequency of illegitimate children, but their own textbooks begin fostering the notion of family without marriage in grades 1 to 4 . . . Not one of the many families described in these books features a homemaker—that is, a wife and mother—as a model . . . There is not one citation indicating that the occupation of mother or housewife represents an important job, one with integrity, one that provides real satisfactions . . . there is not one portrayal of a contemporary American family that clearly features traditional sex roles.[27]

The intense controversy in New York City recently over a curriculum which, in the name of "multiculturalism," sought to introduce schoolchildren to positive images of nontraditional families based upon gay and lesbian relationships was heightened by the resentment of many parents in traditional marriages who did not see their own "lifestyle choices" positively reflected in the curriculum.

Even what was traditionally the educational bulwark of "family values," the home economics program that is part of the curriculum in most American secondary schools (usually for female students who are not college bound but increasingly for young men as well), has succumbed to the anxiety to be up-to-date so characteristic of American education. The American Home Economic Association officially "defines the family unit as two or more persons who share resources, share responsibility for decisions, share values and goals, and have commitment to one another over time . . . regardless of blood, legal ties, adoption, or marriage."[28]

The author once reviewed twelve books on how to teach moral education in schools and found not a single positive reference to the role of families or to the need to reinforce the lessons they have already been teaching through family norms and practices. The general tone of these books was that children need to be shown a better way than that of their parents.

Such messages, whether overt or conveyed through what is not said, undermine the respect of children for their families and their motivation to form healthy families of their own. "Rarely does the notion prevail that families are the first and primary educators whose effects should not be undone, but elaborated on, enriched, and expanded by schools."[29]

The State and Schooling

Is this neglect of or disrespect for the family (or, indeed, for "families" however defined) an inevitable concomitant of government control of schooling? Should there indeed be any government role in relation to the socialization of children and youth, or is that too dangerous a weapon to be left in the hands of the state?

In keeping with the spirit of this volume, it seems appropriate to make the best case for the state's involvement in education before suggesting limits upon that involvement. Every state constitution and those of most European countries make education—in the words of the Dutch Constitution—"a matter of continuing concern for the government." The Constitution of my own Commonwealth of Massachusetts, written in 1780 by John Adams, describes the mission of government in relation to schooling in these terms:

> Wisdom, and knowledge, as well as virtue, diffused generally among the body of the people, being necessary for the preservation of their rights and liberties; and as these depend on spreading the opportunities and advantages of education in the various parts of the country, and among the different orders of the people, it shall be the duty of legislatures and magistrates, in all future periods of this commonwealth, to cherish the interests of literature and the sciences, and all seminaries of them . . . to encourage private societies and public institutions . . . to countenance and inculcate the principles of humanity and general benevolence, public and private charity, industry and frugality, honesty and punctuality in their dealings, sincerity, good humor, and all social affections, and generous sentiments among the people.[30]

As the Dutch example—70 percent of schoolchildren attend publicly funded private schools—shows, government concern for education need not translate into a state monopoly of schooling.

Three primary arguments are advanced for a state role in education, concerned respectively with *unity,* with *justice,* and with *social progress.* We will see that there is something to be said for each, but that in each case a line must be drawn and vigilantly defended, lest a sort of benevolent imperialism intrude too far upon the proper role of the family and the quite distinct role of the civil society, with deeply mischievous results.

As I have shown in *The Myth of the Common School* (1988), the effort in this and other countries to create a state monopoly of schooling derived, historically, from the desire of the rising nationalistic elite of lawyers, academics, and journalists to promote social and political *unity.* These middle-class rivals to the established elites of locality and region, of church and what we would now call ethnicity, saw the state school as the sovereign means to effect what French statesman François Guizot in the 1830s called "a sure government of minds." The school, and the schoolteacher, would be the instrument of the center's hegemony over the periphery, of universalistic over particularistic values, and thus would be necessarily hostile to all forms of pluralism and of loyalties competing with that to the state. Quite simply, the school was to be the state's means of penetrating and neutralizing the civil society. And so we have Danton insisting that "it is in national schools that children must suck republican milk," for the child belongs to the republic and not to his parents, and Horace Mann (more gently but thereby more effectively) insisting that the school liberate children from the "prejudices" of their parents—such as revealed religion.[31]

This agenda is profoundly inimical to a free society, but it is important to note a core of truth in it. There *are* certain shared understandings and habits that are needed to sustain a republican form of government, as the Founders clearly understood. Some of these civic virtues are learned in school, and it is significant that the one set of national education standards that has been widely commended recently is for civic education. Every child in this society needs to learn about the rule of law, the duties of citizenship, and how our system works, and something about the Bill of Rights and why it matters. And it is appropriate that public funds be used to ensure that such fundamentals of citizenship are taught, and taught well. These should be—and usually are—taught in all schools, of course, not just in those operated by government.

But these shared understandings and the habits of civic virtue are also learned through practice, through what we do together to make decisions and to sustain the institutions and cooperative ventures of local life. This, Tocqueville saw clearly and commended. Our policy discussions should be deeply concerned, as he was, about how the overreach of government can undermine these "little platoons" of citizenship. In *Educational Freedom in Eastern Europe* (1995), I show how the totalitarian devastation of civil society, given canonical form by Mussolini in 1925, with his "Everything within the state, nothing outside the state," is being reversed in part through initiatives taken by teachers and parents in hundreds if not thousands of communities to educate children with integrity and effectiveness in nongovernment schools that they have created. Václav Havel predicted, in 1978, that

> the official structures—as agencies of the post-totalitarian system, existing only to serve its automatism and constructed in the spirit of that role—[would] simply begin withering away and dying off, to be replaced by new structures that have evolved from "below" and are put together in a fundamentally different way.[32]

Schools have been among the most common "new structures" emerging during the last years of communist rule and in a flood since its collapse. Groups of parents and teachers have begun to re-create education through school-level initiatives to serve their children more honestly and more effectively, and education policy debates have focused, even more than in the United States, on whether such initiatives should be merely tolerated as an expression of freedom or welcomed and supported in the interest of society as a whole.[33] Such initiatives are an essential aspect of educational reform in the formerly communist nations, where, as Jiří Musil has put it,

> a rich network of independent institutions and organizations has to be formed, that are
> neither state-directed nor state-controlled, that are autonomous social, political, and
> cultural entities . . . Seeking and constituting such social, cultural, political forces,
> capable of attaining such independence and balance, is the process which will decide
> whether a postcommunist regime is successful in its efforts to achieve democracy.[34]

Schools are ideally situated to serve as the occasion for new habits of cooperation, for the development of trust as adults work together in the interest of their children.

Only through such habits, and such trust, can the severely strained civil societies of our countries, East and West, return to health. The creation of new schools or the reforming of existing schools to make them directly accountable to parents is one of the best ways to rebuild trust and cooperation. This is what Mill called "the peculiar training of a citizen, the practical part of the political education of a free people, taking them out of the narrow circle of personal and family selfishness, and accustoming them to the comprehension of joint interests, the management of joint concerns," adding that "without these habits and powers, a free constitution can neither be worked nor preserved; as is exemplified by the too-often transitory nature of political freedom in countries where it does not rest upon a sufficient basis of local liberties." After all, "a government cannot have too much of the kind of activity which does not impede, but aids and stimulates, individual exertion and development."[35]

Do such local initiatives and the exercise of parental choice threaten to disunify society, as is often charged? To the contrary, they serve to overcome the alienation and civic indifference which result from the bureaucratization of aspects of life which should be experienced on a human scale and without the exclusion of natural feelings. Freely chosen and deeply involving schools can help to knit back together the fractured civil society of our cities—yes, and of our suburbs as well.

The second argument for state involvement in education rests upon a concern for *justice.* This was the primary focus of my own work as a state official for twenty-one years, and I continue to believe strongly that government should be vigilant to ensure that justice is done to poor children, and handicapped children, and children whose race or ethnicity or sex may be the basis for denial of opportunity, and immigrant children—the subject of my new book[36]—and children whose families, for whatever reason, do not provide the support essential to their development into the adults they are capable of being. The state does this appropriately by enforcing laws against discrimination of any kind, and by providing extra funding for the schooling of children who are particularly expensive to educate well.

But, once again, there are limits to what the state should do in the name of justice, and these limits are overstepped when it interferes (except under the extraordinary circumstances noted above) with the right of parents to make decisions about their children. As John Coons points out,

> [t]he right to form families and to determine the scope of their children's practical

liberty is for most men and women the primary occasion for choice and responsibility. One does not have to be rich or well placed to experience the family. The opportunity over a span of fifteen or twenty years to attempt the transmission of one's deepest values to a beloved child provides a unique arena for the creative impulse. Here is the communication of ideas in its most elemental mode. Parental expression, for all its invisibility to the media, is an activity with profound First Amendment implications.[37]

As Plato recognized, the only way to create a social system based strictly upon individual merit—however defined—would be to abolish the family. Quite simply, parents help their children more powerfully than any intervention by schooling can "correct." After two generations of preferences for the children of Soviet workers had failed to eliminate that dynamic, Nikita Khrushchev proposed a vast system of boarding schools to ensure that the influence of the Communist Party upon the rising generation would not be undercut by that of their parents. We know enough about child development to say with confidence that even such a totalitarian measure *par excellence* could not have overcome the advantage possessed by the children of educated parents. Under our own system of constitutionally protected freedom, the principle expressed by the Supreme Court in *Pierce v. Society of Sisters*,[38] that "the child is not the mere creature of the state," words that deserve to be carved over the door of every public school, should place a limit upon what the state can legitimately do in the name of justice. As "those who nurture him and direct his destiny" and "prepare him for additional obligations," parents will inevitably have an influence upon their child that confers advantages or disadvantages beyond the reach of public policy interventions.

Strongly as we may feel about the justice represented by the goal of equal educational opportunity unlimited by circumstances, we must judge this stubborn residual influence of parents a very good thing.

Not all parents are a worthy influence on their children, of course, and the third argument for state involvement in education is that society will never progress without encouraging children to surpass the limitations of their families. Schooling seems the sovereign intervention to improve society, by working on the malleable stuff of childhood. Families are often seen as a source of conservative resistance to *social progress*, and the school is charged with showing children the way to a brighter tomorrow.

There is some truth in this. Think of how the children of immigrants learn to function in the host society, learn much that their own parents cannot teach them through their schooling—though it should be noted that Catholic and Lutheran schools, in the last century, were at least as powerfully "Americanizing" as were the public schools.[39] Think of how the progress of agriculture, in this and other countries, has been stimulated by what farm boys and girls learned in school. Schools *are* a powerful agent of social and economic progress, and public policy may appropriately be concerned to identify new directions in, say, vocational education.

But here again a line must be drawn. Not everything that we might agree to be desirable outcomes of schooling should be the subject of government prescription to schools. Citizens of a free society must not be manipulated by their government, even "for their own good." Universal schooling is too blunt an instrument to serve every need that society might have to achieve particular results—especially given its mandatory character, which should raise warning flags about freedom of conscience and opinion. As Stephen Arons and Charles Lawrence have warned,

> If the government were to regulate the development of ideas and opinions . . . freedom of expression would become a meaningless right . . . the development as well as the expression of those beliefs, opinions, world views and aspects of conscience that constitute individual consciousness should be free from government manipulation.[40]

Someone decides, for the best of reasons, that children need to be aware of the danger of sexually transmitted diseases, but when our twelve-year-old daughter comes home from school with a brochure advising her: "When you have oral sex on an anus use a latex barrier, or put a piece of plastic wrap between your mouth and the other person's anus to prevent the spread of germs that can cause STDs," and "use a new needle each time you shoot drugs . . . ," we have a right to feel that our trust in the school has been deeply betrayed and that the sixth grade could find better things to study and more worthy ways of understanding how to deal with the vicious impulses which, as a Calvinist, I have no doubt we all possess.

To sum up, society as a whole does have a stake in the education of every child, and government can legitimately act to ensure that schooling is free, universal and compulsory, and to provide supplemental support to make it more effective for those children who, for whatever reason, are ill-prepared to take full advantage of it. Implicit in government's responsibility to ensure that all children receive an education are two further functions, which our own national government has performed quite well, and to which its role in education should largely be limited: Collecting and making widely available information about the condition of schooling (this should be extended to more effective consumer information for parents), and intervening in cases of racial and other discrimination that denies equal access to educational opportunities.

Government should also (though it does not) ensure that all families are equally empowered to make decisions about the schooling of their children, including the decision to choose a school with a distinctive religious or philosophical character. In most countries in Europe, as in Canada and Australia, public funds "follow the child" to the schools that parents choose.[41]

What should government *not* seek to do in relation to schooling? It should not set itself up as an educator, using its resources and its power to impose a *pédagogie d'état*, a state pedagogy that seeks to shape its citizens. Government oversteps its bounds when it sets out, as in some of the abuses of "Outcome-based Education," to define what children should think and feel about issues on which there are legitimate and deeply held differences within the society.

How should we understand the role of the school? *Not* as an agent of the state or a branch office of government. Also not, I would argue, as purely an agent of the family, as when a private tutor is hired to give lessons. The school, rightly understood, is an expression and a primary locus of the civil society, one of its "mediating structures." Like marriage, which is its cornerstone, the family should be understood in a social context of which it is an expression and agent and without which it would lack the support to function in a healthy and effective way. If the school were only an agent of the family, it could not serve its essential function of helping children to grow into a wider world. It could not be the occasion for families, together with other adults whom they trust, to create and express an understanding of the goals of human development that goes beyond what any one family could provide. This is why even "home-schoolers" commonly link up with others to enrich the educational experiences that they can provide for their children.

No, it does not "take a whole village to raise a child," but it does take a broader community than the family to enable a girl or boy to become a woman or man capable of a decent and purposeful adult life.

What should the role of the family be? First, of course, to educate through the loving disciplines of daily life and through the countless opportunities provided by daily life and by periodic crises to reflect on good and bad, right and wrong, the noble, the true, and the lovely.

Second, to choose an educating community; usually this will include a school but also a rich network of activities and associations that draw the child beyond the family without displacing the family. Only such freely chosen schools and associations have any prospect of possessing the moral coherence which is essential to education and which many public schools so tragically and fatally lack.

Whenever it is proposed—as I am proposing—that public policy in the United States emulate that in other Western democracies by respecting and financially supporting the decisions that parents make about the schooling of their children, there is a great hue and cry about "church/state issues." After all, many of the schools and associations that parents choose will be based upon shared religious beliefs. There is considerable evidence, indeed, that schools with a religious basis are more effective in educating, especially children who are "at risk." Does their religious character mean that they should be unavailable to parents who cannot afford to pay their tuition?

This is not the place to discuss the heated legal and policy question of "equal treatment" of religious convictions and the naturalistic positivism which is the established religion of modernity, except to suggest that the taken-for-granted authority of the latter has slipped considerably since the Supreme Court jurisprudence on the issue emerged in the fifties and sixties.[42]

In any case, framing the question of the fair accommodation of religious convictions as a "church/state issue" rests on a fundamental misreading of American history. It has been more than 150 years since any religious denomination either possessed or aspired to a privileged position under American law or public policy, or to dominate public schooling, as for example the Catholic Church dominated French schooling for several decades under the *Loi Falloux* of 1850. "Church versus state" is a European controversy misapplied to American realities. Here the tension in education has always been between the state and

Charles L. Glenn

families who differ with the state's agenda for the schooling of their children, often but not always on religious grounds. Indeed, it would be more accurate to describe the tension as being between families and the elites who, recoiling from the rich diversity of the American people, have sought to use popular schooling (often not that of their own children!) to shape the children of others.

Schools and Families

But if schools inevitably draw children away from their families toward the broader world, as indeed they should, what can be done to ensure that this does not have the effect of displacing the family?

It is not enough to talk in school about the importance of families, if the educational system is so organized as to deny parents the opportunity to make significant decisions. The present system of assignment of pupils to schools in the United States is almost unique among the nations with universal schooling in its refusal to acknowledge the right of parents to choose schools for their children. This right is spelled out explicitly in the major international covenants protecting human rights.[43] For example, the Universal Declaration of Human Rights (1948) states that "parents have a prior right to choose the kind of education that shall be given to their children." The nations signing the International Covenant on Economic, Social and Cultural Rights (1966) agreed "to have respect for the liberty of parents . . . to choose for their children schools, other than those established by public authorities, which conform to such minimum educational standards as may be laid down or approved by the state and to ensure the religious and moral education of their children in conformity with their own convictions." Similarly, the First Protocol to the European Convention for the Protection of Human Rights and Fundamental Freedoms provides that "in the exercise of any functions which it assumes in relation to education and teaching, the state shall respect the right of parents to ensure such education and teaching in conformity with their own religious and philosophical convictions" (article 2).

John Coons has argued eloquently that American education frustrates parents in exercising this right and duty:

> From top to bottom its structure effectively frustrates the choices of parent and child which the law protects in every other realm of life. Parents choose shoes, food, games, hours and every other important feature of a child's life. In education this liberty is not only opposed but squelched. Ordinary families with all their rich variety in culture and values are forced to accept the form, content and ideology of a politically dictated education. Public schools, as presently organized, chill the traffic in ideas that is generated by free family choices in every other area of life. Though they vest in the mantle of freedom and diversity, in fact they flout this deepest purpose of the First Amendment.[44]

Some assert that government should make the decisions about the education of children because some parents—and poor parents in general—are incapable of doing so and indeed simply don't care.[45] Of course there are some inadequate and irresponsible parents of every social class, and society must have ways of intervening to protect individual children from situations of clearly established abuse and neglect, including that of their need for an education. But policy for the great majority should not be guided by the need to deal with exceptional cases.

Poor parents, perhaps more than others, need to be given opportunities to make important decisions about the well-being of their children; it is the responsibility of policymakers to ensure that, so far as possible, there are no educationally bad choices.[46] It is not as though there were no bad public schools now to which children are assigned involuntarily on the basis of educationally irrelevant factors like where they live.

Research that we have carried out for the U. S. Department of Education shows that inner-city parents of all racial/ethnic groups are keenly interested in making school choices for their children, and use a variety of means of obtaining information and reaching conclusions about which schools would best meet their needs.[47] The major impediment to allowing them to exercise such choices is the disrespect for the family, which is unfortunately widespread among professional educators. Children from middle-class families are easy to teach, it is often said, though their parents may be too pushy and interfere with what educators alone are capable of deciding. Children from working-class or poor families are perceived as difficult, and their parents as not caring about education—which may be just as well, given the widespread belief that schools can't be expected to do much with their children.

What parents *are* is often discussed by educators, and valued or devalued according to whether it is perceived as supporting what teachers do, but what parents themselves *do* is seldom considered to be of much importance. Educators have a tendency to a kind of moral imperialism, seeing themselves as uniquely qualified and appointed to define what education is and how it will take place, adapting how they work to suit the essentially passive raw materials supplied by compulsory attendance laws, collecting "little plastic lumps of human dough from private households and [shaping] them on the social kneadingboard."[48] If challenged, educators might suggest that the patient does not tell the surgeon where to cut.

While it is an exaggeration to refer to "the family agenda of the left" as being to "convince the public that the training and development of children are far too important to be left to the whims and errors of parents,"[49] as does one prominent evangelical, it is impossible to deny an unthinking tendency in this direction on the part of the education Establishment.

Children are not well served by policies that treat their parents as incapable of responsible decision making. The message conveyed by a system in which parents are expected to be passive is that responsible choice, the expression of character or virtue, is exercised *for*, not *by*, the individual—a lesson that encourages personal irresponsibility. An opportunity is thereby lost to engage parents and their children together in making decisions the consequences of which are immediately apparent

234 Charles L. Glenn

to both.

If we have learned anything about equal educational opportunity in these past two decades it is that it is available only in schools that are *effective*, and that good schools are marked by order, a sense of purpose, and the continual cultivation of self-discipline. Often I have found that effective urban schools are led by a rather old-fashioned principal, often a black woman educated in the South or a Latino educated outside the continental United States, with high expectations for the achievement and the behavior of the students and a disinclination to accept excuses based on race or poverty. Sara Lawrence Lightfoot notes as "one of the great mistakes of the sixties"

> when large numbers of humanistic, liberated teachers, mouthing the rhetoric of nontraditional education, invaded black communities. They sought to establish loving, caring, familial relationships with their young black charges. Their goals were often laudable and worthy. Their hearts were more or less pure. But their hippy clothes, missionary zeal, progressive pedagogy, and playful style offended black parents who wanted a more rigorous traditional education that focused on the basic skills of reading and writing. In fact, if ghetto schools are going to begin to be responsive to parental values it may be that the authority structures, pedagogical modes, and educational goals of schools will need to become more traditionally defined with visible and explicit criteria established for child competencies. In the King School in New Haven, when parents became increasingly involved in the schooling process, they negotiated with teachers for more structured and orderly classrooms, and emphasized the rigors of academic work.[50]

It is such teachers and principals that urban parents support most strongly, sensing that they share the parents' own aspirations for their children. Schools characterized by a shared sense of purpose, a sort of educational covenant, schools that have been freely chosen by families, can help in turn to develop in families a sense of the significance of their own efforts. Schools can help families to act more effectively by operating as though what families do is significant—whatever their social class.

Normative judgments are the essential stuff of successful family life, and of successful education. They cannot be avoided. Neither can they be imposed by the state. That is why only a system of schooling based upon family choice of schools would permit the uninhibited expression of particular angles on the truth in schools that have been freely chosen.

A policy supporting parent choice of schools is one way in which government can not only validate the decision making of parents but can also make room within the educational system for differing views of what education is all about. In a society as divided over cultural issues as is the United States, that may be the only basis for a truce in the "culture wars," which divert so much energy from the real work of schools.

The school *can* play an important role in restoring meaning to family life, and thus helping families to function more effectively, but only if we learn to think differently about the school's mission and indeed about what sort of institution it is. We must not continue to conceive of the school as an agent of government, serving the purposes of the wider society according to the principle that educational bureaucrats know best what is good for children, and of parents as a supporting cast whose collaboration is sought so long as they subordinate themselves to the professional definition of what is needful.

Schools deserve to be understood as communities in their own right, responsive but not subordinate to state or church or family, and finally accountable to a shared understanding of the good life for which they educate.

Notes

1. R. M. Clark, *Family Life and School Achievement: Why Poor Black Children Succeed or Fail* (Chicago: University of Chicago Press, 1983), 1.

2. Clark, 122-23.

3. A. de Tocqueville, *Democracy in America*, translated by George Lawrence (New York: Harper & Row, 1966), 291.

4. D. Popenoe, "The Family Transformed," *Family Affairs* 2, 2-3 (Summer/Fall 1989).

5. T. Mashberg, "Worker Poll Shows Family, Fringes Gain Favor," *Boston Globe*, September 3, 1993, 1.

6. G. L. Bauer, "Mothers and Fathers," *Children at Risk: The Battle for the Hearts and Minds of Our Kids,* J. Dobson, G. L. Bauer, eds. (Dallas: Word Publishing, 1990), 165.

7. M. Walzer, "The Idea of Civil Society," *Dissent* 38 (Spring 1991) 293.

8. R. Nisbet, *The Quest for Community* (New York: Oxford University Press, 1953), 271.

9. E. C. Kamarck, and W. A. Galston, "A Progressive Family Policy for the 1990s," in *Mandate for Change,* W. Marshall and M. Schram, eds. (New York: Berkley Books, 1993), 157 (citing D. T. Ellwood).

10. S. J. South, and S. E. Tolnay, "Relative Well-Being among Children and the Elderly: The Effects of Age Group Size and Family Structure." *The Sociological Quarterly* 33 (1992): 115-133.

11. Kamarck & Galston, 159.

12. National Commission on Children (1991). *Speaking of Kids: A National Survey of Children and Parents.* Washington.

13. J. Coleman, "The Family, the Community, and the Future of Education," in *Education and the American Family: A Research Synthesis*, W. Weston, ed. (New York: New York University Press, 1989) 169.

14. L. A. Cremin, *Popular Education and Its Discontents* (New York: Harper & Row, 1990), 53.

15. N. M. Astore, and S. S. McLanahan, "Family Structure, Parental Practices and High School Completion," *American Sociological Review* 56 (1991): 309-320.

16. B. Berger, and P. L. Berger, *The War over the Family* (Garden City, NY: Anchor Press/Doubleday, 1983).

17. D. Blankenhorn, "Ozzie and Harriet: Have Reports of Their Death Been Greatly Exaggerated?" *Family Affairs* 2, 2-3 (Summer/Fall 1989): 10.

18. B. J. Christensen, "War over a Word: Redefining 'Family'," *The Family in America* 1, 7 (September, 2, 1987).

19. M. A. Glendon, *Rights Talk: The Impoverishment of Political Discourse.* (New York: Free Press, 1991), 109.

20. Glendon, 125.

21. Glendon, 137.

22. Cited in "Endangered Family," *Newsweek,* (August 30, 1993).

23. C. L. Glenn, *The Myth of the Common School,* (Amherst, MA: University of Massachusetts Press, 1988).

24. J.S. Mill, (1859) *On Liberty* [A Norton critical edition], David Spitz, ed. (New York: W.W. Norton, 1975).

25. Cited by Christensen (1988), 3.

26. J. Dewey, (1922). *Human Nature and Conduct,* New York: Henry Holt, excerpted in *John Dewey on Education,* Reginald D. Archambault, ed. (Chicago: University of Chicago Press Phoenix Edition, 1974), 62.

27. P. C. Vitz, *Censorship: Evidence of Bias in Our Children's Textbooks.* (Ann Arbor, MI: Servant Publications, 1986).

28. Cited by Christensen (1987), 2.

29. S. L. Lightfoot, "Families as Educators." in *Shades of Brown: New Perspectives on School Desegregation,* D. Bell, ed. (New York: Teachers College Press, 1980), 12.

30. *Constitution of Massachusetts,* Part the Second, Chapter V, Section II, "The Encouragement of Literature, etc.".

31. Glenn, (1988).

32. V. Havel, *Living in Truth* (London: Faber and Faber, 1987), 108.

33. C. L. Glenn, *Educational Freedom in Eastern Europe* (Washington, DC: Cato Institute, 1995).

34. J. Musil, "Czechoslovakia in the Middle of Transition," *Daedalus: The Exit from Communism* 121, no. 2 (Spring 1992), 189-90.

35. Mill, 101-102, 106.

36. C. L. Glenn, and E. J. De Jong, *Educating Immigrant Children: Schools and Language Minorities in Twelve Nations* (New York: Garland Publishing, 1996).

37. John E. Coons, "Intellectual Liberty and the Schools," *Journal of Law, Ethics & Public Policy* 1 (1985): 511.

38. 268 U.S. 510 (1925).

39. C. L. Glenn, and E. J. De Jong, *Educating Immigrant Children: Schools and Language Minorities in Twelve Nations* (New York: Garland Publishing, 1996).

40. S. Arons, and C. Lawrence, "The Manipulation of Consciousness: A First Amendment Critique of Schooling," *Harvard Civil Rights/Civil Liberties Law Review* 15 (1980): 309, 312.

41. C. L. Glenn, *Choice of Schools in Six Nations.* (Washington, DC: U.S. Department of Education, 1989).

42. See my forthcoming "Equal Treatment: Implications for Education," in *Equal Treatment of Religion in a Pluralist Society,* S.V. Monsma and C. Soper, eds.(Grand Rapids: Eerdmans).

43. The passages that follow are taken from the very useful collection entitled *Liberté d'enseignement. Les textes*,(Geneva: Organisation internationale pour le développement de la liberté d'enseignement, no date); texts are provided in French, English, and Spanish.

44. J. Coons, "Intellectual Liberty and the Schools." *Notre Dame Journal of Law, Ethics and Public Policy* 2 (1985): 495-533, at 515.

45. A. Thernstrom, "Is Choice a Necessity?" *The Public Interest* 101 (Fall 1990).

46. C. L. Glenn, "Letting Poor Parents Act Responsibly." *The Journal of Family and Culture* 2, 3 (Autumn 1986).

47. C. L. Glenn, K. McLaughlin, and L. Salganik, *Parent Information for School Choice: The Case of Massachusetts*, (Boston: Center on Families, Communities, Schools and Children's Learning, 1993).

48. M. N. Rothbard, "The Progressive Era and the Family," in *The American Family and the State*, J. R. Peden and F. R. Ghane, eds. [San Francisco: Pacific Research Institute for Public Policy,1986,] 116, citing sociologist E. A. Ross (1912).

49. J.C. Dobson, "Questions and Answers," in *Children at Risk: The Battle for the Hearts and Minds of Our Kids*, J. C. Dobson and G. L. Bauer, eds. (Dallas: Word Publishing, 1990) 59.

50. Lightfoot, 15.

22

The Sex-Ed Wars

Lawrence Criner

I am a journalist who has been reporting on sex education for nearly a decade. It has been a decade in which we have, unfortunately, grown more deeply divided over how to guide the sexual learning of young people. There are those who advocate comprehensive sexuality education, which seeks to "condomize" the young and suggests that they have a "right" to be sexually active. They are opposed by those who advocate abstinence before marriage and fidelity within it.

While this argument rages, the American family has continued to decline. The litany of depressing facts reveals a crisis that threatens to overwhelm us.

One-third of all American children are now born to single mothers, and, as a result, more than 6 million kids live with a single parent who has never married.[1] The divorce rate is about 43 percent.[2]

Allegedly, 3 million children endure physical or sexual abuse each year.[3] Over a million teenage girls become pregnant.[4] Of these, more than 400,000 will choose to have abortions[5] and nearly as many will give birth out of wedlock.[6] Roughly 3 million teens contract sexually transmitted diseases annually—8000 more will be infected by the end of today. Thousands are HIV positive; more than ten thousand already have full-blown AIDS.[7]

This panoply of pathologies has exploded since Amercia embarked on the sexual revolution in the 1960s. Having arrived in the mid-1990s on the far side of this quixotic social experiment—which began with the dream of a golden age of sexual well-being—we can see that the promise of sexual freedom has led not to human liberation, but to a nightmare of broken homes, fatherless children, single mothers, abortion mills, and incurable sexual diseases.

Unfortunately, many of the social programs designed to address these ills are often themselves a product of the sexual revolution. For example, sex education and contraceptive services have increased astronomically since the 1960s, as have teen pregnancies and STDs. The problem and the solution form a vicious cycle.

Nowadays, the classroom is a battleground over condom distribution, alternative lifestyles, school-based clinics, and the right of parents to have a say in what their children are being taught. The standard approach calls for *reducing* the incidence of adolescent pregnancy and STDs *without* reducing teen sexual activity. This feat is to be accomplished by getting kids to feel "comfortable" about sex by persuading them that there is nothing particularly special about it, that it's just another bodily function. "Just remember to use a contraceptive when you do it," goes the common refrain. Presumably, if children learn their lessons well, they will be equipped for life in modern-day America.

The striking concurrence between the introduction of value-free sex education, contraceptive availability, and the explosion in teen pregnancies was well documented by Susan Roylance, J. A. Ford, and Jacqueline Kasun in their testimony before the Senate Committee on Labor and Human Resources, March 31, 1981. Roylance, looking at states with similar social demographic characteristics and rates of teen pregnancy, reported that those states that spent the most on these new family planning programs had the highest increases in abortions and illegitimate births among teenagers between 1970 and 1979. Kasun found in Humboldt County, California, the teen pregnancy rate grew forty times faster after the introduction of sex education programs.[8]

One of the largest studies ever undertaken, based on a survey of 6,000 young women, found that fifteen-year-old girls who had had sex education were far more likely to begin sexual activity than those not having the instruction.[9] A majority of 400 randomly selected family physicians and psychiatrists agreed that the availability of contraceptives has led to increased promiscuity among teenagers. Other studies have raised similar concerns. Yet, the federal government continues to push the contraceptive approach more vigorously, while neglecting a little-known but promising prevention program already in place.

Tax Dollars and CDC

Former Surgeon General Joycelyn Elders provoked a public outcry when she broadcast her readiness to teach teens "what to do in the back seat" of the car—among other things. She embraced the contraceptive message with single-mindedness.

When Elders was removed from her highly visible position, many assumed that her point of view had been demoted as well. Today, however, it is health officials at the Centers for Disease Control who seek to include a "model" K-12 comprehensive sexuality education curriculum in all the nation's public schools.

Longtime sex educator, Professor Ira Reiss, explains in his book *An End to Shame* what a fitting comprehensive sexuality education course ought to teach: "In the ideal program we would . . . present . . . a wide range of sexual acts like masturbation, oral sex, anal sex and intercourse. Contraception including condoms would be talked about, even though we don't expect many preadolescents to have intercourse." Abstinence, he says, " is an outmoded standard of sexual morality."[10]

Since many school districts prohibit discussion of intercourse, homosexuality, and condom use, the CDC is constructing an "infrastructure" to push what amounts to a radical social agenda in the name of health education.

To lead this initiative, the CDC's Division of Adolescent School Health (DASH) has forged "Partners" agreements with twenty-five national organizations, according to its 1995 Project Summaries Report. Included are the National Education Association (NEA), the Council of Chief State School Officers (CCSSO), the American Association of School Administrators (AASA), Advocates for Youth (AFY), National School Health Education Coalition (NaSHEC), Sexuality Information and Education Council of the United States (SIECUS), and other prominent groups.

Each is an advocate with deep financial interests in public education. All are presently receiving huge federal grants to develop curricula, train teachers, hold strategy conferences, and devise tactics for eventually implementing comprehensive sex education throughout the country.

The NEA, which is the nation's largest teachers' union, with 2.2 million members, has at least eight grants from the CDC. One is for a "pilot" program in Farmington, New Mexico. A component of this program involves developing information on "managing controversy and misinformation," presumably ways to deal with obstinate parents. Other NEA grants include money to develop a Teachers' Resource Directory and a manual for Building Community Support—handy organizational tools for developing coalitions—all at taxpayers expense.

CCSSO represents the interests of the state superintendents in charge of education in the fifty states. It has a grant to create a "Directory of Comprehensive School Health Program Staff in State Education Agencies," so they can coordinate their efforts at the state level. AASA, whose affiliates include district superintendents, central office administrators, and principals, has a grant to fund training workshops for its members and state HIV coordinators—there is one in each state paid for by the CDC—to discuss "effective strategies that can be used by school leaders" to advance CDC objectives at a local level.

AFY, formerly the Center for Population Options, has a five-year agreement to develop numerous projects: one for tracking condom "initiatives nationwide through its National Condom Availability Clearinghouse" and another to " develop model policies for school districts considering condom availability programs."

NaSHEC is a coalition of over seventy health and education organizations, and youth-service groups that campaign for K-12 comprehensive health education. A congressional brief by Paul Mero titled "How Congress Supports and Funds Organized Homosexuality" reports that sixteen of NaSHEC's board member organizations have received a combined 104 federal grants from FY93 to FY95 totaling $37,595,944, largely from AIDS grant money. It also states that the groups in NaSHEC employ fifty-nine registered lobbyists to do their bidding on Capitol Hill.

SIECUS has been the driving force behind the push for K-12 sex education in public schools for over thirty years. As a breakaway group from Planned Parenthood, SIECUS moved into sex education with financial support from the Playboy Foundation.[11] Today, it is funded by the federal government. In 1994, the

CDC awarded SIECUS a five-year grant to examine the "strengths and weaknesses of each state's HIV/AIDS" prevention and sexuality curricula, as well as to study each state's infrastructure to support these programs. One aim is to develop new material on AIDS prevention methods and "low-risk sexual behaviors" that can be taught.

SIECUS executive director Debra Haffner states in *SIECUS Reports* what those prevention methods might include. She writes, "Safest sex doesn't necessarily mean no sex." Teens should be taught "behaviors that have no possibility of causing pregnancy or a sexually-transmited disease"—things like "undressing each other, masturbation alone, masturbation in front of a partner [and] mutual masturbation." Then, teens may add their own "list of activities," for sexually arousing one another.[12] SIECUS has been given responsibility by the CDC for developing "training and certification standards" for those who will teach comprehensive sex-ed in the nation's public schools.

The CDC has been less than forthcoming in providing an accounting of the money it has already spent on these projects or in making available to the public copies of the educational materials that have been produced at government expense.

Also troubling are reports of partisan political activities by groups such as SEICUS. Lists of opponents to comprehensive sexuality education have been circulated, and tutorials on ways to remove people from the policy process have been conducted. This amounts to the creation of a kind of "blacklist."

It is not clear, given the national scope and massive funding of some of these groups, that local educational autonomy can be preserved.

The Latex Lie

Condoms are a key component of the comprehensive sex-ed package. But how reliable are they? AIDS is a fatal disease, and condoms are not 100 percent dependable. Studies of condom failure vary, but a number report a failure rate of up to 31 percent.[13] The CDC, however, has chosen to recognize the studies that show a much lower failure rate. Joycelyn Elders once refused to recall defective condoms.

At a meeting of the World Congress of Sexologists, Theresa Crenshaw, president of American Society of Sex Educators and member of the Presidential AIDS Commission, asked 800 sexologists who attended the 1987 international conference in Heidelberg, Germany, this question: "If you had the partner of your dreams and knew that the person carried HIV, how many of you would have sex depending on a condom for protection?"[14] Not one raised a hand. Are we telling our kids the whole truth about condoms?

Many worry that distributing condoms to teens will give them a false sense of security and cause them to become more sexually inconsistent condom users. Robert C. Noble, an AIDS physician, has said, "Passing out condoms to teenagers is like issuing them squirt-guns for a 4-alarm blaze. Condoms don't hack it. We should stop kidding ourselves."[15]

Also disturbing is the fact that sores from syphilis and herpes, growths from human papilloma virus (HPV) and other STD infections are frequently contracted in areas of the body not covered by condoms.[16] Talc-based condoms were recently found to pose a serious medical risk for women.

Manufacturers have been known to release defective condoms, and the mishandling of condoms can render them worthless. A publication of the Department of Health and Human Services titled *Condoms and Sexually Transmitted Diseases—Especially AIDS* warns that condoms should not be "kept in a wallet or stored in a purse for more than two hours"; "never stored in a glove compartment"; used only with a "water-based lubricant." Users are told not to buy condoms from "vending machines that are exposed to extreme temperatures" and not to use them while "under the influence of drugs or alcohol." How many adults, not to mention teenagers, are even aware of, let alone follow, these instructions?

Nevertheless, the CDC is pushing "condom relief" as the national strategy for fighting AIDS. In the homosexual community, the CDC has funded through Project Fire "home-health parties" or "health seminars" (or safer-sex Tupperware parties, according to one health official's depiction), and enlisted transvestite performers to include safer-sex themes in their stage acts.

Curiously enough, the CDC, which manages President Clinton's new get-tough AIDS policy, is offering other kinds of support to the homosexual community as well. The CDC has funded the publication of a booklet entitled "Alone No More," which encourages high school teachers to introduce positive learning opportunities about homosexuality. The CDC has even gone so far as to simply foster homosexual social events in the name of AIDS prevention. The "Great Ball of Fire" gala and the fashion show held in April 1996 in Newark, New Jersey, was touted as the social event of the year by the area's minority homosexual and transvestite community.

No risk reduction study, apparently, has been done to evaluate the CDC's work with this homosexual community. In 1988, the federal government abruptly dropped a $2.6 million safer-sex study at UCLA because condoms were said to be "incapable of providing protection" for the gay male participants.[17] If the CDC-funded projects have not been reviewed, how does anyone know if they are reducing the spread of AIDS?

Yet, the administrator in the Division of STD Prevention at the CDC who handled the original grant for Project Fire has had nothing but praise for the project. When questioned about his decision to fund the program, he told a reporter for the *Trentonian*, April 5, 1994, that the CDC was looking for model "innovative outreach programs" like Project Fire to fight the AIDS pandemic.

The Adolescent Family Life Act

While massive federal support has been allocated for "condom relief" and other kinds of birth control, what funds have been earmarked for abstinence-based education? Abstinence is, of course, the only 100 percent safe way of avoiding AIDS, other STDs, and unwanted pregnancy.

Federal support for abstinence-based education was born in 1981 when Congress passed the Adolescent Family Life Act (AFLA). Before that, the focus of the federal government was exclusively on providing teens with contraceptive services. The statute is unique in that it recognizes the family as the cornerstone of the solution and provides funding for developing values-based approaches to family-life education.

AFLA is the only federal program to subsidize the development of educational materials that seek to take young people beyond the rhetoric of the sexual revolution to a closer understanding of genuinely loving human relationships, and to inculcate the skills and values that encourage self-discipline, strong character, and the will to avoid harmful risk-taking behaviors such as adolescent premarital sexual activity.

Former Senator Jeremiah Denton (R-Ala.), the famous POW who authored the legislation, sought to create an alternative to Title X, the "family planning" statute passed in 1970. Title X provides contraceptive services through roughly five thousand clinics to over 4 million women annually—over one-third of whom are adolescents—but prohibits informing parents if their children receive contraceptives.

Rather than foster conflict between parents and children, AFLA seeks to involve the family in finding a solution to the problem. The statute states:

> Prevention of adolescent sexual activity and adolescent pregnancy depends primarily upon developing strong family values and family ties, and since the family is the basic social unit in which the values and attitudes of adolescents concerning sexuality and pregnancy are formed, programs designed to deal with issues of sexuality and pregnancy will be successful to the extent that such programs encourage and sustain the role of the family in dealing with adolescent sexual activity and adolescent pregnancy.

Eunice Kennedy Shriver, one of AFLA's original proponents, explained during a Senate Labor and Human Resources hearing on AFLA, "To do something helpful about teenage sex and pregnancy, we do not need more money for the mechanics of birth control or more value-free sex education. We need efforts that strengthen family commitment and marriage and get at the problems that lead adolescents into early sexual activity."

From its inception, the statute has received very little support compared with spending levels under Title X. In 1982, for example, the Democratic Congress allocated $11 million to AFLA, while appropriating $124 million for Title X. In 1995, the Republican Congress appropriated $6 million for AFLA, with only one-third allotted for education, but appropriated $193 million for "family planning services" under Title X—over thirty-two times more. The Welfare Reform Act recently signed by President Clinton originally contained a provision to increase federal spending for AFLA to $75 million in 1997; this provision was removed by the Senate. In a last minute House and Senate conference before summer recess, conferees allocated $50 million for abstinence. But the use of the money is unspecified and many worry it will not be used to support real abstinence-based programs.

Despite the scarcity of federal dollars, AFLA has provided seed money to approximately seventy abstinence-based demonstration projects across the country. "Postponing Sexual Involvement," a peer-taught abstinence program developed at Emory University in Atlanta was one of the first programs funded. The study group consisted of eighth graders from the inner city.

A Public Health Service report titled "Adolescent Family Life Program: Highlights from Prevention Projects" showed nonprogram students were five times more likely to begin sexual activity during the school year than were students in the program. When Emory University asked nearly 2,000 sexually active girls what they would most like to learn in an effort to reduce teen pregnancy, 85 percent replied, "How to say 'no' without hurting the other person's feelings."[18]

San Marcos, a bedroom suburb of San Diego, in 1983-1984 had one of the highest teen pregnancy rates in Southern California. Two years after implementing "Sexuality, Commitment and Family," an abstinence program developed by Teen-Aid of Spokane, Washington, reported teen pregnancies fell from 147 to 20.[19]

Hoyleton Youth and Family Services in East St. Louis, Illinois, developed a comprehensive abstinence-based intervention program that incorporated a curriculum titled "Sex Respect," with peer mentoring, class tutoring, and career planning support. The program was introduced into the fourth through fifth grades in four schools, which all fed into the same junior high school. Prior to the courses each elementary school was experiencing two to three pregnancies a year. After installing the classes, the pregnancy rate dropped to zero. When one of the schools dropped out of the program, its pregnancy rate returned to two to three pregnancies per year.[20]

"Project Sister," an abstinence program developed by the University of California at San Diego, reports that not only are the girls in the program postponing sex but they are also less inclined to cut class and use drugs, and feel more satisfied with themselves than those in the control group.[21]

Other successful abstinence programs like "Best Friends," in Washington, D.C., and "Excel" in Conway, Arkansas, were developed without government support.

While there is dispute over some projects' results, evidence of AFLA's potential for reducing pregnancy and STDs is encouraging. Why then has it not received more support? The answer appears to be that AFLA has been targeted by "family planning" advocates who see it as a threat to their social agenda of promoting almost complete personal "freedom" in matters of sexuality.

Attack on AFLA

Ridiculed as the teen "chastity bill," a title fit for the headlines if not the statute, AFLA was immediately dragged into court. In 1983, the American Civil Liberties

Union (ACLU) filed a suit charging that AFLA "on its face" violated the separation of church and state because, among other things, its promotion of abstinence amounted to an unconstitutional advancement of certain "religious" views. According to former Deputy Assistant Secretary for Population Affairs Nabers Cabaniss, the lawsuit was aimed at excluding all but a contraceptive, abortion-oriented approach as the answer to our teen sexuality problem.

Four years later, Judge Charles Richey ruled in favor of the ACLU. He stated in his opinion that AFLA was unconstitutional because the "statutory scheme is fraught with the possibility that religious beliefs might infuse instruction and never be detected by the impressionable and unlearned adolescent to whom the instruction is directed. This possibility alone amounts to an impermissible advancement of religion."[22]

When the U.S. government appealed the case to the Supreme Court, the Court, in *Bowen v. Kendrick* (1988), upheld the constitutionality of AFLA, ruling that the statute did not have the primary effect of advancing religion. However, the court did not address the constitutionality of the statute as applied—that is, whether the program had been administered in an unconstitutional manner. Once the case was returned to district court, ACLU attorneys ransacked HHS files, calendars, computer disks, and phone logs searching for religious references and interrogated staff about the management of the program. Any grant recipient who was thought to have a pro-life orientation was investigated.

Senator Ted Kennedy twice tried, unsuccessfully, to kill AFLA in the 101st Congress by introducing S.110 and S.120. S.110 would have folded AFLA into an expanded Title X birth control program and ended its inclusion of adoption as an alternative to abortion. S.120 would have turned AFLA on its head, eliminating all requirements for parental consent in promoting, counseling, or referring teens for abortion. Ironically, he seems to have run into his sister Eunice Shriver, a strong AFLA supporter.

In 1991, AFLA was threatened when, during debate on an appropriations bill, Representative Pat Schroeder (D-Colo.) successfully eliminated its minuscule appropriation. A few months later, two amendments were adopted in the Senate that restored the funding. Senator Slade Gordon (R-Wash.) sponsored an amendment to reinstate AFLA language that had been struck out of the House bill, and Senator Jesses Helms (R-N.C.) subsequently offered another amendment to transfer $10 million from the National Institute for Child Health and Human Development (NICHD), which was going to be used to conduct a youth sex survey, to AFLA.

Again, in 1994, AFLA was on the chopping block. This time, the Clinton administration without forewarning moved to abolish its funding. The deposed Surgeon General Joycelyn Elders wanted the $7 million designated for AFLA to finance a new Office of Adolescent Health. Government support for abstinence-based sexuality education would have ended with one stroke. The maneuver almost succeeded, until the *Washington Times* broke the story and there was a public outcry to save the tiny program.

Although efforts to rescue AFLA have been effective so far, it is still politically vulnerable. Congress has not reauthorized it since 1985. All this time, however, the most significant attempts to throttle abstinence-based sexuality education were occurring on the local front.

Planned Parenthood's Sex-Ed Storm Front

Jacksonville, Florida, was thrust into the eye of the storm over sex education when Planned Parenthood of Northeast Florida and several parents sued the Duval County Public School District for introducing an abstinence curriculum in the seventh grade. With this suit, the rant over sex education in public schools entered a new phase. At issue was the question: *Who* decides what is taught in the classroom? The duly elected school board, or an outside group with a vested interest in the outcome?

Former Duval County School Board Chairman Stan Jordan was clear that this was the issue: "Planned Parenthood wanted to force its agenda on us and end abstinence-based education throughout the country," he said. Certainly, any time an organization with Planned Parenthood's size and power challenges the decision of a local school board, notable issues are likely to be involved, but the suit has never been thoroughly scrutinized by the press.

Me, My World, My Future, produced by Teen-Aid of Spokane, Washington, had been installed in Duval County in 1990 to comply with Florida statutes that set abstinence as the "expected standard" to be taught in public schools. Steve Rohan, attorney for the school board, said that Planned Parenthood's counsel "indicated very clearly that it would drop the lawsuit, if the school adopted a new K-12 sex education program that included discussion of birth control and safe sex."[23]

Although the eighteen-hour abstinence curriculum provided instruction in such areas as the physical changes of adolescence, fetal development, valuing self, the family unit, friendship and dating, decision making, and communication skills, Teen-Aid's program did not include enough information to satisfy Planned Parenthood. The school district was accused of "censorship in the classroom," for, among other things, not exploring such topics as "abortion, homosexuality, and masturbation," according to the complaint. Allegedly, the school district violated the childrens' right to privacy by "impos[ing] a single viewpoint upon students pertaining to their sexual practices and reproductive decisions, and interfer[ing] with the fundamental right of all public school students to make personal, intimate and private decisions with respect to the autonomy of their bodies."

One of the plaintiffs in the case was asked by a school board lawyer, "What do you think regarding human reproduction should be taught in kindergarten?" The plaintiff is quoted in a deposition as saying, "you need actual instruction on copulation, that type of thing."

Planned Parenthood et al. are in effect arguing that experiencing the joy of sex is a child's right—that children have a right to value-free sex education and a right to express themselves sexually in any way that they choose. Such views lead to the corollary that the family can be bypassed in modern times. When the attempts at social engineering fail, who will accept responsibility for the consequences? The lawsuit presented a deep-seated challenge to parental authority. The legal precedents regarding a minor's right to privacy raise serious questions about the long-standing principle that parents, subject to certain interests of the state, are free to decide how their children shall be educated.

It should be remembered that Planned Parenthood has led the way in establishing minors' rights. In *Carey v. Population Services International* (1977), for example, the Supreme Court ruled a New York law banning the sale of contraceptives to minors was unconstitutional. Today, Planned Parenthood can provide abortions in most states, and in every state, Norplant implants and other contraceptives can be dispensed without parental notification.

Perhaps one reason Planned Parenthood chose to challenge the Duval County School District is its large size. With 123,000 students, it is the fifteenth largest school district in the nation and the biggest in the country to use Teen-Aid's curriculum. By filing this lawsuit and another in Hemet, California, providing legal support for a suit in Shreveport, Louisiana, and threatening legal action in other states, Planned Parenthood in effect has put all public schools on notice that the same fate awaits them. (Similar suits have been threatened in other states.) The small companies that develop abstinence curricula are being financially crippled as a result. School administrators cannot afford to put their schools in legal jeopardy, or purchase educational materials they may not be able to use.

For Planned Parenthood, however, sex is big business. In its 1993-1994 annual report, which covered an eighteen-month period, Planned Parenthood reported a $28 million profit. It provided contraceptive services to more than 1.9 million people. Yet, the "retention rate" of those served was only 57 percent. In other words, Planned Parenthood lost 43 percent of its birth control customers from the previous year, suggesting it found around 820,000 new people to reach with its $693.7 million income for that period. (Comparable figures have been dropped from its most recent report.) Over one-third of its money came from federal, state, and local governments—$30 million from Title X alone.

Where did the new clients come from? According to Jim Sedlak of STOPP International, a Planned Parenthood watch group, "[s]ixty-three percent of its patrons are under the age of twenty-five; 25.5 percent are under the age of 20."

At its crassest, Planned Parenthood's approach to sex education enlarges the market for the very services it provides. Does Planned Parenthood have any incentive to support an approach to sex education that reduces teenage sexual activity? Apparently, it does not.

Planned Parenthood has branded abstinence-based education the product of a radical fringe movement that uses fear and shame to dissuade young people from having sex. Their claim is that these curricula are laden with biases and inaccuracies and attempt to impose a "narrow ideology which is anti-choice, anti-contraception, and anti-premarital sex." An information flyer titled "Real Life" claims these courses have been adopted because the public has been flimflammed:

Right-wing entrepreneurs using "sophisticated marketing techniques prey upon parents' real fears and concerns" in order to sell the curricula.

These objections revolve around questions of sexual politics. It is not that abstinence-based education has not worked, but that it has never really been tried. Recently, Planned Parenthood dropped its suit in Jacksonville when the school board moved to adopt a new curriculum—despite an independent study that suggested there had been a significant reduction in pregnancy among teenage girls.

The lawsuit in Duval County, Florida, represents a strategic move to gain monopoly access to the nation's public schools. Each state and school district has its own specific guidelines for sex education. However, the pressures exerted though the CDC, Planned Parenthood, and other like-minded groups will make it very difficult for any school district to escape teaching comprehensive sex education.

Conclusion

Twenty years ago, in a prophetic essay titled "Sex in the Year 2000," David Mace, a professor and founding member of SIECUS, imagined America becoming a sexual utopia.[24] By the turn of the century, a liberal sexual ideology would be universally practiced. He envisioned a brave new world of cradle-to-grave eros in which kids learned a new morality—one based on freedom from traditional morality. To form a healthy identity, children, Mace said, should learn the "full range of sensual libidinal experiences."

Once exposed to adult sexuality, including "heterosexual and homosexual encounters," adolescents would be fitted to "participate in any kind of sexual" activity, he writes. Marriage as a union between one man and one woman should be extended to include "any group of two or more persons" of either sex.

As a utopian, Mace felt the first step in correcting society's defects required modifying the childrens' thoughts, feelings, and emotions related to sex, placing it at the center of the "New Man's" soul. Freeing them of guilt, shame, and inhibition associated with sex is considered necessary for human well-being. The only problem is that a nation composed of such denizens, each centered on pursuing his or her desires, cannot long remain a civil society.

Little could Mace have known how close to reality his forecast would come, and how devasting the result would be. Mace was right about one thing: How we educate our young in matters pertaining to sexuality and the family will shape the kind of society we inhabit in the twenty-first century. Unfortunately, the federal government appears to have co-opted his vision for the nation.

Notes

1. Margaret L. Usdansky, "Ideas and Trends: Single Motherhood Stereotypes vs. Statistics", *New York Times,* February 11, 1996.

2. The probability that marriage will end in divorce is currently about 43 percent according to Robert Schoen, professor of Population Dynamics at Johns Hopkins University.

3. *Child Mistreatment*, 1994. A publication of the Department of Health and Human Services.

4. "Teen Sex and Pregnancy," July 1996, a fact sheet from the Allan Guttmacher Institute.

5. Linus Wright, "Sex Education: How to Respond," *The World & I*, (Oct. 1989): 505.

6. *San Fransisco Chronicle*, July 15, 1996. A report on the Robinhood Foundation study on "kids having kids."

7. Barbara Nevins, "Sex Ed: A Matter of Life and Death," *Redbook*, (March 1993): 50.

8. Jacqueline Kasun, *The War Against Population* (San Francisco, Ignatius Press, 1989).

9. William Marsiglio and Frank Mott, "The Impact of Sex Education on Sexual Activity, Contraceptive Use and Premarital Pregnancy among American Teenagers," *Family Planning Perspectives* 18, no. 4 (July/August 1986), 151-62. The study's results were published in the form of Logit coefficients that gave the increase in the natural logarithms of the odds ratios for sex activity that occurred when girls received sex education. When these coefficients are exponentiated and applied to the likelihood of engaging in sexual activity at age fifteen and sixteen, the likelihood increased by 40 percent.

10. Ira L. Reiss, *An End to Shame: Shaping Our Next Sexual Revolution* (New York: Prometheus Books, 1990), 50-51.

11. Cliff Kincaid, *"*The Playboy Foundation; A Mirror of the Culture?*"* *Studies in Philanthropy* 13 (Capital Research Center, 1992), 26.

12. Debra Haffner, "Safe Sex and Teens," *SIECUS Report* (September/October 1988).

13. S. C. Weller, "A Meta-analysis of Condom Effectiveness in Reducing Sexually Transmitted HIV," *Social. Science. Medicine.* 36, no. 12, 1635-1644; J. Tussel, D. L. Warner, R. Hatcher et al., "Condom Slippage and Breakage Rates, *Family Planning Perspective* 24, no.1, (Jan./Feb. 1992): 20-23.

14. Theresa Crenshaw's testimony before the Select Committee on Children, Youth, and Families, U.S. House of Representatives, June 18, 1987.

15. R. C. Noble, "The Myth of Safe Sex," *Newsweek*, April 1, 1991.

16. Centers for Disease Control and Prevention, MMWR 1988; 37: 133-134.

17. *The Washington Post*, August 10, 1988.

18. M. Howard and J. B. McCabe, "Helping Teenagers Postpone Sexual Involvement," *Family Planning Perspectives* (Jan./Feb. 1990), 21-26.

19. *The Washington Post*, August 10, 1988.

20. Dinah Richard, "Has Sex Education Failed Our Teenagers?" A Research Report, Focus on the Family Publishing, 1990, 59-60.

21. Patricia Funderburk, "None, Not Safer, Is the Real Answer," *Insight* (May 9, 1994), 25.

22. *Kendrick v. Bowen* 657 F. Supp. 1547 (D.D.C. 1987).

23. Personal interview with the author.

24. Sol Gordon and Roger Libby, *Sexuality Today and Tomorrow* (North Scituate, Mass.: Duxbury Press, 1976), 402. David Mace's essay is one of many on the future of sexuality.

23

Forging a United Front on Family Policy: Premises and Suggestions

William A. Galston

It is my conviction that after a generation of culture wars on family issues among many others, the contending parties are now within hailing distance of some common ground. Many significant differences remain, of course. But intelligent action to implement the points of agreement could help strengthen families across our country.

To make my case, I want to do three things, briefly: First, lay out the premises of my argument about what government can and cannot do to strengthen families; second, outline some policy suggestions that are consistent with those premises; and finally, offer some advice about language and tactics that can foster unity rather than division.

Let me begin on what I think is a note of common ground: Not in every case, but on average, the intact two-parent family is the best arena for raising kids, and it is a form of social organization that also provides important advantages for adults and for the community as a whole. There is every reason to do what is possible and prudent to sustain and to strengthen this institution.

My second point may evoke more disagreement: In my judgment it is neither possible nor desirable for our society as a whole to return to the gender roles and relations characteristic of the 1950s. Some individuals and families may choose to organize themselves in that fashion. But it should not be the deliberate object of public policy to promote that choice to the exclusion of others. And may I add that while the personal is not in any simple sense the political, I for one refuse to recommend, as a matter of public policy, what I could not accept for my own family.

Third, public policy should not create a bias against individuals who wish to make that more traditional choice. In particular, it should not create (as it so frequently does today) a bias against women who chose to invest their energies and work exclusively for an extended period inside the home.

Premise four: While bad public policy has contributed to the weakening of the American family, it is surely not the only force to have done so. Autonomous economic and cultural changes during the past thirty years have had important effects on the family as well. There has been a significant decrease in wages earned by men, particularly less well educated and trained men, and this has had an effect on their eligibility for marriage and their propensity to enter into marriage. There has been a hollowing out of many urban economies that were important centers of manufacturing as late as the 1960s or even the 1970s, a development that has had a devastating effect on the social fabric of our nation's cities. On the cultural front, there have been very significant changes in attitudes toward divorce, out-of-wedlock births, and many other family matters. In short, government is not the root of all evil.

Fifth: Just as public policy is not the sole cause of our problems, it cannot be the full cure. While acting sensibly through government to strengthen families, we should be appropriately modest in our expectations. In all that we undertake we should be guided by the political version of the Hippocratic Oath: "First, do no harm." I take John DiIulio's contribution to this volume to be a welcome and necessary reminder of the implications of that oath.

Premise six: While government can try and in some circumstances should try to lean against dominant cultural trends, it cannot get too far out in front of those trends, whatever we may think of them. This is especially true in a free society that governs itself through responsive democratic institutions.

Seventh, and more hopefully: Social and cultural change is not, as many contemporary pessimists believe and as the previous generation of optimists used to believe, linear or unidirectional. Free societies have (perhaps uniquely have) a capacity for social learning and for course corrections that reflect the hard-won lessons of experience. On my hopeful days, I allow myself to believe that we have now reached such a cultural turning point.

With these seven premises in mind, let me put forward a handful of policy ideas designed to answer one simple question: What could government reasonably do to strengthen American families?[1]

Suggestion One: Create a family-friendly tax code. If we were trying to construct a tax code with the aim of strengthening families, we could hardly do a worse job than what we have now. We need to increase the dependent deduction, the real value of which has been allowed to erode by 75 percent in the past two generations, or perhaps replace it with a generous tax credit, which I would make refundable. We need to reduce the marriage penalty in our tax code, which has risen to scandalous heights. We need to structure the earned income tax credit in a manner that is more sensitive to family size and stability. We should use the tax code aggressively to support adoption. We also ought to consider such measures as education and training credits for parents who choose to leave the paid work force for extended periods to care for their children.

Suggestion Two: Implement pro-family, responsibility-based welfare reform. A long, acrimonious debate at the national level about welfare reform has entered a new phase with congressional passage and presidential signature of a bill in the summer of 1996. Now it is the turn of the states to make wise use of the new opportunities this act provides. I hope we can come together across ideological lines on some approaches that make sense. Can we agree that there ought to be paternity establishment, in the hospital, for every child? Can we agree that there ought to be incentives for ongoing paternal involvement in the well-being and upbringing of their kids? Can we believe that in those cases, which unfortunately are much too numerous, where biological parents do not contribute to the economic maintenance of their kids, that the government ought to play a stronger role in holding those individuals to their responsibilities? Can we agree that while it would have been a mistake for the federal government to mandate such steps as family caps, some states should experiment with such measures and carefully monitor the results?

Suggestion Three: Initiate debates on divorce law reform. There is no federal law of marriage and divorce, but there are flawed laws of marriage and divorce in the fifty states that need to be rethought from the ground up. A number of changes would represent improvements over the status quo. Without going into details, let me say that there are three critical objectives for states to keep in mind as they enter the debate about divorce law reform: First, to reduce the number of divorces, particularly those involving minor children; second, when divorce is not avoidable through the reasonable instrumentalities of the law, to work to mitigate the effects of divorce on minor children (recent research has given us new insights into how to do that); and third, to change the law of settlement and of alimony, to restore fairness for those hundreds of thousands of women and perhaps even millions of women who invested twenty, twenty-five, thirty years in a marriage, only to be left with almost nothing when their husbands decided enough was enough, that it was time for a trophy wife.[2]

Suggestion Four: Get serious about teen pregnancy reduction. While there are limits to what government can do in this area, it can do more than is now being done. When I arrived at the White House in 1993, I was shocked to discover that there was nothing like a national inventory of programs that had been devised by community-based organizations and tried at the local level and that there were few solid studies evaluating the effectiveness of these programs. At the very least, government can create (or help the voluntary sector create) an information clearinghouse; it can disseminate information about programs that work; it can provide modest funding for schools and community-based organizations to adopt and select from the range of programs that work. Government can also provide moral support (as President Clinton has done) for voluntary sector activities such as the recently created National Campaign to Prevent Teen Pregnancy.

Suggestion Five: Regulate television. As a parent, I agree with Michael Medved's point that the medium itself and not just the message is an important part of the problem. Nonetheless, these are distinguishable problems; we ought to be able to work on the message, even as we are struggling to reduce the use of the medium. It is possible, and in my judgment desirable, for government to enforce the already enacted Children's Television Act. It is possible (and likewise desirable) for government (within appropriate constitutional limits) to get serious about family-friendly programming during prime time, which has been allowed to degenerate into a national disgrace. And in my judgment, the V-chip represents an enhancement of parental control and choice rather than an illegitimate extension of government power.

Suggestion Six: Use government wisely to strengthen civil society. For example, I believe (and I'm not the only Democrat who believes) that we should experiment with tax credits for community-based organizations that address the needs of poor families. I do not agree that this is the civil society version of industrial policy, where the government ends up picking winners and losers. A step-by-step approach would allow us to learn from experience while redressing unanticipated consequences.

Suggestion Seven: Strike a better balance between work and family. It is time to get serious about laws and regulations that stimulate telecommuting, flex-time, job-sharing, home-based small business formation, and other trends that can help relax the tension between work and family that is central to daily life for tens of millions of adults and parents in our society.

Let me close with a plea: That all of us work conscientiously to forge the broadest and most inclusive pro-family coalition that is possible in this country. We should focus on what unites us, not on what divides us. (I speak as a Democrat who has waged a long and sometimes lonely war within my own party for the principles and ideas that I've laid out in this essay and whose party has moved significantly in this direction during the past decade.)

When I say that we should focus on what unites us rather than what divides us, I mean, first, that it is not useful and arguably not true to claim that morality is impossible without religion. That is certainly not what my own religion, Judaism, teaches. All sorts of people, including atheists, can be responsible parents and good citizens. There are ample secular grounds for individuals, regardless of their faith commitments, to acknowledge these obligations. A broad, inclusive pro-family coalition cannot be built on narrow sectarian premises.

I mean, second, that it is not useful for leading members of the two political parties to employ the rhetoric of family policy to attack one another. We need less ideological thinking and more openness to evidence. We need less public speech actuated by the quest for power and more public speech guided by the search for usable public truth for a democratic society.

Let me offer an example of what I am talking about. At the conference at which this essay was presented, I found a background paper produced by the Heritage Foundation, entitled "Why Religion Matters: The Impact of Religious Practice on Social Stability." It is a masterly marshaling of the social science evidence bearing on that point and tending toward the conclusion announced in the title. The Heritage Foundation is not a conspicuous supporter of liberalism or of the Democratic Party or of the current administration, but the first sentence of the essay in question runs as follows: "By extolling freedom of religion in the schools President Bill Clinton has raised the level of debate on the importance of religion to American life." In so writing, its author, Patrick Fagan, has given us a model of how civil discourse in this country can and should be conducted.

Notes

1. For a fuller discussion of many of these points, see Elaine Ciulla Kamarck and William A. Galston, "A Progressive Family Policy for the 1990s," in *Mandate for Change,* Will Marshall and Martin Schram, eds., (New York: Berkley Books, 1992).

2. For my full thoughts on this subject, see "Divorce American Style," *The Public Interest* 124 (Summer 1996): 12-26.

24

A Conservative Perspective
on Public Policy and the Family

William Kristol

Many of the contributors to this volume are academics who have had time to do serious thought and research and writing. I was once an academic, and I did a little bit of serious thought and reading and writing, and wrote a few articles for scholarly journals. Then I went into government, my attention span shrunk, and I could no longer write forty-page articles—I could only write three-page memos. Then I left government and now I edit a magazine and I don't write much of anything—I just write headlines for other people's articles. Occasionally I am on TV and, as you know, when you are on TV you never say anything for longer than thirty seconds—so I guess I should keep these remarks short.

My credentials for being part of this lineup are somewhat dubious. My real intervention, I suppose, while I was in government, regarding issues of family and family policy was Dan Quayle's Murphy Brown speech, which I helped the Vice President with a little bit. I remember, to show you how brilliant I was about such matters, something that happened on the plane out to San Francisco in May of '92 when he was going to give the speech, which no one remembers anymore—it was actually quite a long, thoughtful speech about the LA riots and family breakup as part of the reason why something like the LA riots happened. He had this one paragraph to make clear he wasn't blaming poor inner-city women and recognized that this was a broader cultural problem, the problem of illegitimacy. And so, to try and make this point, he seized upon this Murphy Brown episode that had been much in the news—about the baby she was going to have on the TV show. So I remember we were chatting about the speech and he was looking at this paragraph one last time and he said to me "this could be misinterpreted; do you think I should leave this in the speech?" And I cheerfully said, "Oh, don't worry, Mr. Vice President, no one will pay any attention to it." One of many brilliant pieces of political advice I've given in my time. . . .

Let me give you my sense of where I think we are in this debate on family issues and civil society and the State. I'll begin by simply asserting, since we don't have time to argue, that I do think we are in a new political—and for that matter sociological, cultural, and ideological—era, and that the '94 elections really were important elections. November 1994 was important because it was the end of six decades of the Democratic party being the majority party in this country. It had been dominant for all those six decades, and even though it faltered in the last twenty years or so at the presidential level, it controlled most governorships and most state legislative chambers. That really did end in November '94. We don't know what the new era is going to be like—but I think the old era is over and we are not going to go back to it. Bill Clinton acknowledged this in January of '96 in his State of Union Address when he said "the era of Big Government is over." I'm not sure he quite meant it, but he nonetheless acknowledged it. To the degree that Bill Clinton has been hypocritical and has sounded awfully conservative over the last year or so, we just should remember that hypocrisy is the tribute that vice pays to virtue. Clinton's conservatism is the tribute that liberalism has to pay to conservatism in this contemporary era.

I think that's important. It's important for this reason: The political collapse of the Democratic Party in '94 really mirrored a deeper intellectual collapse, of liberalism, of progressivism, of the whole set of ideas that animated the New Deal and the Great Society, ideas that really dominated American politics, American intellectual life, American culture for a long, long time. I do think that liberal, progressive era—that era of governmentalism, as it has been called—is over. It's over for a whole bunch of complicated reasons, including the fact that the evidence is in, in certain respects, on how some of these ideas work—both the social science evidence and the evidence in people's personal lives. It's not so clear that all the liberationist movements in the sixties—movements designed to produce an ever more progressive, ever more secular, ever more liberated society—produced happier human beings. I think confidence in those movements is not nearly as strong, let's say, as it might have been thirty or forty or fifty years ago even among the elites, let alone among normal people out there. For whatever reasons, I do think this era is over and it was visible that it was ending before November '94.

I have always thought that Hillary Clinton's speech—ironically enough, since she's considered a great champion of liberalism—her speech at the University of Texas in April '93, where she proclaimed famously that we were in a "crisis of meaning" and we needed a new "politics of meaning," was very revealing. I mean, here you have a Democratic administration, a liberal administration back in power after this twelve-year Reagan/Bush Republican "nightmare," with a Democratic Congress, with liberal control basically of most of the major institutions of society—the key cultural, educational, and media institutions of the society—and you would have thought liberalism would have been confident, bold, energized, and ready to go to work to do all the important things that had been put on the back burner by all those Reagan/Bush types. Instead, to her credit in a way, Mrs. Clinton stood up and said, not sounding confident and bold, that we are in a crisis of meaning, that we need a new politics of meaning, etc., etc. That was a sign that liberalism, whatever its institutional supports, whatever its inertial force in our society, was exhausted—however much it can hang on, especially in institutions like universities, where there's tenure so the turnover lags by a generation or two. (It is ironic that the universities are regarded as progressive institutions, when they are, by definition, the most retrograde institutions, because they embody ideas that were fashionable and strong twenty or thirty or forty years ago, when the majority of the people in them were educated and were formed. And this was true in the thirties, of course, when the universities were considered great bastions of conservatism against Roosevelt in the New Deal.)

In any case, I do think that "crisis of meaning" speech was an acknowledgment that the liberal era, the long era which goes back to '32, or in a certain sense back to 1912, the progressive era, was over. That is good news and bad news for those of us who think that the last twenty or thirty years did a lot of damage to the country. The good news is that it is an opportunity, and the political side of that opportunity came to light in November of '94. The bad news is that it is tougher to govern than it is simply to oppose bad government by the other guys who are trying to do foolish things. It is harder to play offense, if you want to put it this way, than defense. It is harder to reconstruct or to construct new institutions of civil society, sound institutions, than to simply defend them against assaults. It's harder rhetorically, it's harder practically, and I do think the Republican majority in the beginning of January '95 probably hadn't thought through how difficult it is to lay out an agenda and win popular support for a new governing agenda—how to put together a new governing coalition and hold it together and lead public opinion along. That's a lot different from sort of manning the ramparts against the Clinton Health Care Plan, let's say, where in a sense inertia is on your side, where you are defending what people already have and where you simply have to alarm people about this latest and ridiculous effort by the Left to take over yet another chunk of American society or the American economy.

I think the good news is that there really is an opportunity for people who want to strengthen the family now to strengthen the family—not simply to slow down the weakening of the family. I do think that requires, though, a change in the way lots of us think. We all grew up fighting a defensive fight, a very important defensive fight for ten, twenty, thirty years, and now an offensive strategy is required. That's a great opportunity, and also much trickier and more complicated.

I think the family is the center of the battles in American politics today. And let me briefly say why, using Charles Murray's famous October 1993 *Wall Street Journal* article "The Coming White Underclass," as my text to illustrate two or three points that I think can't be glossed over in the coming debates about how to strengthen the family and how to strengthen the institutions of civil society. I'm assuming basically that the liberal faith in governmentalism, in progressivism, is done and that whatever the difficulty in unraveling or cutting through the Gordian knot that has been created, the task for most of us, at least, is to figure out where to go from here—not simply to beat back the last efforts of an old order.

Murray argues in this important article what I think most people would agree with: So many of the problems of America today—crime, illiteracy, welfare, drugs, poverty—stem from one core problem, which is illegitimacy, which is another way of saying the collapse of the family in the most fundamental sense—children being born outside of wedlock. Illegitimacy, Murray says, is the single most important social problem of our time. I think that is true, and that is why all efforts to steer political debate away from family matters, because they are sensitive and often divisive, don't work. You have efforts in both parties to run away from what are called the values issues or the family issues and it is kind of comical to watch after awhile. You have all these political leaders earnestly getting together and in effect agreeing among themselves that they are going to put these issues on the back burner—and then these issues just pop up because they are in fact central to all the problems, not just to the family problems, but really to all the obvious problems of our society—education, crime, drugs, poverty, you name it. Those issues aren't going to go away and the question is: Can they be dealt with responsibly and seriously or will they simply be allowed to fester or will they be dealt with irresponsibly and foolishly?

Murray's argument is first, as Bill Galston said—and here he goes a fair way down the road with Bill Galston—"do no harm." Government does some harm now. The tax code is not friendly to families, the current welfare system isn't friendly to those families that get sucked into the morass of welfare. It's not friendly to the creation of new families by those who grow up on welfare. There is, I think, an increasing—I don't want to say an increasing consensus, but I would say that the debate has moved considerably, really radically in the last three, four, five years toward an appreciation of the extent to which it is legitimate to ask what effect tax policy, welfare policy, education policy have on the family. And those who would put the family first in judging those policies increasingly have the upper hand.

Again, it is harder to make the changes happen than to win debates about what kind of changes should happen, because of the institutional power and the inertial force of lots of large institutions in our society and lots of people who depend on current programs. But still, I think, over the long run, that we're going to see the federal level and the state levels of government move in the direction of the agenda that Bill Galston basically laid out. And Murray has all kinds of ideas about how to do this and Galston has lots of ideas about how to do this and so do people at the Heritage Foundation: There are all kinds of interesting and important policy debates about how to reform welfare, and how to fix the tax code, and how quickly one could move toward parental choice in education—and those are all very important issues.

What strikes me about Murray's article, and the reason I bring it up here, is that at the very end of this piece, in the *Wall Street Journal*, Murray says that these policies by themselves won't do it. He calls for a "more abstract and crucial step . . . to make marriage once again the sole legal institution through which parental rights and responsibilities are defined and exercised. Indeed, a marriage certificate should establish that a man and a women have entered into a unique legal relationship. The changes that have blurred the distinctiveness of marriage are subtly but importantly destructive." That's really a striking statement. And it strikes me as revealing that Charles Murray—who is a very hard-headed policy analyst—after going through welfare reform, tax reform, and the like, comes to this much more abstract issue, which is the status of marriage: The question of whether it can be made again the sole legal institution through which parental rights and responsibilities are exercised, whether it can become again a unique legal relationship, whether the changes that have blurred the distinctiveness of marriage are subtly but importantly destructive.

I think he's right. I think that is the heart of the really serious and deep pro-family agenda over the next, not just years, but decades. I think that these issues are intrinsically more divisive than some of the unifying sorts of proposals that Bill Galston talked about that don't have to be discussed in a divisive way. They are intrinsically more divisive, because they are so much more sensitive. And let me just mention three fundamental issues that ultimately will have to be faced if we are serious about strengthening the family. Murray alludes to these if you look at his article. These are three of the great revolutions of our time, which ultimately have to be confronted in the field of ideas, in the field of civil society, but also ultimately in politics. They all have implications for public policy and for law, certainly for the courts. You can't simply relegate them to the fights in our culture or the fights in our intellectual journals.

The Sexual Revolution

The first is the sexual revolution. Murray explicitly says that public policy should, in a sense, lean against the sexual revolution, which it certainly does not now. If you want to strengthen the family you need to confront issues like abortion. This means confronting the role of the courts, in particular, in legitimating a whole understanding of human life and sexuality that fundamentally undercuts any attempt to make the family distinctive and unique. When you have the theology of *Roe v. Wade*—and I think theology is the right word—as the theology of the highest court in the land, it is very hard, it seems to me, to be serious about what fatherhood is. For example, under *Roe*, fathers have nothing to say about what happens to the unborn child that they conceived. It's very hard, it seems to me, to marry that with any serious attempt to strengthen the institution of fatherhood. Indeed, it's very hard to really be serious about policies that improve the lot of children, when you have 1.5 million abortions a year in the United States. Not that we shouldn't do all kinds of things to help to strengthen fatherhood and to help children while abortion remains legal and while there remain a lot of them in this country, both of which unfortunately will probably be for quite awhile. But still I think at some point that issue can't be ducked or avoided.

Feminism

The second revolution, which in a way is even deeper I think, is the feminist revolution. Feminism is maybe the most powerful political and social movement of our time. You know, families consist of men and women, fathers or mothers, and despite all the efforts of modern political correctness at denying the distinction between the sexes, they exist, and we should be honest about some of their implications for public policy. It's got to become not politically incorrect and not political suicide to at least raise the issue, for example as Bill Tucker did in a recent issue of the *Weekly Standard*, following along the lines of Allan Carlson and others, arguing for a possible family wage. Are we so committed to equal pay for equal work, regardless of people's marital status, family status and the like, that we are willing, in effect, to force women into the workforce and destroy what was once a more or less informal system where preference was given to those who were heads of households and whom families depended on, which in turn allowed the other spouse—it's politically incorrect to say it, but in practice it is the wife or the mother—to stay home and not be pushed into the workforce? I think this becomes a real issue also in welfare policy—Marvin Olasky alluded to this. There's a tension between the conservative push to workfare and the conservative attempt to strengthen the family, and this has caused, of course, very interesting and I think useful debates among conservatives. But again, I don't think that issue can be blinked away. It doesn't have to be confronted right away. That is, there are lots of useful reforms that don't require a verdict on feminism, and here I do want to emphasize that I agree with Bill Galston in some respects. There are lots of useful reforms that we could make in our tax codes and to our welfare system without necessarily engaging in a huge national debate about feminism or about the relation of the sexes. I mean, there are lots of things that would help peoples' lives in the near term. But over the long run we will run up, and sooner rather than later we will run up, against these more fundamental questions.

The Secular Revolution

The third great revolution of modern times, the deepest one—and Bill Galston alluded to it—is, of course, the secular revolution. Again, this is not primarily a matter of public policy, though it has public policy implications, especially, again, with the courts. Now there are moral atheists and there are immoral believers, God knows, and there have been through all of human history. On the other hand, it is hard to believe that ultimately you are going to strengthen the family without having it, for most of the society, somehow or other grounded in religious belief. The status of religious belief in the society is not primarily driven by public policy decisions, I think, but it's not unaffected by all kinds of public policies ranging from vouchers for parents, making it easier for parents to send their kids to religious schools, to court decisions that draw a line of separation between church and state, to executive orders like the one Bill Galston mentioned that President Clinton issued making public schools friendlier to students exercising the right to assemble on behalf of their religious beliefs—treating religious activities at least as on a par with secular activities in the public schools.

So I do think all these fundamental issues—while one wants to, in a sense, avoid them because they are terribly divisive and they are awfully big issues, and I spend a fair amount of my time avoiding them here in Washington, and certainly spent a lot of time in government avoiding them and focusing on what's more doable over the short term—they are key. I think sooner rather than later one comes up against these big issues and maybe the best one can hope for now is at least to legitimize the debate and the discussion of these big issues and to make it not politically incorrect or suicidal to raise questions about these big issues.

I'll close with this thought. What's most striking to me, when you really step back and look at the last ten, twenty years, is that politics matters. I think ultimately you need to make the political changes. I don't think you can just have some social-cultural revolution and leave politics aside as some of my friends are sometimes inclined to think when they get very disgusted with political action. But really, when you step back and look at it, the religious revival in the country, the efforts of people in civil society, if I can use that term, to change their own lot—it's really been remarkable, without much encouragement at all from the public sphere or from politics or government; when you look at home-schooling, when you look at the growth of all these enterprises—with either the hostility of government or at least without much encouragement from government—the extent to which citizens have taken back control of their lives, and in a sense tried to strengthen their own families and their own parts of civil society, I think historians will find this one of the most remarkable aspects of the last part of this century.

I'll use a funny analogy perhaps from economics. I mean you could make the same case, incidentally, in business, right? Government has kind of meandered along in the last fifteen years doing maybe a little less harm than it used to do to the economy. But the whole huge economic transformation hasn't been due to government—it's happened due to free markets and government has not messed them up as much as it might have. In any case, the model I have for this kind of transformation in civil society is what I sometimes call the Federal Express model. And let me just close with this because I think it makes a point.

I remember when I was a young conservative, there was a lot of talk about how we had to get rid of the Post Office. This was a big issue for some reason—I don't know quite why exactly—but you know in young conservative conferences around 1971, it was the symbol of stupid and inefficient big Government, this one million member unionized thing that couldn't deliver mail on time and all that. And conservatives fought against the Post Office and bills were introduced to allow for competition and there were long important articles about "How the Post Office Doesn't Work Well."

Now what, in fact, happened in that sphere of life? What happened is this: Fred Smith founded Federal Express. There was an attempt by the Post Office and by the public sector to crush Federal Express at the beginning, so politics was important. There was a big fight in Congress in '74-'75-'76, and basically—though there was no political support for disestablishing, or fundamentally changing the Post Office—there was enough political support to protect this effort by entrepreneurs from the attempt by the unions and the government employees to make it illegal. Then technology kicked in with the fax machines and computers, and now twenty years later the Post Office is not a big problem in America. It's improved somewhat because of competition from the private sector, though it's still undoubtedly a waste of money and it could be much more efficient. But basically you've had this social transformation in the way we communicate with one another or the way in which we deliver messages to one another, and it's happened outside of government. And ultimately, in fact, it put pressure on government to improve the way it works; and over the long run the forces of Federal Express and the fax machine and now the computers are going to beat the Post Office.

I do think that is the model for social transformation in this country. Political efforts are most important right now to protect the efforts in civil society to revive the institutions of civil society and the family. Over the short and medium term, the most striking thing in the last twenty years and probably the next twenty years is the extent to which you have a sort of Federal Express model prevailing throughout the economy and throughout civil society. What one does in politics is at least to protect these efforts of citizens and families from government. Over the long run, though, one does need to change the government and change public policies to make them not only not threatening to decent families and decent family life, but to make them actually supportive of the efforts of citizens to strengthen families.

Index

economic issues of, 4, 40; education and, 43-45, 222, 224, 232-35; effect of employment on, 221, 262; Ehrenreich's views on, 27-28; erosion of, xi, 11, 17-20, 219-24; father's role in, xii, 79-86; feminism and, xi-xii, 52-55, 63; future of, 51; gender-structured, 58-61; history of, xi, 3-4, 39-48; individual rights and, 27; intergenerational bonds, 40-41, 46-48; land ownership, 40; liberalism and, xii; Locke's views on, 31-34; media and, xiii, 27-28, 29, 173-89; model of traditional, 222-23; Okin's views on, 58-62; philosophers' views on, 29-35; political system and, 32-34, portrayal on television, 178-79; positive behaviors toward, 143; power in, 54-55; public policy and, xiv, 253-57, 259-66; quality of life and, 40-41; Rawls's views on, 55-64; roles in, 52-55, 58-59, 62; school-family relationship, 224-25; sex-society relationship and, 179-83, 185-86; structure of, 57; tax policy and, 193-95, 199-202, 254; television and, xiii, 163-72, 178-79; Tocqueville's views on, 35; values of, 39; welfare and, xiv, 203-11, 254-55; women's movement and, xii, 87-95; women's role in, 58-59; work-family demands, 88-89. *See also* marriage
family form, xi, 11
family law, 87, 90-91; changes in, 4-5; England, 7; individual rights and, 102-103. *See also* divorce
Family Law Quarterly, 130
family life, ix-x, 222-23; effects of television on, xiii, 163-72; instability of, xii, 69-77; Mann's views of, 42; stability of, xi; tolerance of other behavior, 109-

110
family planning, 240, 244-45
Father Knows Best, 164, 174
father-child relationship, 81-84
fatherhood, xii, 79-86, 261
Fatherless America, 136
fatherlessness, 79-81
fathers, role in families, xii, 79-86
Federal Express, 263-64
females. *See* women
feminism, 20, 210; family and, xi-xii, 52-55, 63; marriage-family relationship and, 5-6, 7-8, 34, 91; motherhood and, 89, 91; public policy and, 261-62; women's attitude toward, 91. *See also* women
Filmer, Robert, 6, 31-32
First Wives Club, 129
flat tax, 197, 201
Foner, Eric, 27
food stamps, 214
Ford, J. A., 240
foster care, 130-31
Fox, Robin, 5
Fox-Genovese, Elizabeth, xi, 3-15, 19, 21, 91
France, family and, 21-23, 232
Frank, Barney, 39
freedom, 156
freedom of expression, 112, 230
freedom of religion, 63, 254, 263
Friedan, Betty, 91, 174
Friends, 140, 168
Fukuyama, Francis, 158
Furstenberg, Frank F., 129

Gagnon, John H., 179
Gallagher, Maggie, xii-xiii, 101, 115n17, 127-33, 173
Gallanter, David, 166
Galston, William A., xiv, 74, 173, 193, 251-55, 260-62
gambling, 162n24

Index 271

Index 271

87
interracial marriage, 111-12
Ireland, illegitimacy rate, 23
Islam, 122, 207
It Takes a Village, 39
Italy, illegitimacy rate, 23, 132

Japan, illegitimacy rate, 132
Jarvik, Lawrence, 170
Jefferson, Thomas, 41
Jesus, 101, 207-8
job-sharing, 61
John Paul II, 92, 94n21, 153, 160, 161n12
Johnson, Paul, 149
Jones, Gerald, 183
Jordan, Stan, 247
Judaism, 121, 123, 137, 140, 144-45, 150, 170, 207, 254
justice, 61-62, 228-29

Kaczynski, Theodore, 119
Kamark, Elaine Ciulla, 74, 193
Karst, Kenneth, 100
Kasich, John, 210
Kasun, Jacqueline, 240
Keeping Women and Children Last, 131
Keniston, Kenneth, 87
Kennedy, Justice Anthony, 121
Kennedy, Senator Ted, 207, 246
Khrushchev, Nikita, 229
Kinsey Report, 187n21
Kiryas Joel case, 121, 122
Kristol, William, xiv, 257-64

Labor and Human Resources, Senate Committee on, 240
labor market, family and, 72, 92-93
labor specialization, 153
Laborem Exercens, 93
Lancaster, Joseph, 43-44
The Last Married Couple in America, 139-40

Laumann, Edward 0., 179-83, 187n21
law of coverture, 6-7
Lawrence, Charles, 230
Leave It To Beaver, 140, 164, 170
Lee v. Wiseman, 121-22
Lenkowsky, Les, 210
Lerner, Robert, xii, 173-89
lesbians. *See* homosexuals
Letterman, David, 168
Leviathan, 29-30
Lewis, Anthony, 120
liberalism, 64, 200; evidence of, 258-59, expressive individualism and, 174-79; family and, xii, 64-65; media and, 174-79; moral values and, x; tax policy and, 202
libertarians, 200, 201
Lichter, Linda S., 174, 177-79
Lichter, S. Robert, 174, 177-79
Lightfoot, Sara Lawrence, 234
Lind, Michael, 131-32
Lipset, S. M., 185
Locke, John, x, xi, 9, 29, 31-35
Loury, Glenn, 93-94
love, marriage and, 10
Loving v. Virginia, 111-12
Luddites, 119
Luker, Kristin, 132
Lutheran schools, 229
Lutheran Social Services, Detroit, Michigan, 216

Macaulay, T. B., 17, 20
Mace, David, 249
Machiavelli, Niccolo, 29
Madonna, 121, 122
McLanahan, Sara, 74
McQuail, Denis, 185
Mad Max, 166
Maine, Henry, 102
males, relationship to fathers, 81
Mann, Horace, 41-42, 227
Marcuse, Herbert, 174

About the Contributors

DOUG BANDOW is a senior fellow at the Cato Institute and graduate of Stanford University Law School. He is the author of several books, including *The Politics of Envy: Statism as Theology* (Transaction) and *Beyond Good Intentions: A Biblical View of Politics* (Crossway).

DAVID BLANKENHORN is president of the Institute for American Values and author of *Fatherless America*.

GERARD V. BRADLEY is a professor at Notre Dame Law School, vice-president of the American Public Philosophy Institute, and author of *Church-State Relationships in America*.

ALLAN CARLSON is president of the Howard Center for Family, Religion, and Society and author of *Family Questions*.

LAWRENCE CRINER is associate editor of the *World & I* magazine, a monthly publication of the Washington Times Corporation.

JOHN J. DIIULIO, JR., is professor of politics and public affairs, Princeton University, Douglas Dillon Senior Fellow at the Brookings Institution, and senior counsel to Public/Private Ventures. He is the author (with William Bennett) of *Body Count: Moral Poverty—and How to Win America's War against Crime and Drugs*.

ELIZABETH FOX-GENOVESE is Eleonore Raoul Professor of Humanities, Emory University, and the author of *Feminism Is Not the Story of My Life*.

MAGGIE GALLAGHER is an affiliate scholar of the Institute for American Values and author of *The Abolition of Marriage: How We Destroy Lasting Love*. Her next book, *The Case for Marriage* (coauthored with Linda Wade) will be published in 1999 by Harvard University Press.

WILLIAM A. GALSTON is professor, School of Public Affairs, and director, Institute for Philosophy and Public Policy, University of Maryland, and author of *Liberal Purposes*.

MARY ANN GLENDON is professor, Harvard Law School, and author of *The Transformation of Family Law* and *Abortion and Divorce in Western Law*.

CHARLES L. GLENN is professor of educational policy, Boston University, and author of *The Myth of the Common School*.

BRUCE C. HAFEN is professor of law, university provost, and former dean of the Law School at Brigham Young University. His legal scholarship has appeared in such publications as the *Harvard Law Review, Duke Law Journal, Harvard International Law Journal, Michigan Law Review*, and *American Bar Association Journal*.

GERTRUDE HIMMELFARB is professor emeritus of history, Graduate School of the City University of New York, and author of *The De-Moralization of Society*.

WILLIAM KRISTOL is editor and publisher of *The Weekly Standard*.

ROBERT LERNER AND ALTHEA K. NAGAI received their Ph.D.s from the University of Chicago in sociology and political science, respectively. They have coauthored three books: *Giving for Social Change* (Praeger), *Molding the Good Citizen* (Praeger), and *American Elites* (Yale). They are currently partners in Lerner and Nagai Quantitative Consulting, a social-science research consulting firm.

WILLIAM R. MATTOX, JR., is vice-president for policy, Family Research Council.

DIANE MEDVED is a clinical psychologist and the author of *The Case Against Divorce* and (with Dan Quayle) *The American Family*.

MICHAEL MEDVED is host of a nationally syndicated radio talk show, former chief film critic for the *New York Post*, and author of *Hollywood vs. America*.

JOHN MUELLER is a principal of Lehrman Bell Mueller Cannon, Inc., a financial markets forecasting firm. From 1979 to 1988, he was economic counsel to Rep. Jack Kemp and the House Republican caucus, and in 1995 he was one of five economic advisors to the National Commission on Economic Growth and Tax Reform.

MARVIN OLASKY is professor of journalism at the University of Texas at Austin, the editor of *World*, and author of *The Tragedy of American Compassion*.

DAVID POPENOE is professor of sociology, Rutgers University, and author of *Life Without Father*.

LAWRENCE STONE is emeritus professor of History, Princeton University, and the author of *The Family, Sex and Marriage in England, 1500-1800*.

DAVID WAGNER is associate professor of law at Regent University.

CELIA WOLF-DEVINE is associate professor and chair of the Philosophy Department at Stonehill College and author of *Diversity and Community in the Academy: Affirmative Action in Faculty Appointments* (Rowman & Littlefield) and "Abortion and the Feminine Voice," *Public Affairs Quarterly* (July 1989).

CHRISTOPHER WOLFE is professor of political science, Marquette University, and president of the American Public Philosophy Institute. He is the author of *The Rise of Modern Judicial Review* and editor (with John Hittinger) of *Liberalism at the Crossroads* (both Rowman & Littlefield).